"On the road for the WWF in the 1980s, we watched *GLOW* whenever we could. We loved *Hollywood* and couldn't wait to see what she was up to next. Many years later our mutual friend (*GLOW* host) Johnny C., paid me a huge compliment: '*Hollywood* was *GLOW*'s version of Jimmy Hart: always on time, great work ethic, never was a problem, and was always upbeat, positive, and fun to be around.' Jeanne has achieved something that's very rare: respect and love from both the fans and her team members."

> Jimmy "Mouth of the South" Hart
> Legendary pro wrestling manager

"*Hollywood and Vine* are street kids. They'll do anything to survive!" "One of my favorite memories is the night in New Orleans you and I went to the bars had drinks and soaked in New Orleans together"

> David B. McLane
> *GLOW*'s Creator, Producer, Promoter, and Announcer

"In 1987, the *GLOW* cast was comprised of thirty-five women ... and me. Jeanne *Hollywood* Basone was that one person in our cast that possessed undeniable 'star quality.' When people would learn about my affiliation with *GLOW*, they would almost always ask, 'So you know Hollywood? What is she really like?' And I would tell them the truth. 'Jeanne is the sweetest, most sincere, professional, and conscientious person I have ever worked with.' That still holds true for my friend ... the original *GLOW* Girl ... The One ... The Only ... *Hollywood*!"

> Johnny "Johnny C." Cafarella
> *GLOW*'s Host and Producer

"What *American Gladiators* was to the '90s, *GLOW* was to the '80s. And, as a gladiator, I've had to face many tough opponents, and I'm happy *Hollywood* wasn't one of them! She is the real deal!"

> Lori "Ice" Fetrick
> American Gladiators TV star

"Growing up watching *GLOW,* I thought *Hollywood* was both badass and beautiful. Now that I have met her, I know that she is also beautiful on the inside as well. She has paved the way for women in professional wrestling, and I thank her for what she has contributed. I am happy to call her a friend and proud of all that she has accomplished. And she also makes a mean bar of soap!"
> "The Queen of Extreme" Francine
> Extreme Championship Wrestling

"Jeanne Basone's highly entertaining and fascinating memoir boldly peeks into her behind-the-scenes life in her role as *Hollywood* star of the Gorgeous Ladies of Wrestling television series. She candidly traces her journey from a Burbank medical office to the bright lights of the Las Vegas Strip and the wrestling ring. Her richly detailed narrative romps the reader through her experiences— in the fast-paced world of glamor, women's television wrestling, movie and television stunt acting, female fighting video production—and details how she survived all the mayhem through more than three decades. Jeanne's story makes one thing very clear – she's done it her way and loved every minute of it. Her book will be enjoyed by book lovers, women's wrestling fans, wrestlers, and industry professionals."
> Bob Harris
> Writer and women's professional wrestling archivist

"*Hollywood* never passed any subjects in school. She was too busy stealing apples from the teacher!"
> "Motormouth" Mike Morgan
> *GLOW*'s Moves and Maneuvers Man

"Jeanne Basone is a 'Legend'! Every term that describes that word describes Jeanne. As *Hollywood* in *GLOW*, she paved the way as an original who completely changed the landscape of the industry. It doesn't matter if it's wrestling, modeling, or acting, she is a true star that brings love and passion to everything she does. I am lucky to call her a friend."
> Dave LaGreca
> Host of Busted Open on SiriusXM

"Few could have worn the moniker of *Hollywood* as gracefully as Jeanne! My favorite of the original *GLOW* girls."

> William Patrick ("Billy") Corgan Jr.
> Frontman for The Smashing Pumpkins and Owner/President of the National Wrestling Alliance (NWA)

"WRESTLER. ATHLETE. ACTRESS. LEADER. STUNTWOMAN. TRAILBLAZER. ENTREPRENEUR. REBEL. ICON. STAR. As the O.G. *GLOW* Girl, Jeanne Basone didn't just lead the way ushering in a new era of professional wrestling, she also helped redefine the world of sports entertainment itself. From growing up a Burbank baby, riding her bicycle around the SoCal streets, to starring on smash hit TV shows, to performing stunts for the silver screen, Jeanne *Hollywood* Basone's epic, endearing, and fearlessly authentic memoir sparkles more than the collective wardrobe of the Gorgeous Ladies of Wrestling in their prime. Fans of the squared circle, sensational behind-the-scenes storytelling, and all things pop culture will not want to miss one of the best – and most important – professional wrestling memoirs ever written by a once in a generation talent."

> A.J. Devlin
> Author of the award-winning "Hammerhead" Jed pro wrestler PI mystery-comedy novels

HOORAY FOR HOLLYWOOD!

☆ ☆ ☆ ☆ ☆

HOORAY FOR HOLLYWOOD!

The True Story
Of The Original
GLOW Girl

A Memoir

Jeanne Basone

Hollywould Productions Inc. ☆ Jeanne Basone

Disclaimer

The opinions expressed in this memoir are solely mine and reflect my personal recollection of the events that took place. While I have tried to present these memories as accurately as possible, they are based on my perspective and experiences. This book is my truth the way I remember it ... yesterday, today, and always.

For more information about this book, or to contact the author, go to:
jeannebasone.com

To my family
who brought me up and taught me right from wrong
and supported me and my big dreams
I love you all very much!

In Memoriam

For all the women and men of *GLOW* who are no longer with us, but whose contributions to the show live on in the hearts and minds of both original fans who saw *GLOW* on TV and new fans who find the show through various media. *GLOW*'s legacy will never die, nor will its unique position as the first all-women's pro wrestling promotion in American history. I love all of you.

Sheila Best (Tara the Southern Belle), 1958-2009
Dee Booher (Matilda the Hun), 1948-2022
Lynn Braxton (Big Bad Mama), 1952-2013
Frank D'Amato (Referee), 1957-1999
Emily Dole (Mountain Fiji), 1957-2018
Suzanne Duplessis (Star), 1966-2019
Ursula Hayden (Babe the Farmer's Daughter), 1966-2022
Andrea Laird Micheil (Angel), 1963-2022
Beckie Mullen (Sally the Farmer's Daughter), 1963-2020
Kitty Burke Municino (Bad Girls' Manager), 1926-2012
Deann Murray (Brunhilda), 1964-2016
Cynthia Peretti (Pepper), 1948-2009
Meshulam Riklis (Owner), 1923-2019
Jackie Stallone (Good Girls' Manager), 1921-2020

HOORAY FOR HOLLYWOOD!

My Rollercoaster Ride To Publication

It was Summer 2017. My friend Ruta Sepetys, a New York Times and international best seller and award-winning author of historical fiction, kindly contacted her San Diego- based literary agent Steven Malk of New York's Writers House LLC. agency. She asked him who would be good in NYC to look at my manuscript.

Steven suggested fast-rising junior agent Stacy Testa at Writers House. Ruta emailed her and made the introduction for me. Woo hoo, what a lucky break! Writers House is well known by the Big Five publishers.

Stacy immediately reached out to me and requested a manuscript, synopsis, photographs, testimonials, and a press kit. I flew to NYC for a meeting. After a long chat she suggested I retain Heather Maclean, an award winning author and client of Senior Agent Susan Ginsberg.

The plan was to have Heather write a 72-page book proposal for Stacy to use in her submissions to publishing house editors. Heather and I would work together to produce content that would include a summary of the proposed work, a detailed chapter outline, a discussion of comparable titles, a section on marketing and promotion, my biography, and two sample chapters. Heather would be paid $8,500 for proposal preparation – $4,250 upon signing of the agreement, and $4,250 upon delivery and my acceptance of the proposal.

Stacy mentioned, a very popular and current trend was self-help/advice books. She suggested I take that route. Of course, there are no "hit" guarantees in the book business. I flew home, slept on it and signed the contract. I was thrilled to have representation by a major literary agency.

Heather and I got to work. She really went to town on it (no time to waste if we were to meet Stacy's Fall submissions deadline). Heather wrote a really good presentation. The working title was *Ready, Set, GLOW: Your Playbook for a Kickass Life.* I liked it.

But here's the thing: You know when you get that gut instinct feeling? Well ... let me tell you, when my gut talks to me, it's usually right. The self-help craze didn't sit well. It wasn't the type of book I had in mind. But, what do I know – Stacy's team was enthusiastic, they were the professionals, and I was ridin' with them.

Long story short. Stacy submitted to 28 editors (two rounds). But we didn't reel in a deal. Some editors were soft on my self-help and others were filled up on acquisitions. But here's the thing: Stacy kindly sent me all of the book notes from editors of the Big Five and other publishing houses. I was blown away by their comments:

"... a huge fan of the show and Jeanne....";

"... interested in adding to my list. The strong female voice with a pop culture/business angle was really appealing.";

"... Jeanne's story is so powerful, and refreshing – it really was a joy to read through the proposal.";

"Given Jeanne's wonderful voice, I have no doubt that this project will find a wonderful home at another house...."

What happened? In my opinion, the trend went cold for my genre.

AJ Lee (WWE) launched her book *Crazy Is My Superheroine* in 2017 and hit the bestseller list. Was my $8,500 investment worth it? Yes.

Fast forward – I meet high profile writer Dan Murphy at CAC in Vegas. I pitch him. His reply, "I'm honored to write your story." Dan's ECW Press publisher gives him a nod. Then Covid hit. A 4-year stall. Another ECW pitch. Good interest but Madusa is next. I would have to wait.

But *Hooray For Hollywood!* was in a hurry and here I am.

Contents

February 18, 1990

It's Sunday night and I'm pacing around my apartment in North Hollywood, California. I'm about to appear on one of the most popular television shows in America. I will be in the living rooms of approximately 15 million homes … wearing a barely-there black teddy. And I'm nervous.

It's not what I'm wearing that's giving me butterflies. As Hollywood, a member of the Gorgeous Ladies of Wrestling – the very first *GLOW* girl hired, in fact – my usual ring gear was a bit more provocative; the teddy is tame by comparison. And I had been on TV plenty of times before with *GLOW*.

But tonight, I'm appearing on *Married… with Children*, one of the most popular shows on the bold new Fox network. Mainstream America will be tuning in. Eyeballs from coast to coast will be focused on me, even if just for a few scenes. It is a lot to process.

This episode will be the second half of a two-part storyline. Peg Bundy (played by Katey Sagal) has lost the family savings in Las Vegas. The Bundy family is in dire straits when Peg sees a colorful sign: "Survive Three Minutes with a G.L.O.W. Wrestler and Win $10,000." She suggests that her husband, Al (played by the inimitable Ed O'Neill), sign up and take the challenge.

"What's a *GLOW* girl?" Al asks.

That's when Babe the Farmer's Daughter (Ursula Hayden) and I turn the corner wearing our skimpy little outfits. I tap Babe on the shoulder.

"So, what time's your match?" I ask as we stop directly in front of the table where Al and Peg are sitting. (You've always got to hit your mark.)

"I don't know," Babe says, as she all-too casually examines her fingernails. "I just hope I don't get another car salesman," she says, rolling her eyes. "They bite."

"Count your blessings," I reply. "Lawyers leave greasy spots."

1

We share a giggle and exit to the left as the camera gets a shot of my butt in sexy stockings. I gently caress Ed O'Neill's face as I pass while the studio audience hoots and whistles.

"You mean all I have to do is roll around on the floor for three minutes with one of those?" an excited Al asks.

Of course, it turns out to be a bait-and-switch, and Al has to wrestle my fellow *GLOW* girl Big Bad Mama (Lynn Braxton), who was more of an intimidating figure with her imposing size and black and white war paint.

We shot the episode weeks earlier, and I thought it went well, but how will it look on TV? Did Babe and I hit our mark right? Did I rush my lines or not give the audience enough time to react before we exited the shot? And how was my butt going to look on prime time television?

I have always been my own worst critic. My boyfriend at the time had been opposed to me doing the show. He was sometimes insecure and jealous; although, to his credit, he did go with me to Sunset Gower Studios in Hollywood the day we shot the scene. Maybe that was more a case of him trying to keep an eye on things than just provide moral support. His hesitancy and my own self-criticism and insecurities were pulling a tag team double-team on me.

I was doing great in *GLOW*, but was I "good enough" for one of the top sitcoms in the country, even in a small guest spot role? I was so excited to be asked to take this part. Please, God ... don't let me embarrass myself.

The commercial ends and the familiar introductory theme song comes on. "Love and marriage, love and marriage ..." croons Frank Sinatra. It's on. I take a deep breath and settle into the sofa.

Let's see if the world is ready for Hollywood.

No

Let's see if the world is ready for Jeanne Basone from Burbank.

☆ ☆ ☆

I was being naive when I thought *only* 15 million people would see that episode of *Married... with Children*. Sure, 15 million – give or take a few million – saw the episode on that winter night in 1990, but with reruns and syndication, and later some completely unexpected new things called the Internet and YouTube, maybe 100 million people have seen that clip by now. People certainly seem to like it. It still comes up at just about every fan fest, comic con, and signing I do. Fans come to meet me and tell me they remember seeing me on *Married... with Children*. A lot of guys – and some girls – tell me that Hollywood was their first crush and that they had pin-ups and fold-out posters of me up on their bedroom walls, courtesy of the short-lived *GLOW* magazine.

I always find it incredible to hear these stories. I'm so honored that people still remember *GLOW* and Hollywood, and I love meeting fans. I've heard of celebrities and rock stars who become jaded and standoffish to fans and the public, and I could never wrap my head around that. That's just not the way I'm wired, I guess. I'm just a middle-class girl from Burbank, California. I had dreams of becoming an actress and a model. And those dreams came true in a very unusual way ... through professional wrestling.

Introduction

"HOL-LY-WOOD! HOL-LY-WOOD! HOL-LY-WOOD!"

Hundreds of wrestling fans were screaming my name in a jam-packed venue. As one of the original Gorgeous Ladies of Wrestling, I was beating the crap out of my opponent, a big-haired bimbo wearing Daisy Duke shorts and a red halter top with white polka dots. I was wearing my sexy silver and black corset and black stockings, an outfit my fans would come to know as one of my signature looks over the years. Along with my bad girl outfit came a bad girl attitude. I slammed my opponent's head into the ring apron – WHAM! – causing her to stagger backwards. Then I threw her into the first row of fans. We hadn't even climbed into the ring yet!

Did I truly hate my opponent that night? Nah, not really. But we were both cast members of *GLOW,* the upstart women's pro wrestling promotion that was making headlines across the United States. The 1980s were the start of a golden age of sorts for professional wrestling, and if Hulk Hogan and Andre the Giant could make a quick buck or two, why couldn't the ladies? After all, I looked a LOT better in a bikini than "The Hulkster."

I honestly had no idea where this offbeat wrestling gig would take me. I could never have guessed that a job like this would lead me – your average American girl next door – to a world that would include wrestling, acting, modeling, international travel, collaborating with rock and roll royalty, and a career as an independent business owner.

I had no idea that this little gig would lead me to the rest of my life!

This is my story.

I have been blessed to meet many amazing people on this journey of mine, including fans, filmmakers, photographers, and other terrific individuals. I have asked some of them to share their thoughts and memories as well. If not for them, this crazy trip could never have taken place.

I hope their thoughts and observations can provide additional insight into some of the stories I am about to tell. Those contributions are woven throughout this book in the sections entitled "Another Perspective."

Shot from one of my first real photo shoots.

PART I

JUST AN L.A. GIRL IN THE SOCAL SCENE
HAD FAMILY, FRIENDS, AND MUSIC, I WAS LIVIN' THE DREAM
BUT I HAD OTHER GOALS IN MY MIND
DIDN'T WANNA BE A SLAVE TO THE GRIND

Chapter 1: My (All-Natural) Roots

I grew up in a pretty normal, middle-class family in Southern California – Burbank, to be exact – situated in the southeastern end of the San Fernando Valley, a few miles from the Verdugo Mountains. Burbank was also the home of Walt Disney Studios, Warner Brothers, and *The Tonight Show Starring Johnny Carson*. We lived a few miles from Hollywood and about twelve miles from downtown Los Angeles. What a place to grow up! To me, Burbank had a certain smell about it, a smell that's hard to explain. It's not a bad smell at all; maybe the best way to describe it would be to compare it to the familiar smell of autumn leaves. Once you leave and come back, there's that warm sunny smell again, and you know that you're home.

In terms of ethnic background, I'm half-Italian and half-Hispanic. My great grandmother on my father's side came from Sicily on a ship across the Atlantic and landed on Ellis Island with her dad. They settled in Akron, Ohio. On my mom's side, their records are not as good. When Mom did one of the saliva tests from Ancestry DNA, it said that she was mostly from continental Europe and Ireland. I would have guessed South America or maybe Mexico. Her family lived close to the Mexican border in Brownsville Texas and could speak both Spanish and English.

Grandma's mom died when she was very young, and all my grandmother remembers of her is a memory of her sitting down, wrapped in an Indian blanket. My mother's great-grandmother on her dad's side came from Scotland on a ship that landed in Galveston, Texas. She met a man there and never went back to Europe.

Mom was born Nelda Marie White on January 8, 1943 in Rio Grande City, Texas. Elvis Presley was born on the same day eight years earlier; I find that to be astrologically interesting. Maybe because she was born on his birthday, Mom LOVED Elvis when she was growing up. She constantly sang his songs. Her favorite was "(Let Me Be Your) Teddy Bear."

Mom moved around a lot with my grandmother, Ofelia, and step-granddad, Bill. Growing up, my mom went to a bunch of schools spread out between Texas, Louisiana, Arkansas, and Arizona. In addition to working as a waitress, my grandma also owned her own store and her own dress shop. Grandma taught Mom to cook early in her life … and thank God she did! My family always ate well when I was growing up.

Mom's first paying job was at a vineyard in Arizona where she picked out all the rotten grapes before they were packaged to go out to market. Later, she worked as a waitress, then as a teacher's assistant and as an English as a Second Language teacher in Burbank.

My dad, Peter, was born in Akron, Ohio to Sonti and Samuel Basone. He was the oldest of three children; he had a younger brother named Ben and a younger sister named Jeannie. If I had a dime for every time I heard him talk about walking five miles to school in the snow, uphill both ways, I'd be a rich woman. Unlike Mom, Dad grew up somewhat poor. One time he found a bike in the river, cleaned it up, and made it his own. Being the oldest, he got his share of new clothes. His younger brother wasn't so lucky, though; he got all of Dad's old hand-me-downs.

Dad must have been pretty handy because, in addition to fixing up the bike, he also built his own soapbox derby car. He raced and won one heat before losing. When I traveled back home one year, he showed me the hill they used to race on. Dad played sports, too. He played football, either as right or left end on offense and linebacker on defense. He even tried out for the swim team, but his football coach said he could either play football or swim. Dad eventually quit the swim team, but to this day, he says he wishes he could have done both.

Dad joined the Air Force in 1958 at the age of 19. His job at the time wasn't very good and he wanted to get out of Ohio, so he signed up for a four-year stint. His first two months of basic training were in Texas. He went on to Biloxi, Mississippi for three months of training as an air traffic controller, and his first assignment was in Madison, Wisconsin, where he stayed for nine months. He then got shipped out to St. John's, Newfoundland, Canada. When they closed that base, he was sent up north to Goose Bay, Labrador, Canada for the last two years of his tour. Dad said it was colder than hell there, which made him want to avoid living in a cold climate ever again.

He met mom on a blind date while he was stationed in Arizona. They actually didn't hit it off right away, but on their second date, something clicked (fortunately for me). He had to go to Sacramento shortly after that, so he and Mom wrote letters to each other every day. They didn't have the luxury of cell phones or putting in dimes and nickels in the pay phone booths, so the next best thing was the good old U.S. Postal Service. As someone who learned the ins and outs of a long-distance relationship many years later, I can only imagine how difficult it must have been to communicate only through the mail.

Those "love letters" must have done the trick because Mom and Dad got married in June of 1962 in Glendale, Arizona … in a 102-degree church! Both were wearing white and, from the pictures I have seen, they looked like Elvis and Priscilla. A very hot Elvis and Priscilla, maybe. They were indeed a very good-looking couple. My mother, after all, had been a Homecoming Queen. She had a glowing, genuine smile and big, adorable dimples in her cheeks.

After their honeymoon in Sedona, they decided not to move to Akron, Ohio, but to Los Angeles, where my dad had an aunt and an uncle he had visited as a kid. One thing you have to love about Southern California: There's never any snow to shovel!

Thanks, Dad, for moving and raising your family in sunny SoCal. If you hadn't done that, I probably wouldn't be writing this book right now!

Chapter 2: Growing Up

I was born eleven months after my parents' wedding day. I came into the world at 4:55 a.m. on May 19, 1963. I was the first of three girls. Julie was born in 1964 and Joelle was born in 1969.

I've always had an interest in astrology. My astrological sign is Taurus the Bull, and if you know anything about astrology, then you know that this is what they say about Taurus ...

Symbol: The Bull
Element: Earth
Quality: Fixed
Ruling Planet: Venus, the planet of beauty and love
Body Part: Neck, throat, jaw
Good Day: Patient, organized, supportive, romantic, careful, dedicated
Bad Day: Overindulgent, stubborn, lazy, vain, too cautious
Favorite Things: Photography, the mountains, great music, rich/gourmet food, satin sheets
What They Hate: Being rushed, hotels, wasting money, dirty things, mornings
Keywords: Stability, security, power, elegance, sensuality, stubbornness, persistence.[1]

Hmmmm. Turns out I love hotels. Maybe all of those Taurus attributes don't apply to me because I am also on the cusp of being a Gemini. What does that mean?

Symbol: The Twins
Element: Air
Quality: Mutable
Ruling Planet: Mercury, the planet of communication
Body Part: Shoulders, arms, hands
Good Day: Fascinating, original, resourceful, charming, wise, adventurous
Bad Day: Restless, distracted, two-faced, judgmental, depressed, overwhelmed
Favorite Things: Cell phones, fast cars, trendy clothes, obscure music, guitars, books, comedy clubs

What They Hate: Small-minded people, dress codes, authority figures, silence, routines
Keywords: Communication, Collaboration, Synergy, Cleverness, Wittiness, Inventiveness, Ingenuity. [2]

I suppose you could call me a solid "Taurini." I'm definitely romantic, passionate, supportive, and organized, and I love socializing, clothes, and music.

Looking back at all my baby pics, it looks like Mom always had me out in the beautiful California sun – listening to the radio, going to the beach, and lying out in my birthday suit. It's no wonder I have such a love for the sunshine.

I was about a year old when Julie was born. When she was a baby, my cousin, Paul, and I were playing in the bedroom where Julie was resting in her crib. She started crying, like babies do, but the troubling thing is that she wouldn't stop. Later, my parents found out that her arm was broken. I don't remember any specifics – after all, I was only around one year old myself – but my parents think Paul and I must have broken Julie's arm while we were playing with her. Poor little Julie! Sorry about that, sis.

We were brought up Catholic and went to church every Sunday, either at Saint Finbar in Burbank or Saint Patrick's in North Hollywood. It's not that I really wanted to go, but my parents wanted us to have a good foundation.

You'd think that, as the only man in a house full of females, my dad might've gotten sick of being the only guy around. Fortunately for him, I was a tomboy growing up. I love my sisters, but it always seemed like the boys in my neighborhood had something exciting planned, and I sure as hell didn't want to be left out. My dad was into lots of sports like golf, fishing, and hunting.

As for Mom, cooking was her specialty. She could bake, decorate, can, or whip up just about anything. And it was delicious! She got a lot of recipes from Grandma and Aunt Jo on my dad's side, and of course many more from her own mom. Her sauce and meatballs are the best anywhere – and I mean anywhere. The meatballs are soft enough to keep you coming back for more. I also love Mom's lasagna, which I've pretty much perfected on my own as well. (Please, people, use ricotta cheese, not cottage cheese.)

Mom could also make Mexican food like nobody's business. The sauce she made for her enchiladas was absolutely addictive. My grandma made homemade tamales once a year, which always turned into an all-day affair. This usually took place around Thanksgiving time, when the whole family was visiting my grandparents near Fresno. Grandma and Mom cooked the pork, prepared the corn masa, and rinsed the husks. Then, like workers at a conveyor belt, we kids would spoon the masa onto the husks, add the meat, and roll the whole thing up. We would make dozens of tamales and take home the leftovers to freeze and save for later.

Mom's homemade jams are better than any you'll ever find in a store. Homemade ravioli is another favorite of mine. Mom and Aunt Jo would make these for Christmas dinner, and what a job that was! Aunt Jo made homemade Italian cookies, and my favorites were the chocolate rum balls and her pizzelles. The cannolis were good, too; she put vanilla or chocolate pudding in them just for the kids.

If you like to cook, or bake, or just love food, then I think cooking comes easily. Before I moved out on my own after high school, I wrote and typed up all of Mom's recipes on 4x6 index cards. I still have those index cards today. If any of the dishes I just described sound good to you, you're in luck – I'm working on a cookbook now!

My parents were probably what you would call "social drinkers." Dad would have a Scotch and water at restaurants and the occasional Olympia beer when he was working in the yard, or fishing, or at parties. Mom would have a margarita once in a blue moon; she didn't care for the taste of alcohol very much. We used to go to this Italian seafood restaurant in Burbank called Piero's when I was little. I remember it was so dark inside – what a cool hangout! It had a bunch of aquarium tanks with lobsters and tropical fish in them. My sisters and I would order Shirley Temples. In my mind, I was a grown-up having a fancy cocktail with everybody else.

Grandma and Grandpa Basone would come from Ohio and stay at least a month or two during Christmas time or summer, bringing us a big bag of M&M's each and every time. Grandpa Basone would always go on walks when he visited, so we would walk with him down to what we called the "liquor store," which was actually a little market that sold groceries, cigarettes, and candy. Grandpa always asked, "Why do you want to go to the liquor store? Do you want liquor?" We would laugh and say, "No! We want candy!"

On occasion, my great-grandmother, Nunni, and great-grandfather, Pete, would come and visit from Ohio. They both lived to be over 100 years old. At breakfast, Great Grandpa – in his 90s then – always mixed eggs with milk in a bowl and then drank it, like an athlete before a big event. Gross! It did not look very appetizing to me. He would also bring us collectible money as well: two-dollar bills, old coins, silver dollars ... stuff like that. I still have all my old coins and bills he gave me.

I remember there was always music playing in our home. From a young age, I recall 93 KHJ AM, a Top 40 station, tuned in on the radio. I remember the DJs "Charlie Tuna" and "The Real Don Steele" spinning that vinyl and, boy, was I hooked! "You're So Vain" by Carly Simon, "Superstition" by Stevie Wonder, "Jumpin' Jack Flash" by the Rolling Stones, "Sunshine Of Your Love" by Cream, Creedence Clearwater Revival, Free, The Jackson Five, The O'Jays, Glen Campbell, The Doors, Bobby Sherman, Neil Diamond, The Spinners, Sugarloaf, Carol King, Chicago, Bread, Five Man Electrical Band, John Denver, Elton John, Bill Withers, Cat Stevens, KC and the Sunshine Band, Paul Revere & The Raiders, Van Morrison, The Carpenters, The Allman Brothers, Ozark Mountain Daredevils, Rare Earth, Jethro Tull, Simon and Garfunkel, Grand Funk Railroad, Steely Dan, Deep Purple, Earth, Wind & Fire, Paul McCartney and Wings, Alice Cooper, David Bowie, War, The Eagles, Linda Ronstadt, The Bee Gees, Sweet, Peter Frampton, The Doobie Brothers, Steve Miller, Boston, ELO, Kansas, Pink Floyd, Supertramp, Led Zeppelin, Black Sabbath, KISS. This was the soundtrack to my childhood. These artists helped shape my musical tastes for the rest of my life.

Who could have known I'd eventually meet and party with some of the musicians I listened to growing up in Burbank?

Chapter 3: School Daze

I started preschool when I was 4 years old. On those chilly SoCal mornings, Mom would dress me in a dark red dress, white stockings, and black shoes or some similar outfit and drive me to school in our big black Chevy. I remember a black felt board with letters and numbers in the classroom, riding bikes around an old oak tree, and "healthy snacks" of Wheat Thins and tomato juice. At the time, we probably didn't care if they were healthy or not, so long as we got a snack. After nap time, Mom would pick me up and drive me home. I got to play while she sewed or ironed. I remember Mom watching her soap operas, as well as TV shows like *The Dating Game*; *Love, American Style*; and *Dark Shadows*.

Whenever I smell freshly brewed coffee, it always reminds me of my days at Bret Harte Elementary School on Jeffries Street in Burbank. (Ironically enough, a different Bret Hart would rise to fame in pro wrestling right around the same time that I did in *GLOW,* but I assure you, that is entirely coincidental.) I can still hear the teachers' heels click-clacking down the wooden-floored hallways. I can still see the off-white walls and blonde-colored doors. And of course, I can always smell that freshly brewed coffee that seemed to permeate the hallways, emanating out of the teachers' lounge. The teachers must have needed some strong joe to deal with us kids.

At the age of 5, I remember going to a school that was one block from our house. In those days, I wore a dress pretty much every single day except on Fridays, when I was allowed to wear pants. Mom made sure we always had a good breakfast before she walked us to school. She packed us a good lunch, too, every day except for Fridays, when we received a whopping 50 cents, which was the cost of eating in the cafeteria. What a deal, right?

I started first grade in September 1968. My teacher was Mrs. Willoughby in Room 19. Whenever we did something exceptional in class, like reading sentences or solving some basic math problems, Mrs. Willoughby would place a colored star next to our name on a posterboard hanging at the front of the room so that everyone knew what we had achieved.

My first crush was Chris, a boy in my class that year. One day at recess, I grabbed his red and blue flannel shirt and pulled on it. One of the buttons popped off and he got really upset and said he was going to tell the teacher. I wasn't trying to be mean. I was just trying to get his attention. I guess at that time my favorite sport was chasing boys on the playground. It's not that I was a bad kid. I was just "full of life," you could say. I knew what I wanted, so I went after it. What's wrong with that? For what it's worth, I learned a valuable lesson that day: boys are *way* behind girls when it comes to flirting.

Ever since I was a young girl, I have really loved animals, especially cats. I will always remember our very first cat, a black cat named Charlie. Well, one day he didn't come home. My dad later admitted that he found Charlie dead, but, at the time, he just told us Charlie was lost. I'm so glad he did that. A few years later, I found a gray stray cat. I asked my mom if we could take her home and her reply was, "Go ask your dad." When I asked my dad, he said, "Go ask your mom." Needless to say, it wasn't long before we had adopted this cat, whom we named Smoky. I can't remember what happened to him, though my dad speculated that he may have been hit by a car.

We weren't *just* cat people; we also had dogs in our home. I specifically remember a black lab we had named Bojangles, who used to go hunting and fishing with Dad all the time. When Bojangles died, Dad got a golden retriever he named Brooke. She went everywhere with Dad; she was his little buddy. When she passed, Dad took it real hard and vowed never to get another animal. Years later, my younger sister, Joelle, had a tiny chick that was incubated at our elementary school, a project my class had done as well. She named the chick Mrs. Brown. Unfortunately, Mrs. Brown passed on a hot summer day, when she might have ingested some of the poisonous snail bait pellets Dad had put out in the yard.

For second grade, I was assigned to Room 12 with Mrs. Weiss, a thin woman with gray hair. Our school was very close to what was then called Lockheed Airport – now Bob Hope Airport – and every time a plane flew over the school, we would have to stop whatever we were learning or doing for a minute or two until the plane passed. That's how loud it was.

I'll always remember Fridays in Mrs. Weiss' class. Every Friday was "Sharing Day," when we all took turns standing up in front of the class and sharing a secret or an incredible story that meant a lot to us personally. Well, my share day came along. What I thought would be a super exciting story to tell came crashing down on my little ego. Right after Christmas, I told my class that on Christmas Eve I woke up and saw Santa Claus sitting at our kitchen table eating cookies! I was so excited that he was actually at my house. I wasn't even finished with my story when a kid in my class, Kenny Frank, blurted out, "Santa Claus isn't real! It's your parents dressed up as him!" I was shocked, horrified, and embarrassed. And that is how I found out about Santa. Damn, what a bummer! Thanks for ruining Christmas, Kenny.

That same year I was invited to Kenny's house for his 8th birthday. I had never been to a boy's birthday party before. I felt a little hesitant at first, but Mom reassured me it would be fine. I got dressed up in my party dress and Mom dropped me off at Kenny's, just a few blocks away from our own house. When I got there, I looked around. Where were all the girls? I was the only little girl there. I'm not sure why I was the only one. Maybe the other girls didn't want to go? I felt a little uncomfortable, but even then, I could handle pretty much any situation. I've always been able to roll with the punches and adapt to different, potentially uncomfortable situations. I remember playing Pin the Tail on the Donkey, and that's about it. When you're only 8 years old, you're not thinking about how cool it is to be the only girl at a party. At least, I wasn't.

A few months later, Mom signed me up for the Brownies, the first level of the Girl Scouts. We had a field trip to the L.A. Zoo, where we all went into the petting zoo area to check out all the baby lambs, sheep, rabbits, and chickens. One mean-looking billy goat started running towards me, so I started running for the gate as fast as I could. Every time I looked back, he was getting closer, closer, and closer. I barely made it out the gate before he got to me. Talk about psychological damage! I never thought I would get attacked at a petting zoo.

I was 8 years old when the Sylmar earthquake hit in the early morning hours of February 9, 1971, with a magnitude of 6.5 on the seismic magnitude scale. Sleeping in my lower bunk bed, I was awakened by a huge shaking sensation. My first thought was that a giant had picked up our house and put it in his pocket. Our friends who lived in Sylmar didn't have water after the quake, and I remember my dad filling up huge buckets of drinking water for them. I remember driving on the freeway and seeing bridges broken in half. Our concrete sidewalks cracked, too. Fortunately, my family and I were safe. This would be my first experience of an earthquake, with many more to come.

Around this time, my parents bought us a little organ that came with sheet music. Oftentimes I would sing in my room, trying to learn to play songs like "One Bad Apple" by The Osmonds and "Something" by The Beatles. I went to catechism classes on Saturdays. These classes prepared you to make your First Communion. Before that happens, you have to make your first Penance, which means going to Confession for the first time. Confessing your sins ... what sins does an eight-year-old girl have to confess? But you had to have *something*. You couldn't go into the confessional empty handed. I mean, only Jesus was without sin, and maybe Mary, too. If I went in there without a list of sins to confess, it would be like I was putting myself up there with Jesus and The Virgin Mary! I needed some sins. The only things I could come up with was that I was not nice to my sisters, and I was mean to the cat. It was more of a fib than a sin, but I hoped it would do the trick. A few Hail Marys for penance and I was all set.

Like most children of that age, I was too young to appreciate religion, but according to the Catholic Church, as long as I knew that the bread and wine I was receiving were actually the real body and blood of Jesus Christ, then I was old enough to make my First Communion. This is a big occasion for Catholic families, filled with family and friends and dinner afterwards to celebrate. The girls typically wore a white dress and a veil, while the boys dressed in their "Sunday best." My grandma, Ofelia, was a jack-of-all-trades: seamstress, chef, mentor, gambler, and lover of coffee and cigarettes. Someone in my family decided that she should make my dress. But I didn't want anyone to make me a dress. I wanted someone to go out and buy me a dress. I was afraid I'd be the girl with the homemade dress that the other girls would laugh at. For weeks, I was anxious about what I would be forced to wear on my big day – my First Communion – in front of my whole school and my entire family. As it turned out, I had nothing to worry about. My grandma made me a white dress with pretty lace. It wasn't store-bought, so it didn't have the frilly look like the dresses all the other girls had. I stood out because I was different, and in a good way. From that point on, I actually loved having my mom or grandma sew clothes for me.

In third grade, I was assigned to Mrs. Snail, a short, pretty, round woman with light brown hair. For some reason, there weren't enough rooms inside the school for all of the students that year, so they put us third graders in a bungalow outside the building. Thank goodness it was air-conditioned otherwise it would have been a sweatbox in the spring and summer. I thought Mrs. Snail was pretty cool because she would teach us square dancing on Fridays. I loved dancing and music, and I didn't mind the chance to be social with the boys in the class.

I enjoyed school, but I was easily distracted. When it came down to memorizing times tables or spelling words, I found I would much rather talk to my friends about the latest episodes of *The Brady Bunch* or *Bozo the Clown* instead. I got my share of notes sent home to my parents, the kind of notes with big red check marks in the boxes labeled "Does not pay attention in class" and "Does not use her time wisely." And when it came time to play games like Four Square or paddle ball at recess, I naturally felt like I should be the one who made up the rules. Some of my classmates disagreed. A short brunette in class once got mad about it and told the recess attendant that I was cheating. It wasn't cheating – just an innovative interpretation of the rules. But it did result in another one of those notes being sent home to Mom and Dad: "Does not play well with other students."

I wasn't a bad kid; I just had a strong personality. My parents were none too happy with all those notes coming home with me from school. They sat me down and told me that they would be sending me to a private school if I got in trouble just one more time. A private Catholic school was a terrifying concept. I'd have to wear a uniform. The teachers (maybe nuns!) would be even more strict. Square dancing was definitely out. Heck, they might even segregate the girls from the boys!

I was terrified. My parents had put the fear of God into me. But I also knew that I couldn't finish elementary school without getting in *any* more trouble. I was doomed to private school. And within a couple of days of the private school talk, I got into trouble again. I was sent home with another note for my parents to sign. It's like I was carrying a death sentence in my backpack. As I walked home from school with my friends Tammy and Mary that day, I said my "final goodbyes." I expected to be enrolled in a new school the next day. I waited until morning to show Mom the note, after Dad had already gone to work. She signed it quickly and then … didn't say anything. She handed it back to me, and I never heard another word about changing schools. But I had learned my lesson. From that day on, I only had one more note sent home in all my years of school. I knew I had dodged a bullet, so I guess I must have started to behave myself.

Either that or I got better at not getting caught!

Chapter 4: Adventures with the Neighborhood Bestie

My best neighborhood friend was a boy named Chuck. We were never boyfriend-girlfriend, but we spent a lot of time together doing the kinds of things normal kids did during the '70s: bike riding, swimming, scavenger hunts, making cookies, helping Chuckie mow the lawn, drinking water out of the hose, do kids still do that? and, of course, going to the beach! This was, after all, Southern California.

Our families often went camping together, and Chuck and I had a blast "exploring" for shells, rocks, and arrowheads. We rode our bikes to places that were very far from home, like Travel Town in Griffith Park, a place that housed all the old trains, like the Union Pacific dining car, Southern Pacific Locomotive No. 219, and Southern Pacific No. 1273. It was free, so why not go in and check it out? We were just kids, and we had all the time in the world.

On one of our bike rides, Chuckie and I rode over to a local drug store called MDX, which was kind of like a smaller CVS. It was there that I committed a tiny, little, harmless "crime": stealing a pack of gum. I told Chuckie what I did and, when we got home, he told his mom. She scolded me and said, "You're going to take that pack of gum back right now, or I'm telling your parents!" I hightailed it back to the store and placed the gum back on the counter. Can you imagine how embarrassing that was? I did steal one more time, and that was a red diary that I just *had* to have. When my mom asked where I got it, I told her I had found it.

On one of our family camping trips, we were hiking through some really steep terrain. I slipped and fell, scratching up my stomach pretty bad on some rocks and barely holding on to a few tree roots. Below me were lots of rocks and a small stream, which looked like a raging river to me at the time. Chuckie had to go and get one of the adults to come save me. Luckily, I survived that expedition.

There was another time when a group of us kids were playing outside, and I decided that we should tie a rope from Chuck's bicycle to the three-wheeler Big Wheel I was riding. We got going pretty fast, and the next time I looked up, I was being pulled into about four or five trash cans –

not plastic bins, but the hard, silver, metallic ones. My chest got all scratched up that day, too.

Coming back from the grocery store one day on our bikes, Chuck's brother, Mike, was riding up ahead of me. Somehow, he lost control and fell off his bike, and I had no choice but to run over the top of him. I was horrified because I thought I had killed him! But when I found out he was fine, we had a good laugh about the whole thing.

Whenever *Batman* would come on television, Chuck, his brothers, and I would get our bath towels and swing them over our shoulders and pretend we were superheroes. I'm pretty sure every other kid did that, too. On Halloween one year, Chuck and I dressed up as bums. I remember burning the cork from a wine bottle to rub a "beard" onto my face.

We also loved to bake, often making chocolate chip or peanut butter cookies from scratch, either at my house or Chuck's house. I'll tell you ... it was almost too much fun for a kid to have. Then there was our Kool-Aid stand every summer. Now what kid has never done that? There was always something cool to do on our street. We used to ride our bikes to the toy store called Alvins on Hollywood way. One day we looked in the trash bin outside in the alley of that store and found all kinds of free toys. It seems like our parents gave us a lot more freedom than kids get these days. The main rule was simple: When the streetlights come on, you'd better get back inside your house.

The very first time I heard live music was right in our neighborhood. Scott Cameron, the 17 or 18-year-old guy that lived next door to us, had a band. He must've been their manager because he never played an instrument or sang with them when they rehearsed outside in his backyard. That was some loud rock and roll! A few years later he would have a small area in his yard that smelled and looked like a field of weed ... probably because it was. When his band played, the neighborhood kids would climb the brick wall that divided our houses and sit there, watching and listening to them play. I loved this! I had no idea they were covering other bands' songs, so when I heard "Jumpin' Jack Flash," I thought the guys in Scott's band were the actual Rolling Stones. This would be my true introduction to seeing bands perform live, something I would do a lot more years later.

Unfortunately, tragedy struck our neighborhood a few years later when Scott committed suicide. He was found in the garage with his Honda Prelude running and his face near the exhaust pipe. It's too bad our age difference was so much that he couldn't reach out to talk to me or my folks. This was the first time someone I knew committed suicide.

RIP Scott Cameron. And thank you for introducing me to live music. You forever changed my life in that department. Thank you Les and Betty Cameron for giving us Scott's car.

Chapter 5: More Childhood Adventures

Scott and his band didn't have a monopoly on music in the neighborhood. Truth be told, I was getting pretty good on the tonette, a type of flute they taught us in grade school. If you wanted a ripping rendition of "Hot Cross Buns," I was your girl! Actually, I did try the flute a bit later. Mom took me to the Killeen Music Store in the Burbank Mall, where you could rent any instrument you needed. I loved carrying the beautiful leather case – lined with blue felt inside – around school. But I was an average flutist at best. I would get light-headed and dizzy after playing for a while. I weighed only about 60 pounds. I guess I didn't have air to spare!

Maybe the woodwinds aren't for me, I thought. Maybe I was a guitar girl. My sister, Julie, and I both wanted to learn how to play guitar, so Mom signed us up and drove us to lessons every week. The guitar teacher was a woman named Mary Schmidt. Mrs. Schmidt had long dark hair and reminded me of Mama Cass from the Mamas & the Papas. I loved the way the guitar sounded from the time we learned our first song, "Proud Mary." I had nails on my right hand that I didn't want to cut, so it was harder for me to get the chords correct. Julie, on the other hand, seemed to adapt really well. Of course, I learned "Smoke on the Water" by Deep Purple right away. Unfortunately, I stopped playing guitar because I wanted my long nails. It was a bad decision because I really loved the guitar. I always wanted to play the piano, too, but never took lessons.

The first time I remember hearing the dreaded "F-word" was right about this time. I overheard one of the boys in my class say it to another boy. Of course, I had no idea what it meant, but it must have made some sort of mark in my impressionable young mind because a couple weeks later, I tried it out myself. I was in the family station wagon with Mom, and we passed by a billboard advertising toothpaste. The slogan was "Pucker Power." So I read it out loud in front of Mom, only changing one teensy little letter. The moment we got home, Mom pulled me into the bathroom and washed my mouth out with soap!

After school one day, Julie and I were playing outside in the backyard. I decided to get inside our red wagon and stand up, not realizing that my sister was going to pull on the handle. When she did, I lost my balance and fell backwards, putting out my left hand to break my fall onto the hard concrete. It hurt – *a lot* – but I tried (to use a wrestling term) to "no-sell" it, which means trying not to let anyone know exactly how much pain you are in. I didn't want to get in trouble with Mom and Dad. After dinner that night, Mom asked me to help dry the dishes, but my arm hurt too much to move it.

"What's wrong with your arm?" Mom asked.

"Oh, nothing," I said, gamely trying to play down my injury. But when I woke up the next morning, my arm was so swollen and bruised that it sent Mom into panic mode.

"Pete! Get her to the hospital now!" she yelled. I started crying, both because of the pain and now because of fear. I was terrified of going to the hospital. The doctors X-rayed my arm and discovered that I had fractured my radius. They put me in a cast and sent me on my way. Less than four weeks later, I was back outside playing as hard as I could. You heal fast when you're young!

In fourth grade, my teacher, Mrs. Farlow, let us bring in records (yes, vinyl) on Fridays for "Record Day." That was absolutely the highlight of my week. I loved discovering new songs and bands from the other kids in class. You know how certain songs take you back to a very specific period in your life? Maybe it was the theme from your senior prom or the song playing in the car the night you got your first kiss. My life is chock full of those "memory songs," and one of the first ones came from fourth grade Record Day. Whenever I hear "Stuck in the Middle with You" by Stealers Wheel, I always think of Steven Drojenski. He sat next to me and always brought in the coolest records.

I remember taking a boat trip with the Girl Scouts out to Catalina Island, a place I absolutely loved. I bought one of those big abalone shells that had an arrangement of smaller shells inside it. Collecting shells was one of my favorite hobbies as a kid, and I would make necklaces out of them every time I went to the beach. I also loved making beaded leather chokers, and I sold them to anyone who would buy one. When we were done at Catalina Island, we took the seaplane back home, which was the first time I had ever been on an airplane.

Of course, like all Girl Scouts, I also sold the famous Girl Scout Cookies. My sister and I had to walk door-to-door, asking the neighbors if they would buy cookies. Thin Mints are still my favorites to this day, and whenever I see Girl Scouts selling cookies in front of a store, I always make sure to buy a box or two.

In fifth grade, I was part of a "combination class," which meant that half the class consisted of fifth graders and the other half was sixth graders. I remember wondering if that meant the fifth graders were advanced and the sixth graders were a bit slower, and that's why they put us together. I don't know; maybe the school just didn't have enough room for two classes that year.

Remember Chris, the boy I had a crush on in first grade? The one whose shirt buttons I accidentally pulled off? His older brother, Joe, was one of the sixth graders in my class. Joe was tall, stocky, and blond, and unbeknownst to me, he had developed a crush on me. I wasn't really interested in "older" boys at the time, so he wasn't on my radar at all. But one day when I came in from recess, I opened up my little wooden desk and there was a small present inside. I closed my desk quickly. My face flushed. I felt very warm and nervous – embarrassed, really. When I had gathered up the courage, I opened my desk and opened the box. Inside was a gold necklace with a little heart locket. I opened up the locket and there was his face. He had pasted a picture of himself in it.

I never wore that necklace. In fact, I'm pretty sure I threw it away without even telling Mom or Dad about it. I had never been given a gift from a boy before, and I just didn't know what to do.

That year, the teacher had us all audition for the Christmas play. She had us read the different parts into her tape recorder. When she played my lines back to me, I couldn't believe that was really my voice. Was my voice really that low? I was given a bit part with one line, which was, if I recall, "I can't wait to taste the sugar plums and figgy pie." To this day, I have never knowingly tasted figgy pie, and I'm okay with that. I had to memorize my line and, when it came time to stand up there onstage and deliver it, I was terrified. I was so nervous. When exactly should I say it? Is there one word I should emphasize more than the rest? "I can't WAIT to ... I can't wait to TASTE the ..." Maybe emphasize the sugar and the figgy? Little did I know that I would spend the bulk of my life memorizing and delivering lines that same way.

Later that semester, our teacher had a cool contest where we had to memorize the Gettysburg Address. Every week we would take one paragraph at a time, stand up in front of the class, and recite it. I think I was only one out of five that could recite the whole address. I received a huge candy bar for my accomplishment. If you think memorizing the entire speech is difficult today, imagine doing it at 11 years old. Again, it turned out to be good career prep for me.

My parents decided I needed an outlet for all my extra energy and signed me up for a softball team. The first team I ever played for was called the "Polka Dot Pennies." Our gold uniforms were covered with pictures of pennies. Again, maybe it was good preparation for all the different wrestling outfits I would wear later. Maybe it even could have been the gimmick of a *GLOW* tag team.

Despite the ugly uniforms, I loved softball. I had a lean and lanky frame, and I could play pretty much any position on the field. I even made the All-Star team in my first season. Not too shabby for a girl who had never played sports except in P.E. class! I also talked my way into games with all the boys in my neighborhood. By sixth grade, my dad had put together a new team of girls from my school, which he coached after work. That gave us a little extra time for daddy-daughter bonding – although I quickly learned that the coach's daughter is usually the player who gets yelled at the most. In any case, I was starting to develop an interest in sports that would continue into my adult life.

In sixth grade, I was assigned to Room 12 and Mr. Lukhardt, a tall, lean man who was very much into sports. Every so often, he would pass out fresh-off-the-mimeograph outlines of an NFL helmet without the team logo on it and have us color in the correct logo. Of course, before we started coloring, we had to hold the sheets up to our faces and inhale … HARD. How we didn't create a generation of worksheet-sniffing addicts, I'll never know! We were supposed to color the helmets to match our favorite NFL teams. But I had no idea what color the Vikings or Colts were. I only knew the colors of the nearby Los Angeles Rams. I used to copy off Joey, the kid who sat next to me, to get the correct colors.

That year, one of our teachers got extremely sick. We had substitute after substitute after substitute. We were supposed to be learning our fractions that year, but when you have a substitute teacher, you don't learn anywhere near the amount you would learn with your regular teacher. This was also the year I decided to wear makeup to school. One day the principal, Mrs. Vogel, called me, along with my best friends, Mary and Lisa, out of the classroom to tell us we were not allowed to wear makeup to school. My poor mother had no idea, since we left our homes with fresh, clean faces and waited until we got to school to cover our faces like little vamps! One of my favorite extracurricular activities was the potter's wheel, where I learned how to make little bowls and coffee mugs with clay. I think I asked Mom and Dad for one of these at Christmas, but ours was more like a toy, not like the one at school.

It was in sixth grade that I broke my arm for the second time. This time it was my right wrist. Anthony Angelini, one of my classmates, was making fun of me at recess, telling me that I loved some boy named George. Of course, I just had to chase him down. During the chase he tripped me and – BOOM – I fell! For four weeks I could not pitch for our team, and Dad had to find a replacement pitcher. Yep, I was definitely accident-prone. The very same day I got my cast off, my dad had me pitching again. My arm was still bent in the middle, but it didn't hurt. I just wanted to get out there and play again.

During our spring break that year, my mom had some kind of Girl Scout outing with my sister, Julie. This left Joelle and me home alone with my father for the weekend. That Saturday morning, Dad said, "Let's go for a ride!" We hopped in his truck and headed north on Interstate 5 for about 30 minutes. Dad took the Magic Mountain Parkway exit, so my mind started racing. I got super excited, thinking, *Oh my God are we going to Magic Mountain?*

Six Flags Magic Mountain is an amusement park with the best roller coaster rides ever, so obviously we were pretty excited. Dad pulled into a gas station to get gas, and I wondered, *Surely we didn't drive all this way just to get gas, did we?* Dad finished filling up with gas, got back in the truck, and headed up the road for Magic Mountain. Yes! We all got a big laugh about him trying to surprise us, and it turned out to be a great day for father and daughters to hang out.

Even as a young girl, I had a great relationship with my dad. At dinner time, when I was in grade school, he would get creative and tape record us kids without us knowing about it. He would ask us how our day at school was, and we would tell him all kinds of stories. He asked me about our cat and how I was doing in class. Years later, he played those tapes for us. Wow! Once again, I thought it was funny to hear our voices on tape. I always thought mine was much lower on tape than in real life.

One summer my Aunt Barb, Uncle Ben and cousins from Ohio came to visit us. Our family had all kinds of fun plans for us while they were in town. We took them to Disneyland as they had never been before.

Some of my favorite rides were The Matterhorn Bobsleds, the Haunted Mansion, Tom Sawyer Island and Pirates of the Caribbean. You needed those coupons in the 70's and the "E" ticket was the highest designation for those popular attractions and the best rides! My mother was a fan of, It's a Small World in FANTASYLAND; me, not so much, especially as I got older. The Jungle Cruise in ADVENTURELAND required an "E" ticket. I really thought those hippos were real too.

Us kids had all decided that we would take the raft over to Tom Sawyer Island; it was the only place where we could explore and roam freely. The island featured a shipwreck with a bridge at the top. There was a fort with lots of caves to explore. As I was going from cave to cave I smelled this earthy aroma inside of them, to me it smelled like rope burning only this was not rope burning but rolled up cigarettes. Marijuana. Did I partake? No, I was too young and only just learned about drugs in school. My older cousin MJ was always smoking those homemade joints and cigarettes when we would take walks after a family get together. My mom used to say if you smoke pot you will go on to harder drugs. I always hated to hear those cliches.

Another Perspective: Julie (My Sister)

My amazing sister Jeanne is only 13 months older than me. Mom said it was almost like having twins.

We did everything together when we were young, including Mom dressing us the same or close to the same. We both took guitar lessons and Jeanne played the flute as well! Or at least tried to. LOL!

When we were a little bit older, we were always acting and performing with our little piano. We played and sang with fake microphones in the backyard, pretending we were movie stars!

We had a blast with our neighbor friends and our sister, Joelle, who was 5 years younger. We played softball, roller skated in the streets, and rode our bikes to the "liquor store." LOL! It was actually our go-to candy store. Jeanne was always dominating the conversation. She was so funny and loud!

At night in our bedroom, we would often make up stories and pretend to be famous people. One in particular that I remember was her pretending to be Howard Cosell, a professional commentator for boxing, and Jeanne would say, "And in this corner, we have Butter Balls." with Howard Cosell's New York accent. We were laughing so loud and having fun until we fell asleep!

We played softball together from fourth and fifth grade until we graduated from high school. The first team we were on was called the Polka Dot Pennies. Jeanne was a terrific softball player, playing pitcher and anywhere she was needed, as she was very good at playing softball and sports! Our last team that we played on was for our dad (Pete) and Gus, who coached "the pros' team." We both were selected to be All-Stars that last year!

In high school, Jeanne was kind of a wild child. She would jump out our bedroom window late at night so she could go visit her boyfriend, driving in her hot rod Barracuda! She ordered me to cover her loud car by going into the bathroom and counting to 17 before I flushed, so the toilet noise would cover the roaring V8 engine! So as not to get busted by our parents, I would put a '70s wig Mom had worn in Jeanne's twin bed on the pillow under the sheets and blankets. So, if my mom came in, she would see that Jeanne was supposedly sleeping in her bed!

When Jeanne graduated from high school at age 18, she moved out and worked at McDonald's, for a short time wearing their hideous lime green work uniform! Sometime after that, we were picked to play extras in the movie industry for low budget films. One in particular was called *No Retreat, No Surrender*.

Soon after that, Jeanne auditioned for a part in the *GLOW* girls' upcoming new wrestling show. Jeanne was picked out of hundreds of girls to play the character of "Hollywood." Her dreams of being a star finally came true!

She also played parts in the movie *Sister Act* with Whoopi Goldberg and the movie *Son in Law* with Pauly Shore!

Jeanne is an amazing wrestler and trains all the time to stay strong and in shape!

I remember one time I watched her do this amazing stunt where she ran up to her opponent and did a scissor kick up in the air and, with her legs wrapped around her opponent's neck, took her down to the floor. It was incredible!

She still works hard at her *GLOW* career, doing one-on-one wrestling, going to comic cons and wrestling conventions – where she sells *GLOW* merchandise – and cruising with *GLOW* girls and fans. Also, she is brilliant in her own soap making business and sells her beautiful, natural soaps to many other businesses and does online sales. She has lived an amazing life, living out her dreams, and has traveled around the world doing the things she loves most!

Chapter 6: Adolescence and Dating

In the seventh grade, I joined a volleyball team that played on Saturday mornings, so that was another sport to keep me busy. One of my teammates was a girl named Tammy Radecki, and we became really, really good friends. We did the usual junior high girl activities, like shopping, going to the movies, and having sleepovers, when we'd stay up real late and watch *Saturday Night Live* or *Don Kirshner's Rock Concert*. Tammy, her brothers, and her mom (her divorced dad didn't live with them) were really into professional sports. Not surprisingly, she was an L.A. Rams and Dodgers fan. In the late '70s, Tammy's mom would often take us to Dodger Stadium. Before long I knew most of the players' names and positions: First base was Steve Garvey, second base: Davey Lopes, pitcher: Tommy John, third base: Ron Cey. The outfielders were Dusty Baker, Rick Monday, and Reggie Smith.

Now, it was always better to sleep over at Tammy's house because her mom would go out on dates, and we would have the house to ourselves. Not only that, but we could stay out later than we could at my house. The rule at home was that we had to be inside by the time the light on the light post outside our house turned on. There were lots of rules and routines in my house: dusting, doing the dishes, sweeping the floor every night after dinner, and going to church every Sunday morning. I guess with all the trouble I was getting into at school, a little praying couldn't hurt, right?

Junior high can be a rough time, what with puberty, adolescence, and all that good stuff. Now we live in a time when cyberbullying is pretty prevalent. I guess I might have been a bullying victim, but back then we didn't call it that. Every time I got my hair cut, the boys would make fun of me. I hated that! Plus, I had thick, curly hair, and frequent haircuts meant more teasing and name-calling. My dad got something called a "Hot Comb" as a gift one time, and I tried to use it to straighten my hair with no luck whatsoever. There were even some boys who chased me home from school once in a while, if you can believe it – one of whom was Chris, the boy I had a crush on in first grade. Hmmm, I wonder what all the boys who made fun of my looks would say if they saw the pictures I shot for *Playboy* years later.

All that teasing took place in the third grade, and in junior high school, it started happening even more. Like a lot of kids, I had braces. I even had to wear headgear. Do kids today even know what that is? You can imagine the nicknames: "Brace Face," "Iron Jaw," and (my personal favorite) "Metal Mouth." You get the picture.

Girls at that age hit their growth spurts before boys, and I was growing so fast it was hard for my mom to keep finding clothes that fit me. On the first day of junior high, a boy pointed to my pants – which ended several inches above my ankles – and asked, "Where's the flood?" I told my mom that day, "I am never wearing these pants again!" Kids can be so mean.

It bothered me a lot at the time, but I guess I was lucky. I might have gotten teased and bullied at school, but it stopped when I got home. We didn't have iPhones, iPads, computers, X, TikTok, Instagram, or Facebook to keep us connected 24/7. We had the landline phone at home – and I was limited on how long I could talk on that – and that was it. Well, OK, we had Atari, too, and I enjoyed playing games like *Combat*, *Indy 500*, and *Missile Command*. But the kind of cyberbullying we see today didn't exist back when I was young.

I also learned a lot more about music in middle school, especially rock and roll. In the seventh grade I sat next to a boy in class who had "Led Zeppelin," "AC/DC," and "KISS" written all over his Pee-Chee folders. I was so intrigued. When I asked him about Led Zeppelin, I said, "Who is he?" He replied "HE?" and laughed at me. "It's a band!" I felt stupid, but that didn't stop me from listening to Led Zeppelin. I absolutely *loved* this band. Their sound was like a drug … so addictive! The Doors also had that same effect on me.

And the music back then was awesome. There was no MTV yet, so when you heard these bands on the radio, you fell in love with the song, not what the artists may have looked like.

I listened to 94.7 KMET every chance I got, and I started up a collection of 45s and albums that I still have today. The first 45 record I bought was "Bungle in the Jungle" by Jethro Tull, and the first album I bought was *Wild Cherry* by Wild Cherry. "Play that funky music, white boy" … you better believe it! I bought every Led Zeppelin album I could get my hands on. AC/DC, Aerosmith, April Wine, Black Sabbath, Boston, The Cars, The Clash, David Bowie, The Doors, Fleetwood Mac, Foreigner, Heart, Jethro Tull, KISS, Kansas, Missing Persons, The Pretenders, Rolling Stones, Queen, The Who. These were the bands whose albums I got from 1976 to 1981.

For those wondering, some of my favorite albums of all time are (in no particular order):

1. *Led Zeppelin*: Led Zeppelin
2. *Van Halen* – Van Halen
3. *Alive II*: KISS
4. *L.A. Woman*: The Doors
5. *Houses Of The Holy:* Led Zeppelin
6. *Aerosmith*: Aerosmith
7. *Out of the Cellar*: Ratt
8. *Slave to the Grind*: Skid Row
9. *No Rest for the Wicked*: Ozzy Osbourne
10. *Animals*: Pink Floyd
11. *Paranoid*: Black Sabbath
12. *RCMC*: RCMC (Rock City Machine Co.) – More on this one later!

As for KISS, they may have been the biggest band in the world in the late '70s. Everybody who was anybody was into KISS: KISS hats, KISS belt buckles, KISS T-shirts, KISS dolls … all of which I still collect today. You name it, we had it. My very first concert at age 16 was (don't laugh) The Kinks. It was a fun concert, but I couldn't help noticing that most of the fans were older than I was and wore glasses. My second concert featured The Who and The Clash. Now that was more like it! The venue was outdoors – at the Coliseum near USC. The music was ROCKING, and I was in heaven. As I walked around that venue, I noticed all the good-looking guys. Boy, did I want to be a part of this scene!

My boyfriend in junior and senior high school was named Tony. He had brown hair and light eyes, and as a star basketball and football player, he was quite the catch. Unfortunately, that didn't make me too many friends with the girls; they all wanted Tony to date them, not me. I soon found out that girls could be just as mean as boys, only in different ways. With the boys there was name-calling and teasing, but with the girls, it was a lot more subtle: rumors, gossip, all that sneaky behind-the-back stuff. Oh, well ... in a way, it helped me prepare for my future career. Nowadays, instead of competing with other girls for Tony's affection, I compete with other women for acting, modeling, and stunt jobs.

Our first date was when I turned 16. He told my parents that we were going to see a movie we got in his El Camino only we didn't go to the movies, we drove straight to our junior high school playground, where we hung out with all his guy friends. This would be my first introduction to partying and drinking my first beer. Tony and I wound up dating all throughout high school. He was always going to concerts without me, though. He once told me, when I said I wanted to go see Queen, that the fans have sex in the aisles. I thought to myself, *Hmmm ... maybe he's the one having sex in the aisles!* What a bunch of crap. He didn't want me going to concerts. Not to throw Tony under the bus, but he was very jealous.

One of my favorite memories in junior high is heading into our lunch cafeteria, where the jukebox would be playing cool songs. Every time I hear "Dance with Me" by Orleans. I think of junior high. My grandmother always told me that I dressed like Cher. My favorite outfit was this yellow and white seersucker cropped top showing my belly button and pants to match with my wooden platform shoes. Heck I still dress like that today!

In October 1981, my Uncle Alan, Mom's stepbrother, had an extra ticket to see the Rolling Stones at the Coliseum. When he asked if I wanted to go, I jumped at the chance. Of course, I wanted to go! I rushed to tell Tony the good news and he said, "If you go, I'm breaking up with you."

"Well, I guess we're breaking up, because I'm not missing this," I replied. I called his bluff, but we didn't break up, and he eventually started taking me to concerts with him.

I bought my first concert T-shirt at that Stones show. It had a fire-breathing dragon on the front. I got a tour program, too. At that show, Prince was the opening act, and believe it or not, he got booed off the stage. People threw trash and all kinds of things at his band. My friend Tammy and I had different opinions in this area. While I was discovering hard rock and heavy metal, Tammy was into the Beach Boys and drooling over players for the Los Angeles Rams. She liked those 28 to 30-year-olds. I was more into guys my own age, like Tony.

I actually thought Tony and I would get married. We dated throughout high school, but eventually broke up after graduation. It just wasn't meant to be. After going to those concerts and seeing what was out there, I felt I could never marry anyone from my school. There was more to the world than my little suburban corner of SoCal.

We had lots of fun while it lasted, though. He'd pick me up in his El Camino and we'd go out to eat, getting served alcohol even though we were only 18. There was a restaurant called the China Trader, which served Polynesian/Chinese food. It was really dark inside there, and they never asked us for ID. My favorite drink was called the Piwi, and it was served in a pineapple. We'd go to the beach, to parties, wherever we thought we'd have a good time. My father reacted, I suppose, like any normal father does when his oldest daughter starts to date. I remember one time I was getting ready to leave the house, only to have my dad order me to put on a bra. I didn't see the point, as I was only a 32B at the time. I knew I wasn't going to win that argument, though, so I put on a bra, left the house, and then took it off as soon as I got into my car.

And what a sweet car it was: a 1973 Plymouth Barracuda with a white body, a black top, Corvette lights, and a Led Zeppelin sticker on the back window. Pretty sweet, if I do say so myself! It wasn't new when my dad bought it for me; in fact, it was Army green with a cream-colored top. The inside of the car was a white leather interior but it had this really funky smell like BO that I could never get out of for the life of me. I felt like the coolest kid on earth driving this car. It was super fast. My dad did a side job for my best friend, Suzy's, dad, and in return he painted my car and fixed it up real nice. I could still get it going pretty fast when I needed to. (Not that I ever broke the speed limit to make it home by curfew, of course.)

I swore I'd never sell that car, but for some reason, I did. I wound up buying a smaller, cheaper car with the money I made, but it wasn't the same. I guess we all do crazy things when we're young.

As far as I was concerned, high school was much better than junior high. For one thing, those braces were off. And my hair was longer and straighter now. I had lots of friends, both the popular kids and the not-so-popular ones. I guess I liked being in the "middle" so I could hang out with all sorts of people. Suzy had a pool, so obviously we spent a lot of time there. I was at her house when I saw *The Exorcist* for the first time. Nothing says "friends forever" like a movie about demonic possession and projectile vomiting, right? *The Exorcist* came out in 1973, but it wasn't until 1977 or '78 when I saw it. After that, Suzy and I saw our first R-rated flick in a theater with my parents: *Phantasm*. *Halloween* with Jamie Lee Curtis was another film I liked. I was a rock and roll, horror movie chick. Whenever we could, we would head out to the theater. Tony and I made it to a midnight showing of Led Zeppelin's *The Song Remains the Same*. We were underage, but someone snuck in a bottle of Southern Comfort, which somewhat enhanced our cinematic experience.

Suzy was a junior varsity cheerleader, but that wasn't my thing. It's not that I didn't have school spirit; I just wanted to be able to spend my free time hanging out with friends instead of cheering at football games. And we definitely went to our share of parties … probably more than our share. On Friday and Saturday nights, these parties took place on Clark Street at the home of the Ziegler triplets. Their mom and dad had moved out of state for a job, and therefore there were no parents at their house.

Sometimes people would cut class and head over there to hide out and party. Like a lot of hard-rocking high school kids, it's just what you did. We drank and smoked a little bit. Not smart, of course, but what can I say – we were kids. I learned the hard way that drinking too much could lead to puking your guts out in your boyfriend's El Camino. I'm sure we had a fight about that one. Oh well, at least I felt better after I puked!

Even with all the time I spent working, partying, and hanging out with my friends, there was still time for family. After eighth grade graduation, my mom and dad decided to take us on a long, cross-country trip … by car! Remember *National Lampoon's Vacation*? Dad certainly had some things in common with Clark Griswold. Dad went to the Chevy dealership and bought a brand-new Kingswood Estate station wagon, right out of the store's front window. It was white with brown paneling on the side and a brown faux leather interior, complete with that new car smell. We were off!

We saw a lot of amazing sites as we headed east. The Grand Canyon was pretty awesome. The Grand Canyon National Park, in northern Arizona, encompasses 278 miles of the Colorado River and adjacent uplands. Located on the ancestral homeland of 11 Associated Tribes, the Grand Canyon is one of the most spectacular examples of erosion anywhere in the world. That dark orange color is quite a sight.

We went on a little tour and saw Indians doing an authentic rain dance. I thought to myself, *There's no way it's going to rain*. But within two minutes, the sky turned black and it started raining cats and dogs. We ran as fast as we could to our station wagon parked in the lot. Thank goodness we had plenty to eat in our coolers. Mom made lunch while dad drove through the typhoon-like storm.

Next, it was off to the Painted Desert/Petrified Desert which is located in northern Arizona. This was not as visual as the Grand Canyon, but we did see rocks that had pictographs painted on them. We also went to Meteor Crater in Arizona that day. That night we stayed at a Holiday Inn that mom had booked through the AAA book. The next day we saw Carlsbad Caverns located in the Guadalupe mountains in southeastern New Mexico which were literally 500 feet underground. The temperature was very, very cool, and the place had a weird smell, which our tour guide explained was bat guano (or droppings). Inside the caverns I found a little gift shop and purchased a postcard to send to a friend.

Our first stop in Texas was a town called Sweetwater, where we stayed at a Holiday Inn and swam in their nice, cool pool. The next morning, we hit the Alamo in San Antonio and Dealey Plaza – where JFK was shot – in Dallas. You know how they say everything's bigger in Texas? I have to agree – at least, considering the fact that I came across the biggest cockroaches I've ever seen when we drove down through Rio Grande City. Yikes! On a more positive note, Mom had some relatives in that area that we visited. In fact, the main reason we took the trip was to get together with our relatives for the annual Basone Reunion. My mom's side of the family lived in Texas, while my dad's side lived in Ohio. So, after leaving Texas, we drove up to Ohio. We had a great time at the family reunion, including spending some time with my great-grandmother, Nuncia – "Nunny" for short – (Farando) Scafiti, who would eventually live to be 103 years old! Good for her! I hope that means I'm going to live that long.

Speaking of family history, my grandmother, Sonti – whom everyone called "Sunni" – was quite the looker in her day. She did some modeling, and even won a swimsuit competition sponsored by Goodrich Tires. I've seen pictures of her in one of her early 1900s one-piece bathing suits, and I'm guessing that *lots* of boys came calling back in the day. Little did Sunni know that her granddaughter would be turning heads in a bikini almost 100 years later. Thanks for the genes, Grandma!

After the reunion, we started back on the road to sunny Southern California. The highlight of our return trip was a stop at Mount Rushmore. Actually, it was the highlight for everyone but me. I picked up a flu bug somewhere along the way, and I spent most of the journey puking into rest stop toilets while my family did the tourist thing. Believe me, road trips in the family car are no fun when you have a stomach flu. I felt a little bit better by the time we made it to Yellowstone National Park. The park is open 24 hours and is home to a variety of animal species, including bears, wolves, bison, elk, and antelope. We saw colorful hot springs, bubbling mud pots, and spouting geysers. We also took a ride through Grand Teton National Park. I need to get back to Yellowstone someday; it was absolutely beautiful. However, leaning over Old Faithful was not the smartest thing to do. Have you ever smelled sulfur? To put it mildly, sulfur smells like rotten hard boiled eggs. After that, we headed south to the "biggest little city" of Reno, Nevada. We zipped through Reno pretty quickly, as our trip was ending, and school would be starting soon we then drove down through the redwoods.

As much as I enjoyed spending time with my family, it was good to be home again. The rest of the summer flew by, and before we knew it, I was on to high school.

Chapter 7: "The French Fry Queen," "The Watermelon Queen," and "Miss Winston Tire"

I guess you could say I was a "straight-B" student in high school. I think I was smart enough to have been "straight-A," but I just wanted to do more with my free time than study. B's were good enough for me. I thought eventually I would go to college and start getting those A's but grades weren't the most important things in my world during high school.

I was, however, always getting top marks in Foods class. I guess it was either my appreciation of fine Italian cuisine or maybe I was just more motivated because of all the cute boys taking the class – probably a combination of both. I even took Woodshop and Auto classes just to be closer to the boys. I made a cutting board, but it didn't exactly come out very straight. I still thought it looked pretty cool, though, in my humble opinion.

I did a lot of babysitting during my high school years. I loved earning money so I could buy my own clothes from my favorite stores at the mall, like Contempo, Judy's and Miller's Outpost.

When I turned 16, my dad decided that I was going to get a job. He gave me a month to figure out what I wanted to do. Obviously, I was way too young to jump into the pro wrestling profession at the time – not that I knew the first thing about wrestling back then – so I did what any self-respecting, ordered-to-get-a-job teenager would do in that situation: nothing. In fact, I procrastinated for almost the whole month my dad gave me. Then, at the last minute, I marched into the nearest fast-food joint – a McDonald's – and filled out an application. Luckily (or unluckily, depending on how you look at it), they hired me. The good news was that I had a steady paycheck coming in. The bad news was that I now had a new nickname: "The French Fry Queen!" Great. At least I didn't have braces anymore.

My first instinct was to quit, but somebody had to pay for my Barracuda's gas, right? Eventually, I was "promoted" to taking orders and then to working the drive-thru window. The drive-thru was the best because I could hide in there when things were slow and no one would bother me.

I worked eight hours a day on Saturdays and Sundays, so my weekends – like most teenagers trying to make money – were now screwed! I also worked four hours a day, three days a week after school. Because of this, I didn't have a lot of spare time to hang out with my friends.

Even though I had a boyfriend, I did have a small crush on a boy that cooked the hamburgers. I can't remember his name, and he did not go to my school. Neither did any of the other kids, for that matter. If I hadn't waited so long, I would have done my due diligence and found another job farther away from my school. On the weekends, kids came through the drive-thru, ordering food and heading to the beach. But not me, I was stuck at this job. Some of those kids, mainly girls, would make fun of me. The boys would come in after school before heading to concerts. I remember being heartbroken when my friends Steve, Danny, and Bill came in and told me they were on their way to see Marshall Tucker – and there I was, stuck on fry duty.

One day as I was taking an order – dressed in my green and white uniform, hair pulled back, and white official-looking cap on – I asked the customer, "How may I help you?" With disgust on his face, he replied, "Why don't you buy your boyfriend a hamburger? It looks like he's hungry!" At first, I didn't know what he meant by that comment, but then I realized he had seen the hickey on my neck. I was so embarrassed I think I turned ten different shades of red!

It seemed like every week this one long-haired, blond, older dude would drive through in his blue van and flirt with me. I always felt uncomfortable when he drove in. He reminded me of a weirdo – maybe a rapist, even? In any case, he really creeped me out. You know the feeling you get in your stomach when something doesn't feel right? Well, that's the feeling I always got when he came through the drive-thru. Now, I am an avid fan of "murder porn." You know the television show *Forensic Files*? He reminds me of one of those perpetrators. If you're reading this today, I'm sorry if I misjudged you, dude, but you creeped me right out!

There was another time when we had a special promotion where you had to get the customer's order within 60 seconds. However, I was too busy socializing with the other kids while I was getting someone's order, and I didn't realize I had exceeded 60 seconds. He looked at me while I was handing him his food and said, "So do I get my order for free?" I didn't even remember that promotion was going on. I still remember how embarrassed that left me.

It was around the time of this promotion that I noticed, when some of the kids were on break, they would secretly smoke pot outside or in the basement. I think I took a hit once on a break. Maybe that's why I couldn't get the guy's order to him in 60 seconds! During this same time, I noticed that two of the male employees were taking $20 bills out of the cash drawer and replacing them with counterfeit ones. I didn't want to get involved, so I played stupid when the manager asked us about what was going on. I was not a narc – never was, and never will be.

While I was cleaning up one afternoon, I found a wallet on the floor. *Hmmm … should I take it? Or should I just leave it for someone else to find?* I probably just should have turned it in, but I didn't. I took the wallet into the bathroom and opened it up. It had a license from Boston, Massachusetts and two $100 bills in it. Being a young kid, I took the cash, put the wallet in the mailbox, and used the cash to buy my prom tickets and some paraphernalia. Looking back, this seems like such a stupid thing to do. But, hey … working for $3.10 per hour, it would have taken me weeks to buy those tickets on my own.

When I got off work, I would go visit my boyfriend and, boy, did I smell like burgers and fries! Even though it wasn't an ideal job, I guess it was good for me in the long run. Ever since my days as "The French Fry Queen," I've always appreciated the value of an education … and a hard day's work! And, unlike that one time, returning someone's money!

My senior year, I was voted "Best Looking" student, which completely took me by surprise. Both of my sisters would be voted "Best Looking," too, so I guess we have Grandma Sunni's genes to thank for that. Speaking of contests, my father is a Lifetime NRA member. One summer, he nominated me for the title of Queen in a festival called The Watermelon Festival, which the NRA was involved with. *What the hell is a watermelon queen*? I thought. All I could think about is women with big breasts, and I certainly didn't have very much in that department.

Anyway, I won and earned the title "The Watermelon Queen." Later, I would work for Sam Winston's Tire Company and become "Miss Winston Tire." It was very flattering to win those distinctions, although there are much more attractive titles than "The French Fry Queen," "The Watermelon Queen," and "Miss Winston Tire."

After graduation, I faced the same question that high school seniors face each and every spring, all across the country: "Now what?" I had always thought the entertainment business sounded like fun. After all, we did live in Southern California, and with my outgoing personality, I figured I'd have a good chance to make it. But how to break into the business? I hadn't quite figured that part out yet.

Another Perspective: Joelle (My Sister)

Jeanne, my older sister, was the epitome of cool. Since day one, she's been my guiding light, always there to lead the way and look out for me. I owe much of my love for rock music to her; she introduced me to Led Zeppelin, Black Sabbath, and AC/DC, playing their albums on repeat until they became the soundtrack of our lives. We even had plans to see Led Zeppelin in concert together in 1980, until tragedy struck with the untimely passing of John Bonham.

From our early days in grade school to junior high, Jeanne was a tomboy through and through. She didn't care about appearances; all that mattered was having a blast with our neighborhood crew, which included both boys and girls. Following her lead, my other sister, Julie, and I jumped into the mix, joining in on bike rides, roller skating, swimming lessons, tree climbing, and countless imaginative games. It was clear from the start that Jeanne had a knack for entertainment and was always eager to put on a show and make us laugh.

But high school brought about a transformation for Jeanne. She traded in her laid-back vibe for a more polished look, swapping Chuck for Tammy and Suzy, and capturing the attention of boys everywhere. Yet, amidst her newfound glamor, she never lost her competitive edge. Whether it was dominating on the volleyball court or leading her softball team, aptly named "Dyn-o-mite," Jeanne was a force to be reckoned with.

Her charm and athleticism didn't go unnoticed; she was voted "best looking" in our high school, a testament to her magnetic personality and undeniable appeal. Even during her stint as the "French Fry Queen" at McDonald's, she brought her trademark energy and humor to everything she did.

Looking back, it's clear that Jeanne was destined for greatness. Her passion for music, her adventurous spirit, and her unwavering confidence were just glimpses of the star she would become. As her little sister, I'll always be grateful for the memories we shared and the inspiration she continues to be in my life. Jeanne truly was the coolest sister anyone could ask for.

Another cherished memory I have of Jeanne involves her trusty 1973 Barracuda. It was a sunny afternoon, and Mom had tasked Jeanne with the responsibility of driving me to a friend's house. Little did Mom know that this mundane errand would turn into one of the most exhilarating experiences of my childhood.

As Jeanne revved up the engine of her beloved Barracuda, I couldn't contain my excitement. Here I was, riding shotgun in my sister's iconic car, feeling like the coolest kid on the planet. With the wind in our hair and the radio blasting our theme song, "Barracuda" by Heart, we embarked on our journey through the city streets.

But Jeanne had a mischievous streak, and as soon as we hit the open road, she unleashed her inner speed demon. With a mischievous grin, she floored the gas pedal, and suddenly we were flying down the streets at breakneck speed. I couldn't help but laugh with exhilaration as we zoomed past the parked cars and houses.

In that moment, Jeanne wasn't just my big sister; she was my partner in crime, showing me that sometimes it's okay to break the rules and live life in the fast lane. As we pulled up to my friend's house, I couldn't wipe the grin off my face.

Chapter 8: The World Beyond High School

Now that high school was over, I had to figure out what was next. Step one was definitely getting my own place and a decent job. I love my parents very much, but the thought of living under their rules at that stage did not appeal to me at all. But, in order to get my own place, I needed a better job. And by "better," I mean that it was going to have to be something that paid a little more than The French Fry Queen's hourly wage.

Luckily, Melissa (Bly) McSorely, whom I had played softball with in high school, had already found work at a local medical laboratory. Now, she was a smart cookie … and valedictorian at our high school, thank you very much! She put in a good word for me, and pretty soon I was the new receptionist at Clark-Sarver Lab in Burbank on Alameda Avenue. I put in a little time and, before I knew it, I had been promoted to the position of phlebotomist, a person who draws blood samples for medical tests. It's a little like being a vampire, but not quite as gruesome. The pay was much better than what I got for being a receptionist, so I was able to make rent payments on a small studio apartment about two miles from my childhood home and very close to work. It had a small kitchen in the back on the right-hand side and a small bathroom to the left. I even had my own parking spot, and it was all mine! Rent was $300 a month.

I became good at drawing blood. What I mean by that is people whose veins were hard to find always wanted me to be the one to draw their blood. I was able to find the vein without too much painful poking and searching. This was in the early 1980s, and AIDS had just been discovered. It was hard to see these men coming in week after week and not getting any better; they were deteriorating right in front of my eyes. It was so sad and scary at the same time. I remember one guy saying, "Please wear your gloves. You don't want to get what I have." Before AIDS, we never wore gloves.

I remember getting a series of vaccinations against things like Hepatitis B. Jaundiced two and three-day-old babies were being brought in, and I had to draw their blood. That was the worst. I had to prick the backs of their tiny feet and drain their blood into little tubes. All the while, these poor little babies were screaming bloody murder. The depressing thing about this job was that, even though we did draw blood for things like paternity testing and marriage licenses, most of the people who came in were really sick.

Eventually I graduated to the upstairs laboratory where the bioanalyst and the rest of the technicians were running the tests. Most of the tests could be done on-site, but more advanced testing was sent out to a laboratory called SmithKline. One day, the bioanalyst decided to play a trick on me. On this particular day, I was preparing a patient's stool sample – one of several stool samples in my area of the lab – for the bioanalyst to observe under the microscope. The bioanalyst opened one of the samples, smelled it … then took a huge bite! What the hell? I was totally grossed out until everyone else in the lab started laughing. Apparently they had filled that particular sample with apple butter, which, to the untrained eye, looks remarkably like a stool sample. Everyone was in on the joke except me.

I became very friendly with Lori Flynn, one of the employees that worked in the lab. Lori was dating the bioanalyst, Burt Sarver. Lori and I used to go out after work up to Castaways in the Burbank Hills and different bars for happy hour. Happy hour back then was really cool. They had a big smorgasbord of free appetizers; all you had to do was buy a cocktail (or two or three). I also was invited to go out with her and Burt. They lived in a beautiful condo right behind Bob's Big Boy on Riverside Drive. I frequently went out with them for happy hour after work to different bars and restaurants in the area. It was then that I discovered the joy of gin martinis. At that time, I drank them with Tanqueray gin, but I am not a gin martini drinker anymore. I prefer dirty martinis with blue cheese olives.

Lori had a brother named David, who was the drummer in a rock band back in Quincy, Massachusetts called Trapper. With his Boston accent, it sounded like he was saying, "Trappah." Like every other musician, model, and actor who had huge dreams of making it big, he was moving to California from the East Coast, and she was curious if I wanted to meet him. Sure, why not? My love for music hadn't diminished; in fact, it was stronger than ever. I remember seeing The Outlaws open for Black Sabbath at the Los Angeles Forum when I went with the other receptionist from the lab. Not sure why that kind of band would open up for a heavy metal band, but so be it; it was great. As it turned out, I met Lori's brother even sooner than I had expected. Believe it or not, his mom and dad moved into the house right across the street from my parents. Now how cool was that? I saw this guy even more after my folks became very good friends with his folks, meeting up at pool parties and other local social events and holidays.

One day while visiting my family, I saw David's van parked across the street. He happened to be outside, so I said hello. We hit it off instantly and started hanging together, which eventually led to officially dating. I attended many of his local gigs at places like FM Station, Madame Wong's, Gazzarri's, the Whisky, and the Roxy on Sunset Strip. The Rainbow Bar and Grill – or "The Bow" as locals called it – was a great hang. Every rock dude and rock chick went there to drink, hang, socialize, and party.

I loved the atmosphere of a live show – so much excitement, so much energy, so many interesting people to meet! I'd have to say that FM Station was among my favorites. It was close to home, plus I knew all the bouncers and bartenders, which helped in avoiding "little things" like paying a cover charge or waiting in a long line. Boy, did I love hanging at FM! It seemed I knew almost everyone there; it was like my *Cheers*, except with live music. Nick Menza, who went on to join Megadeth, was there a lot. He stood at the same place at the main bar all the time, and every time he saw me, he offered me a drink, which I gladly accepted.

I remember one night Paul Stanley and Gene Simmons from KISS were there, probably watching Tommy Thayer's band, Black 'N Blue. (Years later, Tommy would join KISS.) But I never gave those two the time of day because, like everyone else, I had heard all those rumors about how many women they had slept with. And I really didn't like older guys at all. I remember hearing about their interview on *Oprah* in the 1980s, where they boasted about all their sexual "conquests." I was never going to be one of those statistics. Gene finally said, "Young lady, why do you keep ignoring us?" I just smiled and kept walking. In my silent voice I was saying, "Nope, that's never going to happen."

Another time my friend, Ana Cartwright, came up to me at a club in the valley called the Reseda Country Club. The band Union was playing that night and members of KISS were there.

"There's a guy here who wants to meet you," Ana said.

I kept thinking to myself, *I hope it's not Gene Simmons*. Guess what? Sure enough, it was. I tried to be polite and brush him off nicely. Years later we would connect as friends and I would be featured in Gene Simmons' magazine, *Tongue*. (More on that a bit later. Thank you, Eric Singer, for making that happen!)

For whatever reason, I've never been interested in dating famous musicians just because they are famous musicians, especially the older ones. And it's always baffled me that so many gorgeous girls do that very thing. I'm sorry, but in my book, there has to be some kind of physical chemistry.

Along with attending the live shows, I was still collecting albums. One Halloween night, I went to our local record store called Licorice Pizza, which is now back in business in Studio City on Ventura Boulevard. I bought Black Sabbath's *Master of Reality* on vinyl. I still have it in my collection, and I have a pretty serious vinyl collection these days.

My experience with live bands wasn't limited to shows in bars; I also loved the big, outdoor, festival-type concerts. On Sunday, May 29, 1983, there was a huge festival over the Memorial Day weekend called the "US Festival." Billed as the biggest heavy metal event ever, it was sponsored by Apple co-founder Steve Wozniak and held at an open-air field and state-of-the-art temporary stage at Glen Helen Regional Park in Devore (later to become home to Blockbuster Pavilion and now the San Manuel Amphitheater, the largest amphitheater in the United States). You remember Woodstock, right? August 1969? Well, picture thousands of attendees outdoors in the hot sun – sweating, scantily clad young adults drinking, smoking, and taking illegal substances. I didn't care how long it took to get there; I was going to this concert by any means necessary. I don't remember telling my boyfriend that I wanted to go or even inviting him. I just knew I had to be there.

The first day was "New Wave," with bands like Divinyls, The English Beat, Oingo Boingo, The Stray Cats, Men at Work, and INXS. I kind of liked INXS, but I wasn't going to show up just to hear one band. The fourth day was strictly country; again, that wasn't the style of music I was into. The second day? Now *that* was a show I had to see: Van Halen, Ozzy Osbourne, the Scorpions, Mötley Crüe, Judas Priest, Quiet Riot, and Triumph. When I found out tickets were only $20, I was sold. Can you imagine paying that low of a price for all those great bands today?

I wound up going with Margi, a receptionist from work, and Wade, the son of the president of our company. Parking was crazy and nowhere remotely close to the venue. Tons of RVs were parked closer for people staying all four days. We got there around 11 a.m., but as we got closer to the venue, Margi said she felt woozy and had bad stomach cramps. After a bit, still lightheaded, she reluctantly turned back to the car, and that was the last we saw of her or the car for the remainder of the night. I was definitely concerned for her, but figured she'd sleep it off in the car and meet up with us later. Plus, with all those great bands, I intended on having a badass time, no matter what.

Wade and I, along with the thousands of other headbangers just like us, headed to the concert from the parking lot, which felt like it was miles away. Walking up a dirt hill, through a stream of water, we felt like a herd of cattle. People were actually mooing as we headed in! I remember seeing hippie-like people holding up signs about the drugs they were selling. It may have been the 1980s, but it certainly had a bit of the Woodstock 1960s feel. I always said I should have been born in the 1950s; I would have loved to have seen Jimi Hendrix, Led Zeppelin, The Doors, and Janis Joplin live.

Needless to say, the bands were amazing. Quiet Riot was already playing when we finally got in. Their set started at noon and they played five songs. Mötley Crüe was up next, and since I didn't really care about them, I sat down. Once I heard them play, though, I stood up and never sat back down for the rest of the day. Next was Ozzy Osbourne, whom I've always loved. They played twelve songs, all of which I knew and dug, ending with "Paranoid."

At this point, as I went to find a bathroom or a Porta Potty, I thought about where Margi might be, hoping I would run into her. But there were around 400,000 fans there that weekend – an absolutely stunning amount of people. Judas Priest's set included Rob Halford riding in on a Harley-Davidson before the encore. Their set was over an hour long, and they did twelve songs. Triumph came on at 6:10 p.m. At that time, it was still hot, but the sun was starting to go down a bit, taking the edge off the heat. It had been so hot out there that they had these huge "outdoor rain" nozzles that sprayed water to fight the hundred-degree heat. The girls were all dressed in bikini tops, shorts, skirts, tank tops, and jeans. I made the mistake of wearing these stupid, cute, gold sandals that tied around my ankles. Fashionable, but not practical – damn, they were cutting into my skin! What was I thinking? I should have worn my Nikes. Of course, had I known we'd have to park so far away, I would have selected more appropriate footwear.

Triumph was a little mellow for me, but they were followed by the Scorpions, who came on at almost 8:00 p.m. I remember some of the fans yelling for them to play "Arizona," presumably because they had come in from Arizona. I was waiting for them to play "The Zoo," which they did.

Then came Van Halen from 10:00 p.m. to midnight. They were pure fire! Little did I know that, 20-some years later, I would become good friends with Van Halen's mind-blowing photographer, Neil Zlozower. I would eventually go to visit Zloz's studio in Hollywood and make a beeline right over to his file cabinet to start looking at the thousands of pics he had taken: Zeppelin, Mötley, Ted Nugent, the Stones, Van Halen. They were all in there. Neil would let me pick out any shot I wanted and blow it up for me. These were old, so we are talking about film negatives, not digital images. I now have several of Zloz's pics in my home. Thank you, my friend!

Anyway, back to the concert. Van Halen did twenty songs: "Unchained," "Runnin' with the Devil," "Jamie's Cryin'," "Ain't Talkin' 'bout Love" … all the hits. They finished their encores (with fireworks, pyrotechnics, the whole nine yards) around midnight. We had been there for more than twelve hours of non-stop rock. I was beat, but thrilled, filthy, and starting to get cold; the temperature dropped considerably once the sun went down. Now there was just the small matter of getting home. Margi had long since split on us, and despite our best efforts at hitchhiking, no one would pick us up. Who wants to pick up a girl with her guy friend behind her?

At 2:00 in the morning, pitch black, in the middle of nowhere, we still had no way home. Finally, Wade walked up to a residence and called his folks. Remember, this was before the convenience of cell phones. By the time Wade's parents showed up, it was daylight, and we were sleeping on the side of the road next to the freeway exit. God, I was a mess – tired, hungover, and dirty, but happy we had a ride home. Then, Wade's parents rode in like the cavalry. They took us out for breakfast, and it wound up being a happy ending to a long day of great music and one of my greatest moments in rock and roll history.

Things were going pretty well in my life. I had my own place, gainful employment, and a boyfriend who was just as into music as I was. What else could I want? Well, in the back of my mind, I was still thinking about the entertainment industry. To be honest, getting into "the business" had always been a goal of mine. With my looks and personality, I figured I'd be a natural. But whenever I mentioned these aspirations to my parents, they were pretty lacking in enthusiasm. I think they were caught in that parenting trap where they wanted to support me, but would have liked to have seen me get into a profession that was a little more stable. To their credit, though, they never openly discouraged me; so at least inside, my dream was alive.

At a pretty young age (9 or 10, I think), I had set three career goals: 1) to act, 2) to be photographed for *Playboy* magazine, and 3) to present an Academy Award. I really liked actresses like Tatum O'Neal, Jodie Foster, and Kristy McNichol, as well as the kids on *The Brady Bunch* and *The Partridge Family*, and figured if they can do it, why can't I? As for *Playboy*, I didn't actually look inside one until years later, but they were always behind the counter at liquor stores and convenience stores, and you didn't have to be that old to figure out what they were about. I felt that the women on the covers looked beautiful. As for the Oscar, I thought that presenting an Academy Award would be such an important and glamorous thing to do in front of a room full of your peers. Everyone would be stunningly attractive and dressed to the nines, and I felt I could do a great job reading out, "And the winner is …" while everyone waited with bated breath.

What's funny is that usually when kids set goals at that young of an age, they're basically pipe dreams – unrealistic goals that you laugh about later in life. I wonder how many 10-year-old boys have dreamed of hitting a home run to win the World Series for their favorite team? As of this writing, my first two goals have been accomplished. The third one? Well, Oscar hasn't come knocking … yet. Still, to quote Meat Loaf, "Two out of three ain't bad!"

I remember my first professional photo shoot in North Hollywood. I needed headshots for my acting auditions. I put together blue jeans, heels, and an assortment of shirts to wear. Boy, was I naive. I was nervous but confident about myself. That is, until the photographer started taking pictures and blurted out that I had "a wide nose." Oh, geez! What did that mean? My confidence was rattled just like that. Probably not a good comment to make to a young girl starting out in the business. You should build one's self-confidence, not tear it down. I would love to find him today. I could really show him what a wide nose looks like after I get done with him.

My second shoot was much better. This woman was so cool! She did my hair and makeup and made me look really pretty. She handed me a straw to sip my drink through so my lipstick wouldn't smudge. To this day, I drink everything out of a straw, even beer. These shots came out so much better. Now I was ready to find an agent.

Yep, I was bitten by the entertainment bug, and it was an itch I couldn't stop scratching. Some of my friends had worked as "background artists" (also called "extras," the people you see in the background of a movie, television show, or commercial), which sounded like a good way to break in. I signed up with Atmosphere Casting in Los Angeles, and they started to call me for work almost immediately. The only problem was that attending some of these casting calls was infringing on my time at the medical lab. As you can imagine, my boss wasn't too thrilled about that. Unfortunately, being an extra didn't pay well enough for me to quit my day job, so it seemed like my dreams of joining the entertainment industry were just out of my reach.

That is, until I received the casting call that would change my career, and life, forever!

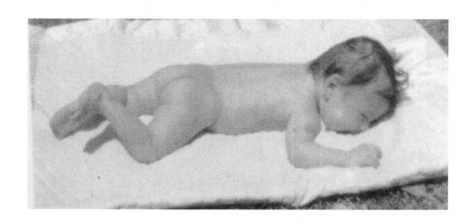

Baby Hollywood Jeanne in 1963.

Top left: Grandma Carney. **Top right:** Grandpa and Grandma Basone.
Bottom: Yes, I did go to Bret Harte Elementary!

BURBANK UNIFIED SCHOOL DISTRICT
Burbank, California

KINDERGARTEN PROGRESS REPORT

Name _____

School _____

Year 19_68_ —19_69_

SCHOOL ADJUSTMENT	FIRST REPORT	SECOND REPORT
Accepts responsibility	G	G
Begins and finishes work	S	G
Follows directions	S	G
Respects authority	G	G
Respects the rights of other children	G	G
Works and plays cooperatively	S	G
Works independently	S	S

EXPLANATION OF MARKS

G — Very Good   S — Satisfactory   N — Needs to Improve

KNOWLEDGES AND SKILLS	FIRST REPORT	SECOND REPORT
READING READINESS		
Enjoys poetry and stories	S	S
Listens attentively	G	G
Expresses ideas clearly	S	S
Speaks distinctly	S	S
Participates in discussions	S	S
Recognizes likenesses and differences of shapes, colors	S	G
MATHEMATICS Understands beginning numbers	S	G
MUSIC Participates in singing and rhythms	S	G
ART Participates in art activities	S	S
HEALTH and PHYSICAL ACTIVITIES		
Practices good health habits	S	S
Shows physical coordination	S	S

FIRST REPORT

SECOND REPORT

Teacher _____   Parent Mrs. Peter Rasona

Teacher Merle Onstott   Assigned to Grade _1_   Room No. _15_

Me as a first grader with my stellar report card.

Me as a second grader and a Brownie with mom. I still have my Brownie book!

Top: Some fond memories of camping. **Bottom:** Camping with Chucky, Mike, Robby, their cousins, my sister, Marty, and Mac the dog.

Disneyland 1975.

Top: 4th and 5th grade. **Bottom:** Team photos from the Dyn-o-mite and the Polkadot Pennies.

Top: Team Dyn-o-mite. **Bottom:** Halloween High school with Julie, Tammy, and Teresa.

Top: Tony Davis & me 9th grade dance. **Bottom:** my '73 Barracuda!

63

Top left: Vacation in the Painted Desert **Top right:** Voted best looking.
Bottom: The Watermelon Queen.

Top: My first high school photo shoot by Jerry. With boyfriend Dave Flynn in 1984. **Bottom:** Christmas.

With my friend, photographer Neil Zlozower.

Top: Mom and Dad on their wedding day and a day at the beach.
Bottom: Christmas 1968.

Top: Grandma Basone. **Bottom:** Another early photo shoot.

PART II

FROM A LAB TO A RING, IT WAS FLY OR CRASH
BUT WITH LOOKS THAT KILL AND GUTS TO MATCH
I TOOK OFF LIKE I KNEW I COULD
HELLO, WORLD, MEET HOLLYWOOD!

Chapter 9: The Audition

I had come home for lunch and there was a message on my answering machine from Atmosphere Casting. It was about an audition. The casting call was for a "sports entertainment show." I was curious. What exactly does the term "sports entertainment show" mean? I didn't know what this was all about, but it seemed like as good a way as any to break into show business. Plus, I would be able to participate because the audition was being held at 6 p.m., after my day job ended. That was key, because if the casting call had taken place during normal business hours, I might never have gone to it, and who knows what I'd be doing today? Surely not writing this book!

I called the casting agency back to confirm and get more details. I was told to wear something I could work out in. I packed a bag with exercise stuff, grabbed my headshot and resume, and took them all back to work. Once 5 p.m. struck, I headed for the restroom down the hall and changed into my audition outfit. My heart was racing, and yes, I was very nervous … as nervous as a cat in a room full of rocking chairs! This would be my first big audition. I drove to the Hyatt on Sunset Boulevard in Hollywood to see what was up.

There were hundreds of girls there, which was a little intimidating. David McLane and his business partner stood at the front of the huge conference room where we had all gathered, and they told us they were looking for twelve girls to star in a syndicated show about women's wrestling.

Well, about one-third of the girls got up and left when they heard that; I guess they didn't want to mess up their makeup or break a nail. To be honest, I was a little concerned, too, but decided to stick around. After all, I had played lots of sports in the past and, if this was a chance to break into the industry, then what did I have to lose? When you're young, you're fearless. I thought I was ready to take on the challenge, nerves be damned.

David McLane had grown up in Indiana and had been a big wrestling fan. He used to run the Dick the Bruiser fan club. Dick the Bruiser took David under his wing and taught him all about pro wrestling promotion, marketing, and announcing, and David had decided he wanted to run his own all-women's wrestling promotion. Dick the Bruiser ran the World Wrestling Association out of Indianapolis, but he wasn't interested in pushing women's wrestling, so David set out on his own. He somehow got together with Meshulam Riklis, a multimillionaire businessman who owned the Riviera Hotel and Casino in Las Vegas. Riklis also owned the Fabergé line of cosmetics, which became GLOW's biggest sponsor.

Riklis put David in touch with Matt Cimber. At the time, Matt was a producer, writer, and director in Hollywood, and he already had a relationship with Riklis. Matt is a fascinating guy. He was the last husband of actress Jayne Mansfield, having married her in 1964 and divorced her in 1966. They had one son together, Tony, who later became an assistant director for GLOW and played the part of Jungle Boy, the boyfriend of Jungle Woman (Annette Marroquin), in the first season. Matt had a background in theater and transitioned into genre films during the 1970s, working on movies like The Candy Tangerine Man and The Witch Who Came from the Sea. In 1982, he wrote, directed, and produced the film Butterfly starring Pia Zadora. The film was panned by critics, but it earned Zadora a controversial Golden Globe for Best Female Newcomer. She also earned a Golden Raspberry Award for Worst Actress that same year for the same role.

Pia Zadora was married to Riklis at the time, and Riklis thought that Cimber could add some sizzle to McLane's women's wrestling project. Cimber added the comedy sketches and rap songs to GLOW. To McLane, the campy bits were probably a necessary evil. Riklis had the money and connections, and Cimber had the Hollywood background and relationships. If the show was ever going to get off the ground, Riklis, Cimber, and McLane were going to have to work together.

All of the girls who stayed at the casting call were asked to state their name, background, experience, etc. into the camera and then sign up for training. At first, I was a bit camera shy. But I gathered up my courage and some intestinal fortitude, battled past the lingering inhibitions, and wrote down my name for the wrestling training. I didn't know it at the time, but the show would eventually be called G.L.O.W., an acronym for Gorgeous Ladies of Wrestling.

I told my friends about the audition, and they were all pretty excited about it. Well, not quite all of them. My boyfriend at the time, Dave, didn't seem too enthusiastic. I wasn't sure why. Maybe because he wanted to make it in show biz before me, so maybe he was a tad jealous? I could tell he was discouraged and didn't want me to go to the training, so I didn't. It's not like I'd had my heart set on being a professional wrestler my whole life or anything. I figured there would always be other chances to become an actress, so why rock the boat?

A couple of weeks passed, and I didn't give it a whole lot of thought. Then one day my roommate, Rick, asked me, "What ever happened with that wrestling audition?" When I told him I had dropped out, he was shocked.

"Are you nuts?" he said. "What if the show becomes a hit? You'll always wonder, *What could have been?* And you'll always resent Dave because he didn't want you to go."

The more I thought about it, the more I agreed with Rick. I had never been the kind of person who shies away from a challenge or the kind that lets other people run my life, so why start now? I picked up the phone, called the phone number from the casting call, and prayed. It felt like an eternity for the call to go through, but then a receptionist picked up and informed me that it wasn't too late to start wrestling training. Whew!

Thank God for my conversation with Rick; thank God for that phone call; and thank God they were still training girls!

I knew next to nothing about professional wrestling. I didn't even watch it on TV. I mean, the only cool TV characters back then for young girls to idolize were Isis the Almighty Warrior from *The Secrets of Isis* and Wonder Woman. I had never had a professional female wrestler to look up to, but that's why they were offering to train us, right? Well, that all sounded good in theory, until I found out where the training was being held: Watts, a neighborhood in southern L.A. that was probably best known for violent riots in 1965 and an increased gang presence in the '70s and '80s. Obviously, I was a bit worried about my safety, but I managed to make it to the training center in one piece.

When I arrived, there was absolutely no one there. I double-checked the address. What the hell? It turns out they had canceled that day's training and forgotten to tell me. I was already anxious about going and now this. This was my first real audition for a part. Up to then, I had only done a little bit of extra work and background stuff. I called again and was told to come back at 7 p.m. on Monday. When I returned, I noticed that there were guards stationed at the stairwell, which made me feel more secure.

When I got to the actual wrestling ring, several girls were taking instruction from a man named Mando Guerrero, who had wrestled all over the country since the mid-1970s and was one of the all-time greats. He was showing the girls some basic tumbling moves: forward roll; backward roll; a three-quarter roll.

Even though I had never wrestled, I figured I could do simple athletic moves like that. It couldn't be all that different from diving and flopping around center field at John Burroughs High School, could it? (OK, pro wrestling turned out to be a LOT different from softball. But, at the time, I was willing to tell myself just about anything to get into the ring.) I climbed into the ring, performed a couple of forward rolls, and just like that, my education as a professional wrestler had begun.

I was so glad I had listened to Rick and gone to that first training session. I kept going back — three nights a week, three hours a session — for the next two months. Boy, was I black and blue from learning how to take a fall! Fortunately, I was paid $75 each time I went in, and gradually I noticed that some of the girls weren't coming back. You have to remember that even though these sessions were referred to as "training," they were technically a part of the audition process. The producers of the show were definitely weeding out the girls who didn't have what it took.

One night, Mando asked for a volunteer to slam her head into the turnbuckle, turn around, and land on her back. Before anyone could bat an eyelash, I raised my hand, darted into the ring, slammed my head into the turnbuckle, turned, and fell flat on my back. David McLane later told me it was that face-slamming move that secured my position as a

GLOW girl, and that I was the first *GLOW* girl hired. Boy, you never know what it's going to take to break into Hollywood!

After two months of intense training, there were twelve girls ready to shoot the show's pilot. David McLane, Matt Cimber, and the show's writers had already come up with creative characters for the show: Americana, Spanish Red, Matilda the Hun, the California Doll, Salt and Pepper, Tammy Jones, Tina Ferrari and Ashley Cartier, The Royal Hawaiian, and Hollywood and Vine. Some of them, such as Matilda, were obvious with regards to who would play them. But for others, we had to figure out which girls' personalities fit with which characters. I was so excited when I was offered the role of Hollywood, which was half of the tag team partnership of Hollywood and Vine, named after the famous intersection that had been relevant in Hollywood – and by extension, show business – ever since the 1920s.

The eleven other ladies who joined me were:

Vine: Janet Bowers
California Doll: Lynda Aldon
Matilda the Hun: Dee Booher
Americana: Cindy Maranne
Tammy Jones: Debbie D'Amato
Spanish Red: Ericka Marr
Tina Ferrari: Lisa Moretti
Ashley Cartier: Nadine Kadmiri
Salt: Charli Haynes
Pepper: Cynthia Peretti
Royal Hawaiian: April Hom

Matilda (the late Deanna "Dee" Booher) had actually started wrestling before *GLOW*. She had wrestled under the name Queen Kong and went on to do a lot of acting. You may remember seeing her in Aerosmith's music video for "Love in an Elevator"; in movies like *Spaceballs*, *How I Got into College*, and *Grunt! The Wrestling Movie*; and television shows like *Mama's Family*, *Night Court*, and *Married... with Children*.

Now, if you know anything about pro wrestling, you know that almost all wrestling conflicts revolve around good guys ("baby faces" or just "faces") vs. bad guys ("heels"). It's this classic conflict between good and evil, and the way the characters play up their roles, that makes a wrestling show worth watching. My tag team partner, Vine, and I were definitely going to be "bad girls." I didn't mind one bit; in fact, I thought it might wind up being more fun that way. Where else are you actually encouraged to be mean, nasty, arrogant, and villainous?

Another Perspective: More GLOW Audition Stories

It's still a little surreal. A casting call went out; a bunch of actresses, dancers, gymnasts, and models answered the call; and the next thing you know, there's a new pro wrestling promotion on television. Once the show got picked up, there was more interest, and women from every walk of life came in and became *GLOW* girls.

I reached out to several of my *GLOW* colleagues and asked them to share a little bit about their auditions and their experiences as Gorgeous Ladies of Wrestling.

Scarlett the Southern Belle (Janice Flynn): I heard about *GLOW* from David McLane. He was in the lobby of the *Playboy* office building in Hollywood. I was leaving because I had been upstairs showing them my portfolio. *Playboy* offered me a job to run across the screen of a movie for $500. I was leaving because I did not give them an answer, and I met David in the lobby.

He approached me and told me that his dream was to have a wrestling team of gorgeous women. He asked if he could look at my portfolio, which I was still holding in my hand. I showed it to him, and he told me more. It was about going to an audition in Las Vegas; they would pay my way; I would be with several other girls; and I would stay for a couple of weeks if it worked out. I went home with his information. I called *Playboy* back and said I would do the job, but they said it was already taken.

I called McLane and told him I would give it a try and go to Las Vegas. I think it was more for a couple of months. I don't think I actually had a job interview. I think that was it. My roommate was Sally the Farmer's Daughter.

I didn't have any experience in wrestling, but David said that was OK and that they would train me. I was excited to go to something that sounded very promising and fun. Plus, they paid you right away, and they offered a bonus after the two months were over. That sounded very professional, so I was excited to give it a try since I wanted to be a model. This was one way to get into the business in some form. I was in the first season of *GLOW* — one of the original girls. I was given the name Scarlett and was one-half of the tag team The Southern Belles with Tara. She was very nice.

Little Feather (Kuno): I was on the same gymnastics team with Ann LaBree (Debbie Debutante) when I was younger. She told me *GLOW* was looking for someone to portray the character of Little Egypt, and she thought I might fit. I went to the Riviera Hotel and watched a demonstration with a couple of the girls and learned a few things like the hip toss and how to fall properly. I wasn't really familiar with pro wrestling except for Andy Kaufman and Jerry Lawler's whole bit. I knew who Hulk Hogan was, but I hadn't really watched it up to that point. I thought it looked fun and would be a way to utilize my acrobatic skills. They decided I wasn't right for Little Egypt, so they came up with Little Feather.

I wish I had incorporated more of my tumbling abilities into my matches. I was just barely 18, extremely shy, and had a lot of stage fright. Every match was really challenging as far as performing in front of people, but there was something exciting about the energy from the crowd and the fact that I was doing something totally different, totally outside of my comfort zone.

For me, the show taught me a lot about life and people. I had so little life experience up to that point, and being on the show was very eye-opening in so many ways. There were a lot of firsts, like going to my first heavy metal concert and seeing AC/DC with Sally, Scarlett, and Hollywood.

If you can imagine living at your job … where your boss was there 24/7 … living and breathing wrestling … that's what it was like. It really was a different world, and I haven't experienced anything else quite like it. There was a certain amount of empowerment through the expression of physical strength that wrestling afforded me, which I hadn't found before, and it was really spiritually freeing in a lot of ways. It was definitely an experience I'll never forget.

Tiffany Mellon (Sandra Margot): My entry into GLOW began in my agent's office in North Hollywood, CA. I was sitting at his desk, and noticed a bulletin on the wall behind him for "*GLOW* Auditions." I told him that I wanted to try out for the show, as I had recently become a fan. He raised his eyebrows and exclaimed, "YOU?" He then arranged a meeting between myself and Matt Cimber. I met Matt at his tennis club in Agoura Hills, CA. We had a nice, long chat, and he then cast me on the show. I have a lot of fond memories of my time as a *GLOW* Girl! And of course, there are some "not so fond" memories... However, the good outweighs the bad.

Lightning (Cheryl Rusa): I heard about *GLOW* for the first time when my boyfriend suggested we watch it. I saw an ad at the end of a first season episode looking for more girls. It was looking for girls "if you've got the stuff." I faked a resume and sent it in with a sexy heavy metal shot.

I had no real experience in the entertainment industry. I had barely started acting classes and did just one industrial film as a stuck-up bikini girl in a kissing booth. Other than that, I was a personal trainer at a gym. My audition was held in a tall office building off Santa Monica Boulevard or Melrose, not too far from the 405. I was totally nervous and excited at the same time, but I tried to be myself as much as possible. I wore a turquoise wrap-around dress with a bikini underneath, in case they wanted to see more. That way, I wouldn't be caught in my undergarments. Since I grew up by the beach and was totally comfortable in a bathing suit, it seemed to be a good choice.

Thunderbolt (Dana Felton Howard): I didn't have to audition. They wanted Sally the Farmer's Daughter to come back, so she said I will come back only if I can bring my friend, Dana. They said OK, and they trained me. I had to get a signed release form from my mom because I was only 17. Matt Cimber decided that I would be Thunderbolt because I was a crazy little firecracker! I would tell Sally that I loved Hollywood and that she was my hero. She would say, "No! I'm your hero." And I would say, "No. I think she's so hot. I wanna be a bad girl like her."

Godiva (Dawn Maestas): I never formally auditioned for *GLOW*. I was friends with Debbie Debutante since high school, and she called me up and invited me to do *GLOW*. I met Matt Cimber at an Il Fornaio restaurant in Los Angeles, and he hired me on the spot. I didn't have any wrestling experience. I wasn't even a wrestling fan. I think we were probably halfway through our filming season before I had ever even seen a match on television, but I was a lifetime athlete and gymnast, and those skills came in handy. I was pretty confident once I got in the ring. Doing gymnastics makes you very comfortable being upside-down, and I figured if I could do a flip to my feet, I can certainly do a flip halfway over and land on my back! I have always been a very physical athlete, and it really led to success in the wrestling ring for me. I went on to become a third-degree black belt martial artist and self-defense instructor. Apparently, combat sports agree with me!

Susie Spirit (Lauri Thompson): I auditioned in Las Vegas. I had moved to town hoping to earn a law degree, but I also needed work. I landed a part as a dancer at the Folies Bergère show at The Tropicana. At my *GLOW* audition, I was told to watch a video of women wrestling in Japan. Women's wrestling in Japan in the 1980s was intense. Once I saw that, I said, "Nope, this isn't for me." and walked. David or Matt — I forget which one it was — ran after me and told me that *GLOW* wasn't going to be quite the same as Japanese women's wrestling, trying to get me to change my mind. I finally said I would do it if they also taught me about television production. I was given a cheerleader character. *GLOW* writer Steve Blance came up with the name Susie Spirit. I wrestled for *GLOW* and continued dancing at the Folies Bergère. I also learned everything I could about television production behind the scenes. I was part of *GLOW* seasons one and two. Today I am an attorney and married with two sons.

Tulsa (Jody Haselbarth): I didn't audition with the first group of girls. I came a few months later. I was in Dallas channel surfing when *GLOW* came on. The beautiful girls, beautiful costumes and amazing action had me hooked in the first few minutes. I knew that I could do that.

My background was rodeo (including bull riding and bareback bronc riding in all-girl rodeos), gymnastics, dance (including belly dancing), and sports. I watched the ending credits and saw it was filmed at the Riviera Hotel, so I wrote a letter, added a headshot, and took it to the post office that night. I even added a rap, but I can only remember the first line: "I'm the Texas Wildcat, and Jody's my name."

Three days later Matt Cimber called me and asked if I could fly to Vegas. I immediately bought a ticket. I arrived in my cowboy boots and jeans and was met by Steve Blance and Johnny C. Steve was quizzing me and asked me to spell what sounded like "tenoid," so I knew that there was a catch. I answered "pnenoid" (silent p), but it is actually spelled ctenoid with a silent c. I should have known that!

I never had a formal interview or audition; I just kind of came in through the back door. I went home to Texas while everyone else went on tour, and I was called back after about a month. Matt named me Tulsa, and I cried. I told him that Oklahoma was north of the Red River and that I was a Texan.

To make matters worse, he wanted me in yellow, my least favorite color. Then, worst of all, he wanted me to be a prairie woman. When Mary Ann, our "wardrobe girl," dressed me in a dull, long, beige and brown calico skirt, I cried again. All the girls were in gorgeous, sparkly, sexy costumes, and I looked like Granny Clampett. I knew that I couldn't fly or climb the ropes in that outfit. I begged her for something pretty — more like a saloon girl — and her face lit up. Then Mary Ann made the most beautiful saloon girl costume for me. Thank you, Mary Ann!

I was a part of seasons three and four, and then the touring we did after the show stopped filming. We were told that there were some internal issues to be resolved and that we would eventually be called back. I am still waiting for that call!

Broadway Rose (Andrea Janell): I heard about *GLOW* auditions while I was at another audition for some other work. I asked my agent, and he gave me Matt's address in Las Vegas and set up the audition for me. Of course, I had to drive to Vegas. This was a problem because I was 19 and my father forbade me to go. I didn't listen and spent my last bit of money driving out to Vegas to meet Matt at his house.

When I arrived at Matt's house — I believe it was a Sunday night — the entire wrestling crew was having a meeting. I was wearing a ripped T-shirt and jeans. Apparently, he saw something in me and asked me to go to the gym to work out with everyone and see what I could do. After that, I was hired as Broadway Rose. I filmed season three with the company.

California Doll (Jayne Adams): I heard about GLOW through my modeling/convention agent in Las Vegas. I was in college and doing gigs to make extra money. I auditioned with Matt Cimber at the Riviera Hotel. I was given the name California Doll, and I was part of the cast for seasons one and two. I didn't have any experience in wrestling, but was definitely already athletic, so it was an easy transition. I had mixed feelings about it. I thought it could be a fun experience that would allow travel, TV time, and fun, and an adventure I could tell the grandkids about some day. I figured I could take a break from school and see where this went. I wasn't an actress like many of the girls and wasn't really hoping to be a star. I actually lost a lot of friends from school because they looked down on the entire endeavor.

I was confident in my abilities as an athlete, but not confident in my acting. The skits were fun, but the other girls were much better at playing to the camera. I love that they did a show about GLOW on Netflix. First, because it allowed some of the girls opportunities to keep working. And also, I think it kind of brought a little more legitimacy to GLOW. I wish our show had been better – better wrestling and less campy silliness. Without a doubt, the best part of the entire experience was the amazing women I worked with, who went through so much shit together, but were there for each other. Amazing women, all!

MTV (Eileen O'Hara): I was in a casting office for a commercial audition, and I crashed the GLOW audition. I thought it would be a good opportunity to get on TV on a popular show as a principal player. I was kind of a rough-and-tumble tomboy and did a lot of athletics, so I wasn't scared at all. Actually, I thought it would be fun and then, when I started wrestling, I loved it. My character was Melody Trouble Vixen – MTV for short. I was in seasons three and four and the bootleg season five that may have aired in Japan or something. GLOW was the most fun I've ever had in my life, and I would still be doing it if I could. When the Netflix show came out, I was kind of disappointed that they didn't tell our stories or let us participate as incidental characters … maybe as a mother of one of the girls. At least give us cameos. But it was a very well-made show, and I really love all of the actors that were in it. They did a marvelous job in their fictional account of the first all-women's wrestling show.

Corporal Kelly (Lily Crabtree): I was watching season one, and they ran an ad saying, "Do you have what it takes to be a *GLOW* girl? Send in your resume." I sent a resume and pictures in and did not hear anything for quite a while. Finally, I got a call asking me to meet with Matt. I met up with him at a Burger King in the Valley somewhere. If I hadn't already seen *GLOW*, I would have thought it was some kind of a scam; I mean who meets at a Burger King? For the interview, I wore one of those one-piece, workout, spandex leotards with booties and a shaker button-up sweater. So '80s! As I was leaving, Justice was coming in, and I thought, *I bet she's meeting with Matt, too.*

I received a call later asking me to come to Vegas to try out. We all met at the clubhouse, and they divided us up, four girls to an apartment. Justice ended up being my roommate, and my mattress was camouflage. It was a precursor of things to come. Although I desperately wanted to be a Heavy Metal Sister, Matt made me into Corporal Kelly.

I always loved wrestling and was training with a friend who was a jobber (enhancement talent; the guys who get paid to lose and make the superstars look good on TV) for the WWF. We rented a ring at a place called Gil's Garage in L.A. It was $10 an hour, and the Lucha Libre guys who wrestled at The Olympic used to practice there, too. Since I was the only girl, they helped me out a lot. Those guys were fearless high-flyers and were amazing to watch run drills. I also sang for a band called The Explosive Broomhandles. We were a punk band and played in L.A. at Club 88, The Troubadour, The Whisky, and Madame Wong's, so I was used to entertaining.

When Matt decided to make me a mean Marine, I almost turned it down. He cut all my hair off and dyed it brown. Corporal Kelly was the exact opposite of my personality, but I couldn't pass up a chance to wrestle, so I decided to try my hardest to be the toughest Marine I could be. I wanted to be a character I had developed called Diamond Lil – kind of a Mae West saloon hall girl heel. I felt like Matt would have used me more if I had been able to adopt that character. I was the second Corporal Kelly, and I was in season three. I broke my arm, came back from that, then blew out my ACL in a match with Sunny. So that was it for my wrestling career. An arm and a leg are enough for any job.

Dementia (Michelle Duze): I heard about the audition for *GLOW* from Hollywood. In 1986 and 1987, I worked at Richard Simmons' Anatomy Asylum (his exercise studio), where a big group of coworkers became friends. Hollywood was in that friend group. She had returned from shooting the pilot and the first episodes of *GLOW*, and she encouraged me to go to Las Vegas to try out. I had never even watched a wrestling match. My audition was in the Riviera Hotel. I don't remember participating in one of *GLOW*'s formal audition events, although I believe they had conducted several by the time I arrived. I returned with Hollywood after a break to work out with the girls and audition after some practice and see if I was able to do it. By that time, the pilot and several episodes had been produced and it was beginning to be sold and shown on several local syndicated television stations.

I had absolutely no experience wrestling. I was athletic and capable and willing to learn. Attaché was my main trainer. We spent our days working out and learning holds and moves in a dark corner of the hotel where our ring was set up. We spent our evenings on her couch in her apartment – she was one of very few girls that did not live in the Riviera Hotel – watching videos of men's matches to learn new moves and become educated about wrestling. I remember meeting David McLane and learning to wrestle with a small group of girls in the slot machine dead storage area of the hotel.

It was an awesome, crazy-fun experience. My grandparents lived in Las Vegas at the time, and it gave me the opportunity to eat dinner at their home each week. My grandpa LOVED wrestling, and they did not miss a Saturday that we were filming. It was fun to live in a community of women that was working on something new and, in a lot of ways, growing up together. We had a few veteran members, like Matilda the Hun/Queenie, who was my roommate. It helped me grow through that season of life, and I loved the experience. In the end, I met my husband, and we raised three beautiful children, so I have good feelings about the experience as a whole.

My character name was Dementia. I worked at the end of season one and all of season two. I then departed *GLOW* and went to work for a wrestling promotion called POWW (Powerful Women of Wrestling) after season two, while Dementia was well represented by another wrestler that I have never met.

It is cool that so many *GLOW* girls are memorializing our experience. In some ways, the experience of actually being a wrestler in the '80s was like a separate lifetime. It's a tough sport and, in some ways, I'm thankful that my career was short. I know my body feels the aches and pains associated with the fact that I used to occasionally suplex someone off the top rope.

Daisy (Helena LeCount): I was in a casting office, and Matt Cimber came out of the back, saw me, and asked me if I wanted to be in *GLOW*. I auditioned in Las Vegas with the rest of the girls. I was nervous. I had never been around that many women in one place in my life. I didn't have any prior wrestling experience, but I was already an athlete. I had seen the show on TV, so I was aware of it and knew what it was. My character was Daisy and I wrestled for two seasons. I was the only one who wrestled every girl in the last two seasons, except for MTV because she was out with a broken arm.

Little Egypt (Angelina Altishin): I was working at a T-shirt store in Las Vegas, and Mt. Fiji came in to have a T-shirt made. She encouraged me to go down to the Riviera Hotel and talk to David McLane. I didn't have any formal auditions. I was put right into training with Attaché as my trainer. I was kind of nervous about it because I wasn't sure how they were going to utilize the women. The only thing at that time that I could relate female wrestling to was mud wrestling, and that did not appeal to me. After I got into training, I realized the girls were taking it seriously, and I got bitten by the bug as well. I was all in.

I was super nervous to step in the ring because I only had two weeks of training. *Entertainment Tonight* was also there, filming a segment about the show. To make matters even more nerve-racking, I had to come out belly dancing, even though I had no formal training in the art. So crazy! That was my debut in the ring. I worked in seasons one and two, and I had over twenty-four matches. I wrestled under the name of

Little Egypt. I got injured at the end of season two with a torn ACL. My first match was with the Heavy Metal Sisters, and my last match was with the Heavy Metal Sisters, which I thought was very surreal.

Stinky (Michelle Jean Javas): Eileen O'Hara (MTV) introduced me to *GLOW*. She was friends with my boyfriend. I had no wrestling experience, only street fighting. I was a fan of *GLOW*. I watched it every weekend on KDOC TV. Hollywood and Vine were my favorites. My audition was in the ring in Las Vegas. I was a little nervous, but when I met the girls, I became eager to start. And I felt this is where I should be. I got my character and started filming live shows two weeks later. It took me some time to really get into my character, and I realized I was a much better stunt woman than actress. I was on the third and fourth seasons in 1988-1990.

Evangelina (Christy Smith): I was living in Hollywood and bought a drama log and circled two auditions, one of which was *GLOW*. I went to the *GLOW* audition, but they wouldn't tell me exactly what it was. I filled out the application, and they said they were interested in me, but I needed to get a headshot and body shot. I went down to the farmers' market, got the photos done, and went back and submitted them. They told me all about the audition/tryouts and that they were going to be in Las Vegas. I agreed to do it, but I did not give up my apartment in Hollywood. I did not have any experience as a wrestler. I was athletic growing up and played all kinds of sports, but my main game was basketball. I had seen the *GLOW* show a couple of times at my friend's house and thought it was pretty cool and entertaining. A gal at the clothing boutique on Sunset Boulevard helped me pick out some new clothes for my interview. I got a blue denim jean skirt, a cute white shirt, and a really cool black leather jacket. I played the character Evangelina in seasons three and four. When I first heard about Netflix doing a show about *GLOW*, I was not happy about it because we weren't going to be in it, and it was our story. But later I accepted it, and I was happy to see it come alive again.

Justice (Norniece Norment): I was swimming at a condo in California and that's where I met Aunt Kitty. She introduced me to *GLOW* and encouraged me to try out. I auditioned in Las Vegas. I had absolutely no wrestling skills. I was scared and nervous, and I had mixed feelings about auditioning. I played Justice in seasons three and four.

Ashley Cartier (Nadine Higgins): It all started with an audition my agent sent me on for a lead role in the syndicated TV pilot for *Gorgeous Ladies of Wrestling*. I walked in, met David McLane, and before I knew it, I was hired. Then came training, where I met Jeanne and the rest of the gang. We all learned the basics of wrestling before heading to Las Vegas to film what turned out to be a global hit!

My memories of Jeanne? All positive – packed with fun, laughter, and a bit of craziness. Jeanne and I were *GLOW* tag team rivals with me and Tina Ferrari (Lisa Moretti) against Hollywood and Vine, which meant we spent a ton of time together, both in and out of the ring. The job was demanding, but Jeanne's infectious positivity and can-do attitude made it a blast. She had this amazing way of turning even the toughest moments into something fun. Those days with Jeanne were some of the best!

Jailbait (Trisha Marie): My dad was a big wrestling fan and bribed me with a donut to watch wrestling with him one afternoon. He let me choose the show. I was flipping through the channels and saw Sally the Farmer's Daughter get branded by The Heavy Metal Sisters ... and I was hooked! I told my dad the show was silly and I could do that (wrestle). He didn't believe me. So I called the Riviera and asked how to become a *GLOW* girl. They gave me Matt's number, and the next weekend I was trying out in Vegas for *GLOW*.

Jeanne is such an amazing woman – so beautiful and hardworking. Best of all, she's down to earth.

Years after *GLOW*, Babe (Ursula Hayden), Jeanne, and I met up, dressed up, and got in the audience for *Let's Make a Deal* with Wayne Brady. Jeanne looked stunning dressed as Wonder Woman. Every head turned as she walked on set. None of us got selected to be contestants on that particular show, but she definitely made an impression.

Major Tanya (Noelle Rose): I did not hear about the auditions for the original seasons of *GLOW*. I was a straightforward actress and spokesmodel, so it would not have come up in my "go sees."

I only heard that seasons three and four were in the planning stage. I had joined the world of women's wrestling through David McLane's spinoff, WOW/POWW, learning there at that time that *GLOW* had ended and was not renewed.

My first professional experience and training with women's wrestling was with the first WOW promotion. They renamed it POWW, and the emphasis was full-on pro wrestling – not so much television and acting – so I completed the promotion, relinquished my crown (lost it in a main event match with Nina), and returned to Los Angeles.

My (scouted) audition was in one of the POWW touring cities – maybe Atlanta, Georgia or somewhere on the Midwest or the Southern tour. I was well into my character and performance as the Russian heel, Natasha the Russian, defending my POWW crown from the star face, Nina, in the main event match.

The writer and producers of *GLOW* would only see a Russian woman fully committed to her Soviet roots and country; dressed in a cape and hat and sash; with a USSR flag and spouting off Russian phrases while dodging beer cans and other paraphernalia thrown at her to distract all efforts in the ring. Those fans really were good at hating this heel!

After the POWW promotion – which also entailed many radio interviews, public appearances, promo events, and the carefully planned and taped interviews of my training as an overconfident Soviet athlete spouting superiority – I had transformed myself for that time, always being Russian in public. That was an important requirement for a *serious* women's wrestling promotion and a great improvisation practice and challenge for a committed actress.

The wrestling training was a two-week crash course prior to hitting the road (puns intended). It became an ongoing process (for me) on the road throughout touring. I built my body more and continued to learn more moves.

I had to do a great deal of this on my own. Fortunately, the referee was also one of our trainers and a part of the tour. I recall his name was Trinidad, which was interesting as my mother is originally from the country of Trinidad and Tobago. It was challenging to get to train as much as I wanted and needed. Most of our extra time was taken up by traveling in tour buses from city to city, as well as by scheduled promo appearances and extra events. The other women had already trained and done this previously. You could say I was *acting as a wrestler* while also *learning how to be a wrestler*.

I felt nervous, scared, and confident all at the same time – times of nervousness before a show or even a final rehearsal. Maybe not so much scared, but there were some moves that could be quite unnerving, and until they were over without injuries, there would be an element of fear about it. But that was a healthy response and kept us alert at all times. Live wrestling is not something you can casually phone in. Confidence came later as the character was locked in; fans were rallying – yes, even for a Russian Bad Girl. The best thing I took away from my *GLOW* experience was a new kind of fearlessness for other performance ventures that came later, both physical and mental.

I didn't really have a memorable interview. I recall meeting with the director once at his tennis club, so I dressed casually. I did obtain a good amount of clothing in RED, mostly when in POWW, since we did a lot of promos and special events, and it was up to us to dress as our character. My favorite was my red leather jacket. I still have it!

Chainsaw (Sharon Willinsky Johnston): I was playing on a football team with my sister Donna and I got an audition from my agent for *GLOW*. I asked if the whole football team could audition and he said yes. Emily Dole was on that football team with me. I remember going in and talking a lot. It turned out that Donna and Emily got hired, but I didn't. So I gave Donna a letter to give to them, and then I got hired. I remember going to the first meeting and seeing the pilot with Hollywood and the Royal Hawaiian and it scared the hell out of me and my sister. We both looked at each other like we were in some serious trouble and we were going to get really hurt by these mean girls. Then to find out that Hollywood was so sweet and awesome. All of the girls were such lovely women, truly.

Chapter 10: Shooting the Pilot

When the *GLOW* executives told us they would fly us to Las Vegas to shoot the pilot, I had to take a week off from my "real" job. They put us up at the Riviera Hotel, which is also where we filmed not only our matches, but also the interviews and comedy sketches that were a prominent part of the show.

During the taping of the pilot — which was shot on December 5, 1985 — they filmed Vine and me doing a promo for our first match, which would be against "good girls" Tina and Ashley. I was pretty anxious about this, considering I had never had a speaking part on a TV show before. I asked the director, Matt Cimber, if there were any restrictions on what we could or couldn't say — specifically, profanity. He assured me I could say whatever I wanted, since they were going to edit the tape before it aired on TV. When the interviewer asked me how I thought we were going to do in our first match, I had an answer primed and ready: "We're gonna kick their asses. They think their sweat doesn't stink. They think they're glamour girls. We think they suck; we think they're sluts. People don't fuck with us. 'Cause if you fuck with us, we'll get our friends on you. Me and Vine ... we're tough."

When the show aired on TV, they bleeped the f-word, but kept the segment. I guess they figured if we were going to be "bad girls" on the show, we might as well talk like it, right? And today, if you go to YouTube and search for politically incorrect wrestling promos, you will see yours truly blurting out the f-word for all to hear!

My partner, Vine, was a girl named Janet Bowers from Toronto, Ontario, Canada. She was a nice gal and we got along pretty well. But the way the *GLOW* people had it set up, we were practically joined at the hip during the first two seasons of shooting: eating together, rooming together, spending "down time" together, and (obviously) filming our matches and sketches together. Any time you're forced to spend that much time with another person, you're going to have the occasional conflict. I don't care who the person is; that's just human nature. Anyone out there ever shared a bedroom with a brother or sister? Anyone ever had an argument with a college roommate? I rest my case.

None of our arguments were earth-shattering — mostly tiffs and bitchy girly stuff. For example, we'd be filming our sketches, each propped on one chair, side-by-side, and one of us would snap, "Hey, get your hair out of my face!" If you remember our '80s "big hair" hairstyles, it's amazing that kind of thing didn't happen more often.

One time Vine asked me why I always came out first when we made our entrances to the ring.

"Um," I said, a bit surprised by the question, "because our tag team is called 'Hollywood and Vine,' not 'Vine and Hollywood.' If you want to go out first, that's fine by me." I wasn't trying to be the top dog. I just assumed we should enter in the order in which we were announced. She said no, and I continued to go out first, but that manner of bickering popped up a lot in the early days.

Vine parted ways with *GLOW* at the beginning of season three. I think she had a conflict with our director, or maybe her visa expired and she had to go back to Canada. We were never the best of friends, but considering I got my start working with her on *GLOW*, she'll always be a cherished part of my professional career.

Anyway, back to the pilot. Some of you sharp-eyed fans might remember that, in addition to the twelve characters I mentioned before, there were three others in the pilot. Those characters were Sara and Mabel, who fought in a match against Salt and Pepper and later became regular characters on *GLOW*, and Jail Bait. So who played those characters? Well, for the pilot, Sara and Mabel were actually played by (wait for it ...) Ashley Cartier and Royal Hawaiian! And Jail Bait, who was only seen briefly and did not appear in a match, was played by Vine. Vine went on to play a different character called Princess of Darkness in later episodes of *GLOW*.

Since it was a first-time television show, we had to promote the heck out of it. We offered free tickets to the taping to all of the guests at the Riviera. We put tickets on the windshields of cars parked outside. We went to shopping malls and passed them out to anyone we could, and by showtime, the room was packed. Even though we had gone through two months of training, this was the first time I had wrestled in front of a live crowd, and I was nervous – so nervous that I couldn't even look any of the audience members in the face.

Our match vs. Tina and Ashley was a blur except for the unexpected slap I received from Tina (Lisa Moretti, who, years later, went on to become a three-time WWE women's champion and WWE Hall of Famer as Ivory). Do you know how it feels to be slapped when you're not expecting it? First, shock! Second, *Well, that's not what we rehearsed!* Third, *How embarrassing …* And fourth, *I'll get you back!*

I was so surprised because that wasn't supposed to happen. But we were all so amped up with the crowd and it being our first match; it's like someone had pressed a giant fast-forward button on the match. Everything went into high gear. And when that happens, sometimes accidents happen, or you lose your bearings as to "what's supposed to happen when." But performing live, you have to roll with it all in real time and make it work.

Of course, it was almost always the "good girls" who won matches, so Tina and Ashley got their hands raised by the referee that night. But eventually I would start getting my fair share of wins as my character's popularity grew and Hollywood became something of a cult favorite. Somehow, we got through all the nervousness and chaos and finished shooting the pilot.

And then it was time to head back home. After a week of pro wrestling before a live crowd, my job at the medical clinic just didn't seem the same. I couldn't afford to quit just yet, though. A few weeks later, David McLane called and invited me to NATPE, the National Association of Television Program Executives convention in New Orleans. This was a huge opportunity, both for me and for *GLOW*, because we had to use the pilot to convince the network buyers to syndicate our show. Even if we were the best wrestlers or actresses in the world, if we could only get an airtime of 4 a.m. on local cable access stations, the show wasn't going to last. We had to make an impact at NATPE if *GLOW* was ever to see the light of day.

Chapter 11: Getting GLOW on the Air

I wasn't the only girl invited to the convention. Matilda the Hun, Tammy Jones, and Americana (with whom I roomed) were also asked to go. As you can probably imagine, the convention was huge. Hundreds of TV actors and producers were there, all hoping to convince an executive to give them that all-important break, pick up their pilot, and give them the security blanket of a contract for a regular time slot ... for one season, at least.

Among all these hopefuls pitching their projects, the *GLOW* girls were up on a small platform with pink ropes around us, simulating our wrestling ring at the Riviera. A TV monitor showed the pilot, which included Patti LaBelle's hit song "New Attitude."

For four days, the other girls and I worked the crowd, trying to lure the buyers and executives over to the booth so we could show them our pilot. We took pictures with O.J. Simpson, Mr. T, and a few other big-name celebrities. I remember being introduced to the executive producers of *Married... with Children*, a show I would appear on a few years later.

One night, David McLane took me out to dinner at a place that resembled the White House from the outside – pretty classy – and I was fairly sure I was being wined and dined. He walked me back to the hotel and invited me up to his room; of course, I declined (after all, I had a boyfriend back home and I'm a loyal person). I wasn't offended or anything. David was always doing nice things for me, like buying me ice cream or the occasional rose from the airport. And it wasn't like he expected anything in return, either. Or maybe he did, but I just ignored it. You hear all those horror stories about "casting couches," where producers expect you to sleep with them if you want to get a certain role. I was lucky that was never the case with David. I've certainly seen that kind of thing happen with other girls, but that was not going to happen to me. Nothing ever happened between me and David beyond some innocent flirting.

I recently received David's remembrance of me at that time, and he kindly said: "One of my favorite memories is the night in New Orleans.

You and I went to the bars and had drinks and soaked in New Orleans together! Love, David".

It might surprise some people to hear this because David was so good in the comedy sketches we did, but originally he had envisioned *GLOW* as a pure wrestling promotion without comedy or rap or any of the other embellishments we did. He was a fan of old-school pro wrestling. He ultimately left *GLOW* after season two and went on to start POWW (Powerful Women of Wrestling) in 1987 and WOW (Women of Wrestling) in 2000. But he didn't want any of us former *GLOW* girls to be involved when he started WOW. I think he wanted a fresh group of young girls that had very little experience so he could control them. It's too bad, though, because I think some of the other *GLOW* girls and I could have been a big help with WOW.

While we were in New Orleans, the *GLOW* girls took over Bourbon Street. We hit Pat O'Brien's for a few Hurricanes (okay, more than a few) and a rock club called The Dungeon. On a future *GLOW* tour, we ended up in New Orleans at the same time as Mardi Gras, and we girls wound up wearing lots of beads by the time the visit was over. But I'll leave it up to your imagination to figure out how we got them! Of course, we also visited the Hard Rock Cafe so I could get a T-shirt.

It was on our first trip to New Orleans for NATPE that we met Joanne Cooper painting random people's faces on the street. Joanne eventually ended up becoming *GLOW*'s makeup artist. Matt took out a $100 bill, tore it in half, and said to her, "Meet us tomorrow at 9 a.m. with your suitcase, and if you bring the other half of this bill, I'll give you this half. We want you to be our makeup girl for the show."

Once the convention was over, I went back to my day job again. This time, though, I had the thought percolating in my head that our show might get picked up. The convention had gotten me excited and made me optimistic that this little women's wrestling show might be a game-changer for me. Sure enough, the *GLOW* people called me and told me the good news: we had been picked up! I was excited as hell and could not believe this was actually going to happen. They told me to pack my bags for Vegas. We were going back to the Riviera to shoot an entire season's worth of episodes. I gave two months (not two weeks) notice at the medical lab and never went back to it – or any other "regular" job – ever again.

Chapter 12: Early Years

By 1986, I had officially broken into show business. The *GLOW* pilot was good enough to be picked up, and I had left my job at the medical lab to begin my career as an "actress." I flew to Las Vegas for the taping of season one, and soon after I arrived, I ran into David in the lobby of the Riviera Hotel.

"So," I said. "What's going on?"

"Not much," he replied. "Except that you're going to be wrestling a 350-pound woman in the first episode of the season."

Relax, I thought to myself. *He's probably kidding.*

"No way!" I said, waiting for the punchline.

"Yeah," he replied. "Tomorrow I'll introduce you to Mountain Fiji."

Hmmm, not exactly what I was expecting. But what the hell? Since when has my life been a slow, quiet, calm, walk in the park? A 350-pound wrestling opponent? Bring it on!

And so it began. Vine and I opened *GLOW*'s first season by wrestling Mt. Fiji in what the producers called a "handicap match." In wrestling, a handicap match is when one wrestler faces off against multiple opponents simultaneously; hence, the "handicap." Let's see ... Vine and I weighed a combined 231 pounds, while Mt. Fiji weighed 350 pounds all by herself. Who the heck was supposed to be handicapped, anyway? Andre the Giant had made handicap matches quite popular in the World Wrestling Federation. Apparently, the *GLOW* producers wanted to create our very own Andre with Mt. Fiji.

To be more accurate, Hollywood and Vine opened the season by teaming up and beating down Mt. Fiji's storyline "sister," Little Fiji. Again, it was a totally stereotypical battle between good and evil — the two bad girls teaming up on Little Fiji, unaware that her big sis, Mt. Fiji, was watching the whole thing.

This episode also featured the famous *GLOW* theme song for the first time, which was written by Hank Doing and had all of us dancing and rapping in the ring.

WE'RE THE GORGEOUS LADIES OF WRESTLING
WE'RE ALL CHAMPIONS IN THE RING
WE COME FROM THE STREETS
WE COME FROM THE CITY
WE COME FROM A WORLD WHERE THERE IS NO PITY

SLAM, BAM, IT'S A WRESTLING JAM
COME ON, LADIES, GIVE US A HAND
IT'S A BIG BAD BATTLE IN THE RING
WE'RE GONNA HAVE FUN AND DO OUR OWN THING

Okay, you've made it this far into the book, so we might as well address "The Question." Most people who have seen a professional wrestling match have the same question: "Is it real?"

I'll answer that question with a question of my own: "What do you mean by 'real?'" If you mean authentic athletic competition where the outcome is in doubt, then of course pro wrestling doesn't fit that definition of "real." It's not a win-or-lose battle, and most people pick up on that fairly quickly. However, if by "real" you mean is it a situation where human beings are involved in highly athletic activities that the average fan: a) could not perform, and b) is willing to pay part of his or her entertainment dollar to see, then hell yeah, it's real! That's as real as it gets.

Let's look at this example: What if John Q. Public, the average wrestling fan, got picked up by a 350-pound wrestler and was thrown out of the ring (a 15-foot drop!) onto a hard concrete floor? He'd probably lie there until his head cleared, and what next? He'd probably take a couple days off from his job to recover. Well, guess what? That WAS my job and that DID happen to me when Mt. Fiji threw me out of the ring onto that not-soft-at-all concrete. Gravity is most definitely real. And so is a concrete floor!

Welcome to professional wrestling! When I got knocked on my butt, I had to pop right back up – no sitting around waiting for sympathy. You have to be in position for your next spot. There are no time-outs in pro wrestling.

Was there the risk of real injury? Of course! Any time you've got that much running, jumping, kicking, slapping, punching, choking, head-locking, and clotheslining … well, you get the idea. Go back to the audition stories and read about the very real injuries a few of my former cast members suffered. The injuries are most definitely real.

Luckily, we practiced five days a week before the live show on Saturday. It was so important to know what was going on, both inside and outside the ring, at all times. You had to know what holds or maneuvers your opponent was going to perform so you could respond in a way that not only looked realistic to the fans, but also minimized the risk of injury. When I look at tapes of the old matches, I can't believe how freaking flexible I was! I was like Gumby with heavy metal hair. I could twist and turn in all directions without getting seriously injured. At 5-foot-7, 115 pounds, I didn't have enough time to keep any fat on me – in the wrestling ring six days a week, plus spending what little free time I had in the weight room working out. God, I miss that metabolism of my 20s!

Even with all the practice, there were still injuries. One time Susie Spirit (obviously a "good girl," as you can tell by the name) had an accident during a match against The Headhunters and dislocated her elbow. She had to be helped out of the ring and missed a few weeks while she recovered. They must have shown slow-motion replays of the injury more than 100 times, and I'm sure Susie got sick of that. Many years later, I heard that the show had been short on content and had to fill time, which is why they showed that segment over and over. But it was effective. Years later, many people still remember that match and the injury.

At the time, most *GLOW* fans assumed it was all part of the act – a "work" in wrestling lingo – and part of the storyline. But it was, in fact, a legitimate injury. I challenge anyone out there to watch a video of that match and tell me that pro wrestling isn't real.

☆ ☆ ☆

While Mando Guerrero trained the first batch of *GLOW* girls for the pilot, training duties were later handled by Dallas (Debi Pelletier) and Princess Jasmine (Cynthia Peretti, who had played Pepper in the pilot). Matilda was friends with Debi, who was already a wrestler and was dating fellow wrestler "The Alaskan" Jay York. Debi lived in Los Angeles and Matilda told her *GLOW* could use another trainer, so Debi drove to Las Vegas to meet with the producers and was hired as a trainer.

Debi had wrestled in California for promoter Karl Lauer under the name "Debi the Killer Tomato." Shortly after she started with *GLOW,* she pulled me aside and told me I needed help with my dropkicks, so she worked with me to get them right, which was greatly appreciated. She had been working as a trainer for about three months when Matt Cimber saw her wearing a cowboy hat that she had picked up at a rodeo in Vegas.

"You look really cute in that cowboy hat," Matt said. "We ought to make you an on-screen character. Your *GLOW* name will be Dallas." Just like that, we had a new *GLOW* girl, doing a Dallas Cowboys cheerleader-type gimmick.

But Debi only stayed with *GLOW* for the first season and decided to jump ship. They had us wrestling in a boxing ring, which is more rigid and less forgiving than a pro wrestling ring. She had had enough experience in wrestling to know the difference, and she felt the producers were putting the girls in an unsafe environment. Girls were getting hurt left and right and she complained about it, but her complaints fell on deaf ears. It wasn't the ring, some said; the girls must not be falling right. She also saw a lot of unwanted sexual tension going on within the company. She was in a relationship and had a four-year-old at home, and she figured it just wasn't the right place for her, so she left. I remained friends with her and even did a tour of Panama for her and "The Alaskan" years later.

Dallas taught me how to execute a dropkick, which became one of my signature moves – at least, one of my signature "legal" moves. Heels gotta heel, after all. Later on, *GLOW* girls Ninotchka, Americana, Debbie Debutante, and Royal Hawaiian would train the rest of the girls.

On top of the physical demands of pro wrestling, there was also the entertainment aspect. Let's be honest, if all we did was show up and throw each other around the ring without showing emotion or interacting with the crowd, then pro wrestling wouldn't be nearly as popular as it is. Fans are just as interested in the characters and the storylines as they are in the physical act of wrestling itself – even more interested, most of the time. And the *GLOW* writers had plenty of characters to work with. First, there were the "good girls," which included Tina and Ashley, the lollipop-licking Tammy Jones, the ditzy-but-cute California Doll, Americana, Scarlett and Tara the Southern Belles, Little Fiji, and Little Egypt. Then there were the "bad girls," which included Hollywood and Vine, Matilda the Hun (a 6-foot-4 wrestler who squashed plenty of opponents; the natural adversary for Mt. Fiji), The Heavy Metal Sisters, Spanish Red, and Attaché (a kick-ass Marine who loved to beat up the good girls).

GLOW's good girls were managed by Jackie Stallone, the mother of Sylvester and Frank Stallone. Sylvester, obviously, was famous for his Rocky and Rambo movies. Frank, while he did some acting, wasn't nearly as well-known to the general public – unless you watched *Saturday Night Live* back when Norm Macdonald was on Weekend Update. Jackie showed up in promos and even had her own rap. The good girls she managed were called "Stallone's Sweethearts."

The bad girls also had a manager, Aunt Kitty. She was a large, blonde-haired woman who watched the matches ringside and defended us against the booing, goody-two-shoes fans. Aunt Kitty was actually Matt Cimber's real-life aunt, and he had found a role for her as *GLOW*'s resident heel manager. Aunt Kitty didn't have any problem approaching the ring and handing us "illegal" weapons when the ref wasn't looking. To emphasize our villainous nature, the bad girls were called "Kitty's Killers."

Early on, I really hated the outfit that the wardrobe had given me. It was pink with black sides, and it made me look really flat-chested. It was just not a flattering look for me at all. So I went shopping at the "stripper stores" — Frederick's of Hollywood and Playmates over on Hollywood Boulevard — and picked up some clothes that I thought looked hot. I'd buy an outfit for me and a matching one for Vine, and those outfits became our new ring gear. I never asked permission, either. Why ask when someone might say no? That's why Vine and I had several different outfits and different looks. One show, we might wear animal prints. Next, we would do corsets. Then next, we'd have cute little leather miniskirts. Sometimes I would wear a black choker that I thought looked very heavy metal. I was trying to mimic the looks of the video vixens on MTV because I loved that rock and roll, heavy metal look. I think those outfits and that rock and roll fashion sense really made Vine and me stand out early on. Once I had some outfits that I thought were more flattering, I felt more comfortable in my own skin and more at ease in the ring.

Our biggest rivals during the first season were definitely Tina and Ashley. While Hollywood and Vine were always introduced as "street punks," Tina and Ashley were promoted as the sophisticated beauties who always looked like they had just gotten done shopping on Rodeo Drive. Their initials were "T&A" — hmmm, I wonder if that was intentional? Vine and I were always announced first, and we would usually do something "evil" when we came out, like vandalizing the arena with spray paint or pretending to steal the fans' watches and jewelry. Tina and Ashley, on the other hand, would come out posing and preening for their adoring fans. Of course, that just gave us a great opportunity to attack them outside the ring before the match officially started.

Like any other job, the more you do it, the more comfortable you get. With every new week of the GLOW tapings, I felt more and more at home. When we filmed the pilot, I was so nervous I couldn't even look individual fans in the eye. Before long, I was not only looking at them, but I was also interacting with them.

"Hey! Anyone over here have a belt I can borrow?"

"I do! Take mine, Hollywood!"

The first guy who could whip off his belt the fastest gave it to me. I then put it around my opponent's neck and threw her into the audience, where I would punch, kick, and choke her. I would also grab fans' drinks – a beer or Coke perhaps – take a sip, and then throw the rest in a good girl's face. An interactive fan experience! Sometimes I would ask the cameramen to lay out extra cables around ringside and have them tape the cables down with neon-colored tape. During the match, I would find the non-essential cables that had been marked for me, pull one up, and wrap it around my opponent's neck and drag her out through the audience with it.

And it was GREAT! Vine and I would enter the arena to a blasting rendition of Mötley Crüe's "Looks That Kill" being played on a boombox by a couple of male fans waiting for us to come out. Again, great music continued to play a huge part in my life. With such a hard-rocking introduction, the fans always reacted to our entrance. The fans who liked the bad girls cheered, and some even held up homemade signs – their support was awesome! Then, of course, there were the fans who liked the good girls (BOR-ing!), who booed when we came in. Either way, it was great theater.

None of the matches on *GLOW* were freestyle. Every single match was scripted. The wrestlers wrote down exactly what moves they wanted – based on the concept for the match and some input from the writers – and then we had to memorize the moves and rehearse them. Rehearsals also gave the cameramen a chance to think about the best shots.

The matches themselves usually followed a familiar script: 10-20 minutes of give-and-take action between the babyface(s) and the heel(s). There were always several near-pins – when the ref slapped the mat two times, but the girl on the bottom managed to escape just before the required three-count. And the heels always did plenty of things that were against the rules (let's be honest – who's ever seen a pro wrestling rulebook?) to try to gain an advantage. Most of the time, the babyface would overcome the heel's illegal tactics to win and the crowd cheered the triumph of good over evil.

I absolutely LOVED my role as a heel and played it to the hilt. I would get to the gig early and hide all sorts of props under the ring before the crowd came in and before any of the talent got there. I mean, the look of surprise on their faces was priceless — spray paint, an extension cord, cups of water, and handcuffs, which we used a lot. (Let's see, a bunch of young, in-shape, athletic women wearing bathing suits or wrestling tights who also liked to put handcuffs on each other? No wonder *GLOW* had such good ratings!) On the rare occasion when I was allowed to win, I waved to the crowd and flashed my "cherub-cheeked" smile (as one of my loyal fans calls it) to the crowd. When I lost, as heels usually did, I sure as hell didn't go down quietly. Sometimes I'd kick my opponent in the stomach when the referee was holding up her hand in victory; sometimes I'd be dragged out kicking and screaming; whatever it took to play up my bad girl persona for the fans. Once in a while, another heel — like Matilda the Hun, Attaché, or Envy — would come out and help us attack the babyfaces. David McLane even got into the act one night, dragging Vine out of the arena.

In addition to wrestling, *GLOW* was also known for its comedy skits. Remember the old TV show *Hee Haw*? Our skits were a lot like that – campy as hell, but totally in line with the show. I think it added a little sex appeal and cheeky humor, too. Here's an example of the dialogue in a skit where Aunt Kitty and I knocked on David McLane's hotel room door. The idea behind the skit was that Aunt Kitty wanted me to marry David so she could take over *GLOW*. The room that you see David come out of, Room 575, was actually the room David was living in at the Riviera Hotel.

Aunt Kitty (to David): "Hollywood's got such pretty skin. I gave her $100 to get a facial."

David McLane: "Oh, yeah? What did she do with the money?"

Another one had Aunt Kitty carrying a pie for David while I smiled next to her ...

Aunt Kitty: "David, look what this girl did for you. Have a piece."

David: "Alright, I will." (He takes a piece and makes a face as he eats it.)

Aunt Kitty: "She baked it with her own two hands."

David: "It tastes like she baked it with her own two feet!"

Then Aunt Kitty smashes the pie in David's face!

There was another skit where I was getting examined in the office of Doctors Fiel and Grope. (Yeah, you read the names right. I told you it was campy.) Believe it or not, Dr. Grope was an actual doctor for our director, Matt Cimber. He did some acting on the side.

Doctor: "Tell me, my dear, what is the difference between love and a hamburger?"

Hollywood: "I don't know."

Doctor: "Good – then meet me for lunch tomorrow!"

Even the play-by-play, ringside commentary was cheesy. For example, later on in seasons two through four, the announcer, "Motormouth" Mike Morgan, would say something like, "And there's a clothesline! But we all know Hollywood will never come clean." Or as two girls circled each other, he might say, "A little game of cat and mouse to see who's the 'Big Cheese.'"

See what I mean by campy? But it was also a lot of fun, and it was my first real chance to break into show business, which I had wanted to do ever since I was a little girl. Besides, who the hell was I to complain about cheesiness? I was a former French Fry Queen!

But GLOW wasn't all fun and games. We were still making a television show. We had to keep to our times in our matches and make sure everything looked good and was safe. We had to remember our lines. And producing weekly content can be stressful, for both the performers and the executives. Our director, Matt Cimber, was always yelling and screaming at us to get this and that right. I was always getting yelled at in that first season. I really am pretty tough, but I remember one night, after a season one show, he laid into me so badly I started to cry. Years later, I can't even remember why he was yelling at me. This taught me that you'd better have tough skin in the entertainment business. If you don't, this kind of work is not for you.

We also had to stay in shape at all times. Matt was telling everybody about how they had to be thin, so all the girls were on a strict diet. I was very blessed with my metabolism; I was able to eat whatever I wanted and not gain weight. But he really got to some of the other girls. In seasons three and four, he was on Godiva's butt all the time. Godiva was never fat. She was absolutely beautiful and had curves like Marilyn Monroe — which is awesome — but he made her feel bad and wanted her to diet. The atmosphere at *GLOW* made a lot of girls feel insecure with their bodies and how they looked.

It was during the second season that Vine, me, and a few other girls worked on a sitcom called *We Got It Made* and *The Kenny Rogers Special.* In our trailer was not one, but two Screen Actors Guild contracts for each of us — one for cable and one for "free" TV. This was my first union contract. I was working Taft-Hartley. That means whenever a signatory producer hires a performer that is not a member of SAG-AFTRA, they must report such hiring to the guild. After that, the SAG department mails the actor a letter informing her that she is now able to join SAG. I think you have one year before you have to join. Back in 1987, there was a $1,200 initiation fee, followed by annual dues. Today that fee is much higher. Unfortunately Vine and I never filmed anything that day with Kenny Rogers because the show ran over time, but we were paid our union wages.

During our downtime, the producers always had something going on to keep us busy … so they could keep an eye on us. On January 1, 1988, during the third season, we were invited to the Riviera Hotel to see Mr. Riklis' wife, Pia Zadora, sing in the main showroom. The actress and singer first appeared onscreen in the 1964 movie *Santa Claus Conquers the Martians* as a Martian child. She became nationally known in 1982 when she accomplished a very rare feat. She won the Golden

Globe for New Star of the Year and two Razzie Awards (the opposite of the Oscars) for Worst Actress and Worst New Star —all for the same movie, *Butterfly*. She later appeared as a beatnik in John Waters' cult classic *Hairspray* and as herself in the third *Naked Gun* movie.

Pia was much more famous — and acclaimed — for her musical career. Everyone glammed up for the big event — girls in dresses and guys in suits and ties. Pia was the headliner, and legendary comedian Alan King was the opening act. King grumbled about being an opening act again after all these years but added, for what he was being paid, he'd open a toilet!

I was not into Pia's type of music, so I wasn't really looking forward to it. And of course, they would not let me out of it. Ultimately, I convinced myself that going out with everybody would be fun.

I don't think I had been to a Las Vegas show of that type before. The venue looked exactly like when Elvis Presley played the Las Vegas Hilton in 1976, with everyone sitting in their red, tablecloth booths with white napkins, having drinks, and watching a show. We all sat at a big table to the side of the stage.

When Pia first went on, me being young, I tried not to laugh. We had already been through an hour of Alan King, and now I just had to sit there listening to Pia belt it out. To be honest, I was pretty darn bored, but I could not leave while Mr. Riklis' wife was performing. That would've been very disrespectful and rude. But by staying, I was able to attend the VIP afterparty with all the executives.

That was the only time I saw Pia sing. I met her again 35 years later through people with Shatner Universe, a production company connected to the famous actor William Shatner. They wanted to use her as a guest on a new reality show, but the show never happened.

Another Perspective: Keith Ishii (GLOW Fan)

Like many male teenagers of the '80s, I was obsessed with many things: video games, girls, television, rock music ... and wrestling. There was no better way to end a Saturday night than to turn on the TV and sit down to watch *Saturday Night's Main Event*. Randy Savage dropping elbows from the top rope; Greg Valentine applying his figure four leglock; and Hulk Hogan screaming into a microphone while tearing his shirt off! It was a weekly ritual to watch the WWF on the weekend, and I usually never missed it. Then one night, as I sat on the couch watching the glory of two gigantic men throw each other across the ring in the final match, there came a teaser for the next show. Normally the programming after wrestling was nothing interesting, but on this particular night, the announcer mentioned something about "the gorgeous ladies of wrestling," which would be coming up. I had no idea what he was talking about, but the words intrigued me. Of course they intrigued me! I was a teenage boy with hormones flying around like a cyclone in the Midwest. Gorgeous ladies? Wrestling? I didn't know what it meant that they apparently had an entire show based on this, but I was in!

Then I started watching it, and I have to admit that at first, I was puzzled. What exactly was this? It started off with a bunch of girls rapping, and it intermingled the wrestling with cheesy jokes and sketches ... it was bizarre. But even as I whispered to myself that this was ridiculous, I couldn't bring myself to turn it off. There was something almost hypnotic about it. Years later, I came to realize what that was. The first time you see anything groundbreaking and brilliant, you're stunned by it. It doesn't fit into the normal, everyday reality of what you see, and your first reaction is to cringe and wonder what's going on. But *GLOW* was doing something that was both unique for its time and remains unique today. The coupling of *Laugh-In*-type quick-fire sketches with the popular style of rapping — which was just finding its audience at that time — combined with colorful characters and athletics was genius, not to mention trailblazing for women's wrestling. And I, like almost anyone else who watched it, appreciated it on the deepest level for its entertainment value and what it did for women in the sport.

I have to say my favorite character was Hollywood. She was brash, sexy, street smart, outspoken, and tough! What's not to like about that? I've always found that the more appealing characters were the villains, and she was great at playing that role. From attacking the Farmer's Daughter outside the ring before the bell, to dressing up as a German and parading next to a German flag, she was the perfect balance of a villain you wanted to see get her just due, while at the same time making you love everything about her sexy demeanor and conviction in whatever she was doing. Over 30 years since its abrupt end, there still hasn't been anything quite like it, and *GLOW* was one of those shows that I always remembered vividly and loved because of its uniqueness. The action was great; the skits were so cheesy that you had to laugh; and the characters were awesome! I got invested in them as much as a housewife who watched soap operas all day and talked to her husband about them as if they were real people. Like most teenage boys, I had a crush on a few of them (*cough* *Hollywood*). After all, they were the *Gorgeous Ladies of Wrestling*! But thankfully, the sex appeal of the women wasn't all there was to it. There was so much more, and that's what made the show so memorable. It wasn't just a bunch of beautiful women flaunting their bodies, standing around in a ring. They were performers in every sense of the word — from the physical punishment they took, to the skits they performed, to the interviews they gave on talk shows, to simply staying in character day and night. They were dedicated actors and athletes, and I think I speak for everyone who is a fan when I say that we sincerely appreciated that!

Chapter 13: Adventures in Japan

When season two of *GLOW* ended, I didn't want to go back. I really thought I was done. I was missing my family, my friends, my boyfriend, my home, and all the fun things to do in California. I felt like I badly needed a break. My relationships were strained from not being home full time. But another opportunity presented itself. And despite my homesickness, I felt that I had to take advantage of it.

That spring, I had an interview for a modeling gig that was headed to the Far East, so I decided to go to Japan with eleven other models. We were supposed to be gone for two months, and I would be required to do a fashion show every night. The promoter for this was named James Adams. I had never met any of the other girls before. They weren't wrestlers; they were actresses and real models. In a way, they reminded me of the original *GLOW* girls – some were nice, but others were a bit catty.

I had never been to Japan, and the only piece of advice I got was to keep my passport with me at all times. It just so happened that the night we did a fashion show at a club called The Red Lantern was also my birthday. James had a birthday cake for me, and we celebrated until the early morning with the girls and some of the Japanese promoters. We went from club to club to club — definitely one of my most unique birthdays!

Every place we went to we were escorted by the Japanese mafia, the yakuza. At one club, there was a man they called Chin-Chin Man ("Pee-Pee Man"). One minute, Chin-Chin Man was dancing on top of the table wearing something that looked like a diaper. The next minute, I saw him spinning a 45 record on his penis! Then he put his privates into an ashtray and just kept right on boogying away. It wasn't the kind of thing you saw every day ... at least, I didn't.

At another club we went to, I saw the most beautiful looking women I had ever seen. As I got closer, though, I noticed that their voices were deeper than most women I knew. It turned out that they were men in drag. At that point, I'd never been to a drag show before. I mean, I knew they existed, but had not been to a club where men dressed as women. They were all very nice, too — both the ones with breast implants and the ones without.

On another evening, I remember us going to dinner with one of the businessmen, and while I thought I had ordered crab, I had actually ordered crab *brains*. Another time, I had shark fin soup — a delicacy in Japan, for sure, but not something I'd eat on a regular basis. On one of our free weekends, they even took us to Tokyo Disneyland. It was so much cleaner than the one in Anaheim, California. I took many photos that day because, let's face it, I was pretty sure I would never get a chance to go to Tokyo Disneyland again.

Now, once we got done with the fashion shows, the customers would call the models to spend some time at their tables to eat, drink, and socialize. Usually there was a hostess sitting on a stool next to the customer acting as an interpreter for us. I drank Hennessy because I noticed that's what everyone else was drinking. When we were done with dinner, they would tip us for our time and company. There was no talk of sex or anything like that. Thank God, because I was not there to do anything else besides modeling.

The promoter, James, said that we needed to give him the tip money we received to put in the kitty and split with all the models. However, I noticed that the same two girls were never getting called to those tables, but we still had to split our money with them. Most of the models did not like this, and neither did I. Why should we have to give some of our tip money to girls who weren't working? After being there for three weeks, another girl and I decided that we had had enough, and we started looking for a way to get back to the U.S. But every time I called the airlines to switch my flight, they would tell me that all the flights were sold out. I kept thinking, *I'm never going to get out of here!*

At another venue, the Chippendales (the male exotic dance troupe) were appearing on the same dates as we were. When we ran into them at a tanning salon one day, I told one of the guys about my desire to go home and my problems with the airlines. He told me to tell the airlines that my working visa was about to expire. I did what he said, and sure enough, they had me on a flight as soon as I wanted to go.

I decided to sneak out with the other girl who wanted to leave. Wrong thing to do! We left for Japan's Narita Airport during broad daylight (around 11 a.m.) in front of staff and guests. We stood out like sore thumbs because we were so much taller and lighter-skinned than everybody else. When we got to the airport, we decided to sit somewhere out of sight. Just when I started to think we were in the clear, out of nowhere came James, running into the room we were sitting in. My heart dropped! I was surprised and totally embarrassed at the same time. Why didn't I just tell him I wanted to leave instead of sneaking out? He asked what he could do to change our minds.

"Nothing," I said. "We're going home!" And that's exactly what we did. Japan had been a unique experience, but it was just time for me to go back home.

Chapter 14: Strained Relationships and Backstage Drama

As I previously mentioned, Vine left the show at the start of the third season. Even though our tag team partnership helped me to establish the "Hollywood" identity that has been part of my life ever since, I felt like going solo actually helped my career. It wasn't just the fact that Vine and I didn't get along very well outside the ring. I mean, we roomed together, ate together, and did sketches together. We were always side-by-side. With all due respect to Vine, it just felt freeing to do something a little different and go my own way.

Doing more singles matches allowed me the freedom to be more creative. Along with training sessions, I also watched WWF (now called WWE) matches to pick up new holds and moves. One of my favorites was the flying head scissors. It was a great finishing move that I started to use a lot during *GLOW*'s third season. I recorded WWF programming and carefully watched how the move was executed: how to time the jump, how to roll through, and how to land safely, both for myself and my opponent. I worked through the move with Tulsa, who proved to be a terrific and willing "practice dummy." If I wanted to learn something new, I did my due diligence on my own time, watched it on TV, and worked it out.

Just like any job you have, there are going to be some of your fellow coworkers you get along with really well and others that … you don't. (Have you ever seen the sitcom *The Office*? I rest my case.) Outside the ring, I hung out with several of the other *GLOW* girls: Godiva, Daisy, Lightning, Major Tanya, and MTV, to name a few. We would all hit the rock clubs and have a pretty good time. One of the girls I DIDN'T get along with was Sally the Farmer's Daughter. We were both from the same high school, and that's probably the main reason we were always trying to outdo each other. (I was voted "Best Looking" my senior year. How about her?)

The ironic thing was that some of my most action-packed singles matches were against Sally. I wrestled her more than any other babyface since the office knew that those matches were going to be good — because we genuinely did not like each other. One of my most memorable matches against Sally was one in which we didn't even make it into the ring – we began brawling outside the ring and the Riviera's security guards had to separate us. I threw her into a pillar; she reversed it and threw me into the pillar and it broke. I threw her into the audience; she threw me into the audience. We were dragged out of the arena without having an official match.

The next week, we fought in a Texas Barroom Brawl. The fighting could take place anywhere in the arena, but to win the match, we had to pin the other girl in such a way that she couldn't get to her feet for a full 10-count. I kicked her ass, by the way.

One thing that really bothered me about Sally was the fact that she clearly didn't care about my safety or well-being during our matches. It might not be obvious to the average spectator, but when two girls are involved in a pro wrestling match, it is incredibly important that they work together. Sure, to the viewing audience, we're "opponents." But if you step back and look at things objectively, it should come as no surprise that the two combatants work as partners. After all, if someone is going to lift you over her head and slam you onto the mat, you should probably have a decent working relationship, right? Well, that relationship —and the trust that went with it — never existed between Sally and me, mostly because she refused to drop her initial negative attitude toward me and work together in a professional manner.

One time during a match in Nebraska, Sally tossed me out of the ring in the general direction of the audience. However, she was so careless in doing so that my feet caught the top rope of the ring, and I fell awkwardly onto the arena's hard concrete floor. Needless to say, I was pissed off. Who wouldn't be? In spite of the pain, I bounced off the floor and arm-dragged Sally back into the ring, where I stomped on her belly so hard it knocked the wind out of her. In wrestling, that's called giving a "receipt" –a bit of payback, if you will.

At the end of the match, we left the arena screaming at each other. Mt. Fiji and Big Bad Mama had to break us apart. Little did the fans know how "real" that conflict was!

Speaking of "real" one afternoon after we finished with our dress rehearsal, which was on Fridays.

Some of the *GLOW* girls and I walked across the street to Circus Circus. We were still dressed in our workout bodysuit gear. Let's just say we weren't wearing a lot.

As we walked past a group of girls, I heard one of them say, "Put some clothes on!" I knew they were talking about us, so I turned around and said, "What did you say?"

I went into Hollywood heel mode. I tried to dropkick her, but hit air. That was embarrassing.

The next minute she and I were in a ball on the ground. This was a real competitive fight, something I was not used to.

Security came, pulled me back, and a patron from the casino pulled the other girl back. She cut loose from him, and while my hands were still being held behind my back, she cold cocked me right in the eye. I had a huge black eye.

The cops came and asked if I wanted to press charges. I said yes.

A few hours later, the same girl called me and apologized. I did not press charges.

I learned the hard way pro wrestling and real fighting is not quite the same.

☆ ☆ ☆

There was one match/interview where I had to wear Broadway Rose's outfit.

Now everybody remembers in season three and four that my wrestling gear consisted of black lingerie and fishnets.

This particular show would not allow it, it was too risqué and so they made me change. And that is why I was wearing Broadway Rose's purple one piece.

☆ ☆ ☆

A great memory is meeting the late great George Pérez. an American comic book artist working for Marvel comics and DC comics. I had the honor of working with him at one of the wrestling companies in Los Angeles. He would have storyboards of wrestlers and the matches he would direct

He named my character Blonde Vixen.

George drew me the most beautiful portrait of that character that I still keep on my wall today.

Sadly, Jorge passed away on May 6, 2022 of inoperable pancreatic cancer.

Hollywood as Blonde Vixen, drawn by the late George Pérez.

Another Perspective: Mark Chervinsky (Filmmaker)

I first met Hollywood at the premier party for the documentary *GLOW: The Story of the Gorgeous Ladies of Wrestling* at the Dresden in Los Feliz, Los Angeles. I was there to support my friend Jason Connell, who produced the film, and to meet people I could use in my own documentary *At What Cost? Anatomy of Professional Wrestling*.

After schmoozing with Little Egypt, Jungle Woman, and Ashley Cartier, I finally crossed paths with Hollywood. Dressed in a long, crocheted dress, she looked stunning. It was clear during the photos taken before the movie and during the Q&A afterwards that she still was the troublemaker of the girls – my kind of person! One good thing about making movies is you always have an opener to talk to good-looking women. I introduced myself and told her about my film, and we talked for a little while. Before she left, she gave me her card, told me to email her, pointed out wrestler and actor "Mr. Outrageous" Al Burke, and told me I should talk to him. I did just that, and not only is he now in my movie, but we are still friends.

The night concluded with me being cock-blocked by The Heavy Metal Sisters, my wingman bailing on me, grabbing breakfast with some *GLOW* girls, and enjoying a quick make-out session with a *GLOW* girl, who will remain nameless. Not bad for a weeknight!

A few weeks later, Hollywood was back in Hollywood. This time, she was in front of my cameras, and I knew her well enough to be calling her "Jeanne." Wearing a leopard print sweater, she let me interview her for an hour. She told me about the audition process for *GLOW*, Mando Guerrero, learning how to be a great heel, getting in trouble in Tijuana, and what Sylvester Stallone's mom was like. I asked her questions like: "Did Britney Spears steal your look?"; "Are you the queen of catfight videos?"; and "What's on your Amazon wish list?" She also showed me a script for a custom video she was in town to shoot. I was fascinated by how detailed it was — and also by the fact that gut punches are very popular with her clientele.

All in all, I was glad to see that this once very popular *GLOW* girl from the '80s was able to turn her experience into a career using the skills she learned, which so few people do. I was happy to meet her, put her in my film, and call her a friend.

Chapter 15: GLOW on Tour

Some of my craziest travel experiences, no doubt, took place when I was still a *GLOW* girl. We took the show on the road in 1986, flying to Miami and then taking buses to different venues in the Southeast.

Touring was one of my favorite things to do. We would try to stop at the local Hard Rock Cafe in every place that we toured and pick up a Hard Rock T-shirt from that city as a souvenir.

There were two different buses: one for the "Good Girls" and one for the "Bad Girls." Our tour was organized by the same company that used to promote the Harlem Globetrotters. Even better, the heel bus was an old touring bus once used by the 1970s blues-rock band Foghat. For someone like me, who had been following rock music since before junior high school, this was even cooler than the Globetrotters connection.

Since our show was still new, we needed to work very hard to promote it. We performed a lot of shows, ate way too many meals at Shoney's and Waffle House, and were followed every step of the way by a growing legion of *GLOW* fans. After our first show at the James L. Knight Center in Miami, some of these fans followed us back to our hotel. When one of them knocked on the door to our room asking for an autograph, Vine freaked out. I wanted to open the door, but she wanted to call security, so we compromised and had him slide his pen and paper under the door.

Even though all this promotion work was fun, it was also kind of exhausting. One of my final memories of that first tour was falling asleep in the darkened catacombs of the Bad Girl/Foghat bus, then waking up to a "Good News, Bad News" situation. The good news was that we were in Alabama on a bright, sunny day. The bad news was that we were near a paper mill. How could I tell? If you have to ask, then you've never been near a paper mill. The smell is unique, to say the least. You will never forget that fragrance!

Our first *GLOW* tour was limited to Miami and Alabama, but as the show became more popular, we went out on the road more and more.

During seasons three and four, we toured the Midwest, the South, and also the East Coast. And as much fun as those tours were, they also came with their share of problems. The night before we were scheduled to appear on *The Sally Jessy Raphael Show* in New York, Vine and I missed our connecting flight out of Chicago. This was a big problem, of course – how could the *GLOW* girls go on a major daytime talk show without their most well-known villains? Thinking fast, Vine and I caught a different flight to New Jersey and called Matt Cimber from the plane to politely explain the situation and request transportation whenever we landed. When our red-eye flight arrived, there was a limo waiting; unfortunately, this didn't include our luggage (costumes, toothbrushes, etc.). Still, we managed to make it to the show — although Vine ultimately appeared in the audience, not with me, MTV, and Godiva in the ring they had set up. If I had to describe the way we got there, I would use the phrase "by the skin of our teeth."

On a tour during season three, Godiva and I were driven to a rock club in Rhode Island called JR's Fast Lane. Matt told us that we'd be judging a Halloween costume contest. As tired as we were, Godiva and I were still excited about the idea. As it turned out, we were smart to be excited. When the limo dropped us off, we walked into a totally kick-ass, rock and roll club. The costumes were awesome, incredible, and unique. These people knew how to rock a contest. I had never seen costumes like these; they were very creative and everyone was dressed to the nines. I had never seen that in L.A. Even better, we met up with a few fans afterwards who were VERY interested in us, and I ended up bringing one of those fans back to my room. The next morning, I went to breakfast with that fan, and I could have sworn I saw Matt glaring at me from across the room.

When I got back to my room, I realized that my interpretation of Matt's glare was accurate.

"Don't you know you're not supposed to bring fans back to your room?" he shouted at me.

"No!" I shouted back. "I only work Wednesday to Sunday, so how could I know this rule?"

I was also upset because I saw other *GLOW* girls violate this rule all the time. Big Bad Mama and Stinky were doing it. Well, maybe not "all the time," but I'd seen it enough to know it wasn't a hard-and-fast rule. I didn't see what the big deal was. It wasn't like I had been caught dancing with a Chippendale dancer. (That happened somewhere down the line.)

Matt wouldn't get off my case, though. He threatened to send me home without pay. Even worse, I was going to have to miss *The Phil Donahue Show*, which was a huge deal at the time. I don't know what got into Matt, but eventually someone must have talked some sense into him because I was not sent home, and I was allowed to go on the *Donahue* show with all the other girls. Phil Donahue himself was really great. The funniest thing was when we showed up at the show, he was wearing jeans, a T-shirt, and a black leather jacket. He looked more like "The Fonz" than the professional, suit-and-tie-wearing interviewer I had seen on TV over the years. He wore this outfit for our segment of the show.

This incident wasn't the only time I clashed with *GLOW* management. One time in Chicago, Gabe Elias — our PR guy who was always using our frequent flier miles for himself — booked Mt. Fiji and me at a Boys & Girls Club event at the Fairmont Hotel. There, we met greats like Michael Jordan, Scottie Pippen, and Willie Mays. Once Gabe was sure we were there, he bailed out, leaving us with no per diem money or anything. I had one of my friends send me $50 through Western Union. But once we showed up at Johnny Rockets, the whole wait staff knew who we were and comped our entire meal.

All of these run-ins with management got me something of a "reputation," I guess. One time in San Diego, we were all in a cast meeting when the director pointed at me and said, "No one is going to Tijuana tonight. We have a show to do tomorrow!" To reinforce the point, he said that if he found out anyone had taken Stinky to Tijuana, we would be "double-fined." After the meeting, the other girls were kind of bummed out, but I said, "Hey, we made plans to go to Tijuana BEFORE we knew the rule. We're still going." I wanted silver tips for my black cowboy boots and a Hard Rock Cafe T-shirt from Tijuana, and I was going to get them. So Godiva, Daisy, Stinky, and I wound up making the trip, with a minor detour on the way back to tour one of the Navy's nuclear submarines. (Believe me, security was tight.) When I finally got back to the hotel, Daisy came running up to me.

"They know we went to Tijuana!" she yelled, panicking.

So, more drama. Johnny C. saw the "Hard Rock Cafe: Tijuana" bag I was carrying and grabbed it out of my hands.

"Look! They went to Tijuana!" he shouted.

My God. What a narc!

Matt threatened to dock my pay, along with the other girls' pay. Needless to say, no one was happy. But the funny thing was, they didn't dock my pay one cent. And I think I know the reason why. For all the "rule-breaking" grief I gave the producers, I was 100% professional when it came to being on the show. I was never late, never missed a taping, and never missed a meeting. In fact, I usually showed up before the shows to hide props (chains, etc.) and talk to the cameramen about specific shots. I wanted to give the fans a great show, and I wanted all of the "spontaneous" things that happened during a typical *GLOW* match to go smoothly. And they usually – if not always – did.

That night we went ahead and did the show in San Diego (at our full rate of pay), and afterwards a fan came up to Godiva and me and handed each of us a package. I swear, I thought mine had drugs in it! But when I opened it, I saw that it was a HUGE blue Topaz heart ... 14 carats! It was a really nice gesture from the fan.

Years later, I reminded Johnny C. about the time he narc'd me out. He didn't remember it at all. "Oh, my God, did I really do that?" he said, acting surprised. Yep, you did. We had a laugh about it. There were no hard feelings, especially since no one docked my pay.

As for Stinky, she actually bought a leather jacket that night in Tijuana, but she was so afraid someone might find out that she had been in Tijuana with us that she kept it hidden from everyone for the entire tour.

☆ ☆ ☆

Sometimes even the "bad" events wind up having funny conclusions. One time Mt. Fiji and I were staying at a hotel in Calgary. Usually the heels didn't room with the babyfaces. It was the 1980s and even *GLOW* tried to maintain a little bit of "kayfabe," which is a wrestling code meant to maintain the illusion that the heels and babyfaces were rivals and that wrestling was a legitimate contest. But on this particular night, Fiji and I were paired up together. In the middle of the night, I heard a distant chiming, like a clock going off somewhere in the distance. It was really annoying, and I couldn't sleep. When it struck thirteen, I realized that it probably wasn't a clock.

"What the hell is that noise?" I asked.

All of a sudden, we heard sirens out on the street. We looked out the window and saw a bunch of fire trucks, ambulances, and paramedics down below us.

"I wonder where the fire is?" Fiji said.

Cheryl "Lightning" Rusa called our room. "You guys have to get outside. There's a report of a fire in the hotel!"

Even though it was four in the morning, we got out of the room in a hurry and went down maybe twenty-five flights of stairs to safety because the elevators had been shut down. Fiji was a 350-pound woman, and I was trying to get her down those stairs as fast as we possibly could. We finally got outside, and everyone was standing around in robes and pajamas. Fiji still had her curlers in her hair. Fortunately, it turned out to be a false alarm — but man, what a wake-up call that was!

That Canadian tour almost landed me in some serious hot water. When we were crossing the border, the customs agents decided to interview all the girls. They pulled us into little interrogation rooms, one at a time. They asked me all sorts of questions: who I was, where we were going, our purpose in Canada – all the standard stuff. I remember

I was wearing a cool black leather jacket at the time. They eventually let us into Canada and we were off on our merry way.

It wasn't until a few days later when we were attending the Calgary Stampede rodeo event that I noticed something in one of the many pockets of my leather jacket. I stuck my hand in and noticed that there was a little hole in the bottom of the pocket. I reached down into the hole and found this little paper bindle, and there was – shall we say – a white powdery substance inside. I had drugs on me, and I had no idea how they had gotten in there. I don't know if someone had slipped it into my pocket or if I had been holding it for someone once and lost it in the hole of the pocket or what. Canada is super strict when it comes to drugs, and I had unknowingly carried some across the border. I was extremely lucky I didn't get busted.

Another Perspective: Douglas Dunning (GLOW's Sir Miles Headlock)

The best way to describe my time on David B. McLane's *GLOW, Gorgeous Ladies of Wrestling*, which aired from 1986 to 1990, would be to say that it was one the most memorable experiences of my life. I would characterize it as an experience not unlike Alice stepping into the Looking Glass of the world of women's wrestling.

I was surrounded by very beautiful ladies, such as Jeanne Basone and Trudy Adams. I was hired to portray Sir Miles Headlock, an offshoot of the immensely popular *Max Headroom* television show of the time. I was presented through a combination of live action video and Paintbox software, which was an early form of computer-generated imagery (CGI). My character was chroma keyed in and out by this technique.

The thirteen episodes that I appeared on were shot in 1986 and 1987 and were directed by Matt Cimber, a director known for *The Witch Who Came from the Sea* (1976) and *Butterfly* (1982) with Pia Zadora, as well as *Hundra* (1983) and *Yellow Hair and the Fortress of Gold* (1984), both of which starred a friend of mine, Laurene Landon.

Fortunately, I never sustained any injuries. However, I cannot say the same of the ladies! One I recall, Susie Spirit, took a horrendous fall and sustained a serious compound fracture where the broken bone actually broke through the skin. This horrible incident was used numerous times in flashbacks on successive episodes, which I personally considered to be in bad form, playing off someone else's pain.

All in all, being on *GLOW* was like being in a candy store with different flavors!

Chapter 16: Playboy Magazine

By 1988, *GLOW* had started to take off a little bit, despite our late-night programming slot in many locations. We were starting to get attention from both television viewers and magazine editors. *Playboy* magazine came calling — not for me specifically, but to the *GLOW* staff. They wanted to coordinate a shoot with several of the *GLOW* girls in a pictorial called "Lethal Women."

Surprisingly, they gave the *GLOW* producers free rein as to which girls they would pick to appear in the magazine. I guess they figured the producers knew us better than anyone, considering they worked with us on a daily basis. I'm sure *Playboy* insisted on having the final say-so, but the initial choices were made by our producers.

And, in another remarkable case of "right place, right time," I was one of the girls chosen to appear. It was one of my childhood dreams come true! There was only one problem. After I was told that I was one of the lucky girls, one of the members of our production staff told me I needed to come in for a meeting. Being young and naive, I was pretty excited. I figured we'd be going over all the details for the shoot: where to go, what time, what to wear, or NOT wear — that kind of thing. However, I would soon find out that this was going to be a very different kind of meeting. As I entered the room, I saw one couch and one chair. I made sure to sit in the chair, which was made for only one person. Once I sat down, the staff member spoke first.

"Before I okay you for the *Playboy* shoot, I'm going to have to see your body," he said.

See my body? What the hell was that supposed to mean? Didn't he and everyone else see my body each and every day during training and rehearsals, decked out in skimpy wrestling or workout attire?

"What do you mean?" I asked, although I was starting to figure out where he was coming from.

"Well, *Playboy* wants girls to be naked for their photo shoots, so I'm going to have to see you naked."

So that was it – the infamous "casting couch" scenario I'd heard so much about but had (thankfully) never experienced firsthand. I wasn't about to go along with this guy's scenario, and I decided to act quickly. I decided to turn on the water works. I started to cry.

"I came here to wrestle for *GLOW*, not to be treated like this," I said, with tears running down my cheeks. And that was true. I wasn't going to let anyone take advantage of me. I was making my stand. And I knew that it could very well have ramifications that could affect my position in *GLOW*.

"Well, if *Playboy* wants to see me naked, fine. But I don't think I should have to get naked for you. You work for *GLOW*, and you've already seen as much of my body as you need to," I said.

The staff member stood up and stepped closer to me. It seemed like he wasn't going to take no for an answer. Before I knew it, he was all over me, trying out holds and moves that you would never, ever see in a *GLOW* match. I was very insistent, though, and pushed him away. I left the room that day feeling both mad and down in the dumps – mad that this guy would try to use his position to get me to take my clothes off, and down in the dumps because maybe I had just missed an opportunity to pose for an internationally famous magazine that I had dreamed about posing in for years.

Still, I knew I had made the right decision. After working in the entertainment business for a few years, I already knew many girls who had "climbed the ladder" and received promotions or great roles by using their bodies as a bargaining chip. I absolutely did not want to be one of those girls.

The thing is, that kind of behavior was fairly common back then. This is way back before the #MeToo movement. But it still felt wrong to me; it felt wrong in the gut. And I have learned to trust my gut. It tends to lead me in the right direction.

Call it karma, fate, or whatever you like, but soon after that infamous meeting with the staff member, *Playboy* ultimately made the decision and invited me — along with two other *GLOW* girls, Godiva and Thunderbolt — to their studios to shoot some Polaroids and set up a shoot date. I was thrilled because I had been able to stick by my own personal set of standards and morals without missing out on a wonderful professional opportunity. When I left the initial meeting with the *Playboy* people, it definitely felt like I was walking on air.

On the day of the shoot, I was both nervous and excited. I had never posed nude before, so I had no idea what to expect. One of the first things that jumped out at me was how many people were there. I guess I had thought of it as being more "private" – like the model, the photographer, and that would be about it. Instead, it seemed like there were six or seven people around at all times: the stylist, the wardrobe person, the lighting expert, the makeup artist, etc. You might think that having more people around would make a person more nervous about taking her clothes off, but in a funny way, it made me less nervous. Yes, there were a lot of people around, but not one of them looked at me like I was a piece of meat or an object, and that really helped me settle down. If this photo shoot was just a normal, business-as-usual job for all these people, then maybe I could treat it that way, too.

The hardest part of the whole experience wasn't taking my clothes off. It was holding the same pose – perched on the side of a bathtub – for so long. God, it felt like hours! Because *Playboy* is such a high-class operation, of course they wanted to get the photos just right.

"Arch your back! Bend! Bend! Bend!" the photographer kept urging me. They wanted more curves, they said. Curves? Hell, I was as feminine as the next girl, but at that point in my career, I was more long-and-lean, Gumby-flexible wrestler than full-figured, voluptuous model. So I bent and I arched as hard as I could for a pose that they asked me to hold for what seemed like hours! When I woke up the next morning, I had a nasty looking bruise on my leg, but that was a small price to pay for appearing in *Playboy*, in my opinion!

We did the photo shoot in 1988, but the photos actually appeared in the December 1989 Issue. I had no idea what pics they were going to print: non-topless, topless, bottomless? I'll never forget the way I felt when the issue first hit newsstands. I felt proud of myself. I did not particularly like the pic someone at *Playboy* had chosen of me, since they had taken rolls and rolls of film that day, but I was very happy I was in it and had a full page in the magazine. I remember they had given Thunderbolt a quarter page. I think some of the other *GLOW* girls had to be jealous. It was such an honor to be asked to pose in *Playboy*!

My parents, however, had a slightly different reaction. It's not that they didn't support me. They've always encouraged me to follow my dreams and be my own person. It's just that they came from a different, more conservative generation. Plus, they were (and are) pretty devout Catholics. Remember when they threatened to send me to a private school if I didn't stop misbehaving? So, while it's not like they shunned me when the magazine came out, it's also safe to say that it wasn't a conversation starter at family get-togethers, either.

I felt really lucky to be associated with *Playboy*. In fact, I did three more photo shoots: a "Career Girls" spread in 1992 and two *Playboy's Book of Lingerie* shoots in 1993. Along with being the fulfillment of a childhood dream, there were other perks, too. I got to visit the Playboy Mansion quite a few times during the 1990s and attended some of the legendary parties there. Years later, in December 1998, I was invited to their annual New Year's Eve party. Although I had recently broken my leg (more on that later), I still thought, "Hell yes, I am going to go!" There was no way I was going to let that broken leg keep me from attending, so I wore this long, gold, cut-out, sexy dress and toted my crutches to the party. I had to sit a lot, but still, I had to go.

But just like everything else in Hollywood, once I stopped shooting, the invitations stopped coming. I don't mean that in a negative way; it's just that show business is definitely a "What have you done for me lately?" kind of profession. But another cool perk came when I got to meet Hugh Hefner. He autographed my December 1989 issue of *Playboy* at Glamourcon, a convention in L.A. for well-known models and their fans. Meeting Mr. Hefner was cool, but he was swarmed by so many fans, friends, and bodyguards it was hard to get any conversation going at all. I remember he looked happy and always had a smile on his face.

Posing for *Playboy* opened up some new doors for me as well. Because it was such a famous magazine, it looked pretty good on my resume, and I was able to score some other modeling gigs. I made the cover of *Easyriders* magazine in April of 1995, as well as the covers of some other "hot girls and hot cars" types of magazines and a few calendars, too. I appeared in Gene Simmons' *Tongue* magazine in 2003 for a spread called "Headlock Hotties." Don't you just love some of these titles?

Speaking of Gene, he came over to my house one day to personally scout things for the photoshoot we were doing the following day. I had a ring set up in my backyard, and we would be taking the photos in my ring. That day, however, I was also filming a boxing match with a wrestler named Candi. Since Gene was there already, we had him be my cornerman for the boxing match. So there I am boxing and going to Gene Simmons of all people for pugilistic pointers between rounds. During one break, Gene grabbed a bottle of water and poured it all over my chest — wet T-shirt style — to "cool me down." Funny, I never saw Cus D'Amato do that with Mike Tyson!

On the wrestling end of things, I was also on the cover of *FIGHTING Females* magazine several times in the mid-to-late 1990s. *FIGHTING Females* magazine was published quarterly by Tribeca Publishing in New York. One of the contributing editors for that magazine, Bob Harris from Vancouver, was always on the lookout for cover models and stories for his three-page spread. When he would put out an email for us girls to send him pics, I would get back to him almost immediately with a few to choose from. He would then submit them to the editor, who would pick which ones to use. I think I was on a total of four covers for them. This was a great magazine. It promoted all kinds of female wrestlers: pro, mud, oil, one-on-one, WWF, and stuntwomen. It also promoted all of us producers and allowed us to buy ads to advertise our companies. Bob was the best! When he wrote articles, he would always make sure he mentioned me and my video production company, Hollywould Productions. He was always giving me a plug here and there. We've known each other since 1998, when we met at a wrestling convention in San Diego, and we've been friends ever since. Bob still sends me a Christmas card or round-robin letter every year, describing his past year's events.

Another Perspective: Steve Blance (GLOW's Head Writer, Referee, and Commissioner)

My friend Jeanne has duly been called "The *GLOW* Original." As Hollywood, she was the only *GLOW* girl to appear in the pilot and all four seasons of *GLOW*. I had applied for a writing position on the show and was given a one-week tryout. At the end of the trial, as I was nervously waiting to hear my fate, Jeanne invited me to catch some sun with her by the Riviera Hotel pool. Who could turn this beautiful girl down? Hollywood was the first cast member to be nice to me, and we've been friends ever since.

In the ring, Hollywood was fearless. She was the first girl to take a backdrop from the towering Mt. Fiji. During the match, one of the participants missed her spot and, rather than let the bout fall apart, Jeanne rushed the giant and took the fall. Whether it was a singles match, tag teaming with her partner, Vine, or a flat-out free-for-all, Hollywood was up for anything in the ring. When I booked a clothes-ripping match, where two teams had to relieve each other of their garments, I knew Jeanne would be perfect for it. As it turns out, a fan kept one of her high heels as a souvenir.

When we were on tour, Hollywood was always the last one out of the arena. She wasn't being a diva. It's just that crowds of fans wanted her autograph, and Jeanne didn't want to let anyone down. Before it became cool to cheer the heels, Hollywood was the bad guy everybody loved. When we decided to include anti-drug public service announcements during *GLOW*, Hollywood was the natural choice to deliver them. She was a favorite of the entire viewing audience.

One of my favorite matches featured Hollywood and Vine vs. The Showgirls, Bambi and Babette. They were actually male dancers disguised as lady wrestlers. They took the match to get close to Hollywood and Vine. Once the dancers had their wigs ripped off and their identities discovered, they were rewarded with hugs and promised a date. As they left the ring, they realized Hollywood and Vine had stolen their watches and wallets.

Jeanne and I regularly keep in touch and get together when she's in New York. I'm proud to have introduced her to matzo ball soup and corned beef at Ben's Deli. She still travels all over for wrestling appearances and conventions. I've had the pleasure of accompanying her to autograph sessions and webcasts, and she still makes time for all of her fans. My friend Hollywood is truly an original.

Chapter 17: Later Years

As I mentioned earlier, David McLane left *GLOW* during season two. In September 1987, we were introduced to Johnny Cafarella ("Johnny C."), who came in at the start of season three. Ostensibly, he was an onscreen replacement for David McLane, who had served as the main announcer and interviewer. I, like most of the other girls, thought he was an on-air talent. Unbeknownst to us at the time, he had come onboard as a producer, too.

Now, there was a little bit of political back-and-forth going on behind the scenes, which I wasn't aware of at the time. I didn't really hang out with the production crew, so I didn't know a lot about what was going on. The girls hung out together. I didn't get very involved with any of the production aspects. Johnny C. had been involved with an outfit called "The Glorious Ladies of Wrestling" on local television in Minnesota. I think there were some legal conversations about trademarks and branding going on, but they ended up bringing in Johnny C. to essentially replace David.

Johnny was a nice guy. I thought he looked the part – maybe a thinner version of David McLane. We got along ... for the most part.

As I mentioned before, the good girls of *GLOW* were managed by Jackie Stallone. But in one of my matches, you can actually see her nine-year-old grandson, Sage, cheering like hell for the bad girls!

Years later, in one of those supermarket tabloid magazines, somebody wrote an article about me and Sage under the headline, "Sly Stallone's Son Falls for Lady Wrestler." The article, which took up a whole page, included a photo of Sage sitting right next to me. Yes, he did have a crush on me, but we did not date. He was a little kid. I still have a copy of the magazine.

Honestly, there were a lot of fans who rooted for the heels. Watch tapes of old *GLOW* matches and see who gets the biggest cheers. Not to brag, but if I had a nickel for every one of my matches where fans chanted "HOL-LY-WOOD! HOL-LY-WOOD!" loud enough for the broadcast to pick up the audio, well ... I'd have an awful lot of nickels.

But back to Jackie Stallone. One night, the *GLOW* girls went out to a club in Beverly Hills to do some kind of promotion. At some point, we met her son Frank, who apparently had a big crush on me. After that night, he called the *GLOW* director numerous times in an attempt to get me to go out with him. It was flattering, but I already had a boyfriend, and while I was a "bad girl" in the ring, that didn't carry over to my personal relationships. Sorry, Frank!

Then, in the third season, along came Broadway Rose. She was my on-screen "cousin" from New York City, who I did a few tag team matches with. She was a very good rapper. That girl could really move!

I was living in Las Vegas during the taping period, but on occasion I would sneak out of Vegas and head home if there was some cool event I didn't want to miss. When I did, I would fly back to Vegas from the Burbank airport early Saturday morning to make sure I was back in time for TV tapings. I remember one time the wind was so strong coming in that we almost had to head back to Burbank. We must have circled the airport three times trying to land. I was a nervous wreck – not just because of the wind and turbulence, but because I would have missed the taping if we had to turn back. And if I missed the taping because I had snuck out of town, I figured I'd get fired on the spot. Fortunately, we landed safe and sound, and I made the taping without a problem, but those were the kinds of risks I took at the time. When you're young, you sometimes do stupid things.

In the summer of 1988, four of us *GLOW* girls flew to London to promote our show overseas. It was Babe the Farmer's Daughter, Debbie Debutante, Mt. Fiji, and me along with our publicist, Gabe Elias. We stayed in the Kensington area in central London. This was my first visit to Europe, and it was summertime, so the weather was lovely. We each had our own room at the Hilton — something we rarely got — and the promotion company was awesome. Melissa Lombardi was our host. We did promos at HMV stores, did photo shoots, went out to dinner, and took a train to the seaside town of Cardiff. To this day, I've never had fish and chips as good as the ones I had in London. There is a pub on every corner, and each one has its share of regular customers.

I thoroughly enjoyed this city, partly because it made me realize that New York City wasn't really that old, which I had previously thought before traveling to the UK. I remember going shopping on Oxford Street, Piccadilly Circus, and in very cool hippie shops in Soho. I couldn't wait to buy Doc Martens there. I remember taking photos of Big Ben and trying to get the attention of the Beefeaters during the changing of the guards at Buckingham Palace. Walking through Hyde Park to go shopping at Harrods reminded me a lot of Central Park in New York. Taking the underground was new for me. Every street corner had fresh flowers, and I fell in love with flowers called freesias. The scent of those flowers is heavenly, so I made sure to have them in my hotel room whenever possible.

Back in the U.S., another way we promoted *GLOW* was by going on the classic TV game show *Family Feud*. We did three tapings between 1988 and 1989. Each taping had five episodes, so we shot fifteen episodes altogether.

I was our team captain for two tapings (they did an alternating captain gimmick for the first taping) and shared the stage with Godiva, Jackie Stallone, Babe the Farmer's Daughter, Sally the Farmer's Daughter, Daisy, Liberty, Justice, and Mt. Fiji. Along with promoting our show, we also raised money for charities like Athletes & Entertainers for Children, Children of the Night, and others.

They paired the *GLOW* team up against teams of male wrestlers from World Championship Wrestling, the former Jim Crockett Promotions (an affiliate of the National Wrestling Alliance), which had recently been purchased by TV mogul Ted Turner. The WCW teams featured the likes of Sting, Lex Luger, Tom Zenk, Brian Pillman, The Steiner Brothers, Tony Schiavone, Road Warrior Animal, Brad Armstrong, and Jim Ross.

People always ask me questions about *Family Feud*, specifically when it comes to Sting, the team captain for the WCW squad. He was flirting with me pretty heavily in every episode, and I guess I flirted back a bit myself. I'm often asked if things went any further — if there was anything more than a bit of back-and-forth harmless flirting. My stock answer has always been: "You'll be able to read about that in my book." Well, now that you're reading my book, here's the answer ...

No. Nothing ever happened between Sting and me. I've been told that we had good chemistry on-screen, and he was very nice to me, but I was still in a long-term relationship with my boyfriend, Dave. I've always been a very loyal person, so I never tried to pursue anything. Maybe Sting was interested or maybe he was just playing for the cameras. I just know I had a boyfriend, which meant I wasn't interested. (Or was I?)

Family Feud had a team on set to do our hair and makeup, which was a nice treat. We all did our own hair and makeup with *GLOW*. The *Feud* crew were just caking our faces with this really heavy foundation. I thought it was overkill at the time, but they must have known what they were doing with those cameras and lighting because it ended up coming out great. I didn't think any of the girls looked overdone.

As for what I would wear, I went with the signature Hollywood look of black lingerie for the first taping. Between the first and second tapings, I had my breast augmentation surgery done. The second time I was on, I wore a red dress with a neckline that plunged way down there, showing off the girls. The host, Ray Combs, even said that I looked different somehow. I think I know what he was referring to.

Sometimes people watch those old episodes on YouTube and give me grief for some of my answers. Honestly, it was one of those things where you're playing against the clock, trying to beat the other person to the buzzer to give the first answer. I would buzz in right away, even before I had processed the question, and would try to come up with an answer afterward. Sometimes it worked; sometimes it didn't.

As always, some of the answers to the *Family Feud* questions were pretty funny — sometimes on purpose, sometimes by accident. Here are some of my favorite exchanges from those episodes ...

Ray Combs: "Give us a question you do not like to be asked."
Hollywood: "Is this color real?" (referring to my hair)

And then from Jackie ...
Jackie Stallone: "Is this your own nose?"

Ray Combs: "Name a sport whose players might have pot bellies."
Hollywood: "Poker players."

Ray Combs: "Name a gift of clothing you can buy for someone even if you don't know the exact size."
Hollywood: "A baby."

Ray Combs: "Name something a man wears to bed at night."
Hollywood: "The thing around their eyes. An eye mask."

Ray Combs: "Name something you buy that is almost always white."
Road Warrior Animal: (looking at Godiva) "Underwear."

Ray Combs: "Did it not bother your concentration to stand across from that beautiful lady?"
Animal: "That's how I thought underwear."

Ray Combs: "Name something that bees do."
Jackie Stallone: "What else do they do? They don't make clothes."

Ray Combs: "Name something that is towed."
Liberty: "A frog."

Ray Combs: "Name something a man stops for before picking up his date."
Mt. Fiji: "Condoms."

Ray Combs: "Name something that you take to a hotel."
Mt. Fiji: "A camera."

Despite the additional national television exposure from all those appearances on *Family Feud*, the end of *GLOW* was very near, even if we didn't know it at the time.

We would find out soon enough.

Chapter 18: My Favorite GLOW Matches

Over the years, a lot of fans have asked me what some of my favorite *GLOW* matches were. The following are the ones that usually come to mind. All of them can be found on YouTube — on channels such as Mike Rand, Adrian Duarte, Wrasslin' Tapes, DustyOldTapes, TimeOut TV Wrestling, SaborAmericano, and others — so please check them out. I actually wrote down these comments while watching them myself.

1) Texas Barroom Brawl with Sally the Farmer's Daughter

It's awesome for me to see the young men out of their seats at the beginning of this match, trying to get attention and a high-five or handshake from their favorite bad girl. Steve Blance was the referee in this one. I immediately took charge in the match and, like in so many others, Sally and I ended up outside the ring, where I threw her into the audience. There's a great video inserted in this one where I tell Sally, "You know, you may wanna get the phone number of Tiffany and Roxy's plastic surgeon, 'cause you're gonna need one when I get through with you!" Sally pins me a couple of times, but I get up before the ten-count. Then, after I bulldog Sally into the mat, I pin her for a ten-count and win. But Sally continues fighting and ends up riding on my back as I run out of the arena!

2) Sumo Match with Big Bad Mama, MTV, and Me vs. Mt. Fiji, Lightning, and Zelda

In this one, I team up with MTV and Big Bad Mama against Mt. Fiji, Lightning, and Zelda. The fans go crazy when Mt. Fiji comes out in her sumo outfit. I'm wearing a silver ankh in this one, which was given to me by a fan in Texas. Benny Diamond is the referee and, while Aunt Kitty is distracting him, he accidentally gets elbowed by Fiji and falls outside of the ring. While he's out there, Fiji body slams Mama outside of the sumo circle, but the ref doesn't see it! Then Mama throws some "voodoo powder" in Fiji's eyes, temporarily blinding her. Mama takes advantage and pushes Fiji out of the sumo circle. By this time, the ref is back in the ring and raises Mama's hand for the win. Zelda is very upset about this and tries to explain to Johnny C. that Mama is a cheater. I go after Zelda and MTV goes after Lightning, and it's pure mayhem again, with Fiji throwing me out of the ring and then going after Mama.

3) "Battle for the Butler" with MTV and Me vs. Roxy and Tiffany

This match was to see who would keep Tiffany's butler, Jeeves, whom MTV and I had kidnapped and renamed "Blaze." Jeeves rides in on a Harley with me in the front and MTV on the back. Definitely one of my best entrances ever in *GLOW* and a fan favorite! Jeeves is hilarious in this one and looks like a demented Tommy Lee. MTV and I spray paint "We K A" (We Kick Ass) on a pillar before getting in the ring and mocking Tiffany with a variation on the Rolling Stones' "Satisfaction." I tell Tiffany, "His name isn't Jeeves. It's Blaze. Remember?", followed by a kick. Then MTV and I clothesline Tiffany and Roxy and proceed to stomp on them. I handcuff Tiffany to Roxy in the middle of the ring, after which MTV and I prance around the ring, modeling their stolen coats. But eventually Tiffany and Roxy escape and turn the tables on us to win Jeeves back.

4) Gestapo Match with Matilda the Hun, Vine, and Me vs. Mt. Fiji, Little Fiji, and Americana

This was probably the most infamous match *GLOW* ever did. First off, when we found out that we would be doing this match, Vine and I went shopping at a prop house in L.A. with Matt Cimber. We bought whips, chains, billy clubs, gas masks, etc. – just an everyday shopping list for *GLOW*! The wardrobe department (in other words, me and Vine with a sewing kit) sewed patches on our hats and jackets, and then we had to learn the German national anthem – the one with the famous line "Deutschland über alles" – which we sang as we entered the arena, with Vine waving a German flag. Then the good girls entered with Americana waving an American flag and Little Fiji waving an Israeli flag. This was an "anything goes" match and, if a white flag in one of the corners was waved for any reason, that would signal the end of the match. Matilda and Fiji start off by trading blows with billy clubs, then move on to whips. At one point, I torture a handcuffed Little Fiji outside the ring by putting a "foreign object" under her fingernails, then Vine joins the fun with a gas mask and pliers. Vine starts talking into one of the gas mask's hoses and David McLane comments, "She's blowing into it!" What did he think ... she had eaten garlic?

Anyway, while Fiji is choking Matilda against the ropes, I run in and unthinkingly grab the white flag of surrender and start bashing Fiji over the head with it, which gave the match to Team U.S.A. Now, did I feel stupid waving that flag? You better believe it! Hollywood would certainly have more street smarts than that! But somebody had to wave the flag and let the good girls win, so I took one for the team. It all ends with Fiji throwing me off the top turnbuckle, body slamming Matilda, and then tearing a swastika armband off Matilda and stomping on it while leading the crowd in a chant of "U.S.A.!" I'm often asked, "How did you feel about all of this?" Well, when you play a heel, you have to do your job, and we certainly did ours that day. But I did feel a little uncomfortable, to say the least. Surprisingly, after the matches were over that night and I was walking back to our room at the Riviera Hotel, I noticed that someone had scribbled swastikas all over the pool's diving board. Now that really did frighten me.

5) Alley Fight with Vine, Attaché, and Me vs. Little Egypt, Tara the Southern Belle, and California Doll

This match was a six-person tag team event. No rules ... which means anything goes, even stripping a wrestler out of her clothes! Vine and I are wearing some funky looking rock and roll outfits we had put together, and we enter with a trash can full of weapons. As usual, fans were chanting, "Hollywood and Vine!" as we entered, which always put a smile on my face. I mean, at the time, this was the only way we knew if we were popular or not. There was no social media to look at, and the sad fact is we did not receive most of our fan mail. Vine and I were so evil that we started spray painting Tara's hair while Attaché was being double-teamed by Little Egypt and the Doll. I actually liked these "alley fights" with the weapons and clothes coming off because they were different – and boy, did they show off our personalities! This match was also one of those rare moments when the heels won.

6) Tag Team Match with Vine and Me vs. The Showgirls, "Bambi and Babette"

This was a really fun match, narrated by Susie Spirit and Sir Miles Headlock. In addition to doing *GLOW*, Susie Spirit worked as a dancer at a Vegas show called Folies Bergère at the Tropicana and knew all the dancers there. She had Matt Cimber hire two of the male dancers, who dressed as women — in red costumes, feather boas, and wigs — just so they could wrestle with me and Vine. I was way into '80s rock and roll-type animal prints at that time and bought our outfits in Hollywood. This would be the first time that we wrestled men in the ring. Every time Vine or I get in the ring and put a move on one of them, he reverses the move and starts kissing us. Susie Spirit keeps repeating things like, "There's that strange move. I wonder what those two showgirls are up to." We eventually find out by pulling off their wigs and seeing that they're men. We also learn that they were just hoping to get dates with Hollywood and Vine, so we tell them yes and that we'll meet them later. After we leave the ring, they realize that we stole their watches, so ultimately we got the last laugh!

7) Singles Match vs. Sally the Farmer's Daughter (Revenge for Vine's Concussion)

I think this season one match was my first match without Vine. The story was that, in a previous match, Sally had thrown Vine into a pillar and given her a concussion, so I was out to get revenge. The action is intense right from the start and, as always, goes outside the ring. I hit Sally with a billy club, throw her into a ringside chair (that I pulled a hapless fan out of ... sorry, dude), and both of us end up rolling around on the ground. This was one of my favorite matches against Sally, and you can tell by the looks on our faces that neither one of us wanted to lose. Some of the moves we did were quick, precise, and involved lots of reversals.

One of the best was a spinning kick to Sally's head while she had my other leg in the air, twisting my ankle. Ultimately, though, Sally pinned me after a sunset flip and was declared the winner by the ref, Frank D'Amato. Once her hand is raised by David McLane, I come up from behind and trip her, then the action moves outside the ring again and we start cat-fighting. It actually felt like she was pulling the hair out of my head, so I yelled, "You bitch!" before throwing her into a pillar. But I rarely used profanity during a match, unless I knew that something was being done to me deliberately. We ended up in a ball again on the outside of the ring and David, as he often had to do, called for Riviera Hotel security to break us up. Fans definitely got their money's worth with this match!

8) Caribbean Cruise Match with Big Bad Mama, MTV, and Me vs. Mt. Fiji, Lightning, and Zelda

This was another great match where we could wear different outfits. A number of kids greet me as I come in – a sign of our growing popularity with children. I'm in a black corset and have an animal print bikini bottom underneath. The winners of the match are supposed to get a free Caribbean cruise. I love all the props they made for us for this match. I bravely go toe-to-toe with Fiji, but, as always with Fiji, end up on the losing end ... getting what the announcer, "Motormouth" Mike Morgan, refers to as a "keister buster." The match descends into chaos and Johnny C. says the match is over and there is no prize. But then Babe the Farmer's Daughter comes out with a packed suitcase, and it appears that she and Johnny C. had secretly planned to go on the Caribbean cruise by themselves. We respond by tearing the clothes off Johnny, revealing a Hawaiian shirt and shorts!

9) Texas Tornado Match with Godiva and Me vs. Sally and Babe the Farmer's Daughters

This match involved four wrestlers battling it out in the ring at the same time. Godiva and I came out on a horse led by Beastie. Sally has to call out to Babe to get her to stop flirting with a ringside spectator and get in the ring. It's a pretty quick match, but has a lot of back-and-forth action. I briefly gave Sally a face claw, which was unusual. I also got to bulldog Sally into the mat and dropkick her out of the ring – sweet! It was really great to finally tag-team with other wrestlers after Vine left at the beginning of season three. But, of course, the good girls win again, with Babe pinning Godiva.

10) Singles Match vs. Tulsa for the United States Championship (1993 *GLOW* PPV Match)

Tulsa looks very beautiful and makes a spectacular entrance on a pretty Appaloosa horse. Of course, I needed a grand entrance, too, so I called Harley-Davidson of Las Vegas and asked them to send someone down who could bring me to the ring on a Harley. The fans loved it and I got a lot of cheers. Since this was 1993, I already had breast implants, and this was the first time I got to show them off in *GLOW*. I certainly don't look like the 115-pound wrestler in the first two seasons and have definitely grown into this character and look more professional, including my working the crowd. The blonde hair, which started years before in *GLOW*, stayed with me until 1999, when I went back to being a brunette. This match lasts close to fifteen minutes, with a lot of back-and-forth action, including me dragging Tulsa around the ring with her lasso. I even kick the ref – the appropriately named Nutsy Fagan – in the balls! Unbeknownst to the ref, I have turned one of *GLOW*'s good girls, Lightning, into a new heel character, Party Animal, who helps me win the match.

Another Perspective: William Taylor (GLOW Fan)

The 1950s offered us James Dean. The 1960s, Hugh Hefner. The 1970s, Arthur "The Fonz" Fonzarelli. The second half of the 1980s redefined cool – and finally from a female standpoint – when TV audiences first witnessed a *GLOW* star in the making named Hollywood, who was the very personification of cool.

With her own gradual evolution of costuming during that inaugural 1986-87 season, she became the iconic combination of sneakiness, good looks, smooth presence, and decisive (if not divisive) ring strategy.

It was a mixture of ingredients that fans were drawn to – for in everyday life, they would love to get away with what she did in the ring. Hollywood stated she often was the last person on the tour bus after matches due to autograph requests.

She displayed a sense of humor that appealed to students ranging from the free-spirited college crowd to those in elementary schools who copied her lines as a way to get back at others' insults at recess – a role model via the comeback line. A good example was when the *GLOW* doctor stated that leeches were used in early medicine, to which she replied, "Yeah, now they have their own offices." On the flip side, give her credit for showing her serious side in public service announcements encouraging people not to use drugs.

Her matches with Vine in *GLOW*'s first two seasons generated excitement and emotions ranging from cheers to boos combined with a reassuring smoothness that they would get the job done, even if they had to fight fair. They spray-painted the walls of the Riviera Hotel's showroom, they shoved hot dogs in announcer David McLane's mouth, and – along with Matilda the Hun – dressed as German soldiers leading into a match versus Mt. Fiji, Little Fiji, and Americana – a match that Fiji's team won and that saw Americana destroy the German flag.

Hollywood has a mystique which would be a perfect box office smash if she'd star in a remake of *Easy Rider*, the classic 1969 film starring Peter Fonda, whose character, Wyatt, displayed free living and toughness with a touch of reckless abandon.

Another thing that made Hollywood so cool was her unique ability to reach out and connect with fans in a rather loving way. It's a great example of how even the toughest of characters can show their soft side without losing their "reputation."

Her body temperature might be 98.6 degrees Fahrenheit like the rest of us, but Hollywood's symbolic coolness easily invigorated the atmosphere at any appearance. Other female wrestlers can try to emulate and imitate, but will never duplicate, because she is one original that simply can't be copied.

James Dean and The Fonz had their leather jackets. Hugh Hefner had the smoking jacket. But Hollywood didn't need such apparel, because there's no reason to warm up when you're naturally so cool.

William Taylor is a life long follower of the weather. He got his degree in meteorology and by the late 1980s became known as the unofficial New Orleans Saints historian for his research on team history.

Chapter 19: My GLOW Raps

The individual raps that preceded the matches on *GLOW* were unique to each wrestler and were a great way for the girls to express themselves as their characters. These raps were usually written by the wrestlers themselves, sometimes with input from *GLOW*'s writers and/or from other wrestlers. If someone had a good idea, they were happy to share. Anyway, for the record, here are my seven individual raps that appeared on *GLOW*.

HOLLYWOOD'S THE NAME AND DON'T FORGET IT
IF YOU GET IN MY WAY, YOU'RE GONNA GET IT
WHEELIN' AND DEALIN' IS HOW IT GOES
I'LL PICK YOUR POCKETS JUST LIKE THE PROS

CHEATING AND STEALING IS NO SIN
WHEN I'M IN THE RING, I FIGHT TO WIN
I'M REALLY SLY AND I'M A SNEAK
I'M A TOTALLY DIFFERENT KIND OF FREAK

HOLLYWOOD AND VINE, WE ARE SO FINE
WE'LL BEAT YOUR BUTTS ANYTIME
I LOVE TO ROCK, I LOVE TO ROLL
WHEN I'M IN THE RING, I TAKE CONTROL

ROCK AND ROLL IS WHAT I DO
IF YOU WERE ME, THEN YOU COULD TOO
SO SORRY, BOYS, IF IT DON'T ADD UP
IF YOU WANT TO WRESTLE ME, YOU GOTTA BE TOUGH

I'M HOLLYWOOD AND I'M FROM L.A.
NOW YOU LISTEN TO WHAT I GOT TO SAY
IF YOU STEP IN THE RING, I'LL STEP ON YOUR FACE
THEN YOU KNOW YOU HAVE BEEN DISGRACED

*WELL, HOLLYWOOD IS BACK TO RULE THE RING
BEATIN' ON PEOPLE IS MY THING
ANOTHER YEAR OF HAVIN' FUN
AND MAKIN' MY OPPONENTS RUN

I'M TOUGH, WILD, STRONG, AND SLICK
AND I KNOW EVERY DIRTY TRICK
I'LL HURT YOU EVERY CHANCE I COULD
YOU JUST DON'T MESS WITH HOLLYWOOD

And as a bonus, for the first time ever, here are three more raps I
wrote but never used on the show.

**I'M JUST TOO HOT, I WON'T COOL DOWN
WHEN YOU'RE WITH ME, YOU'RE GOIN' TO TOWN
YOU KNOW THAT I'M UP TO NO GOOD
THAT'S WHAT YOU GET FROM HOLLYWOOD

**I RULE THE STREETS WITH MY PAL VINE
THE TWO OF US ARE REAL FINE
AND IN THREE YEARS WE'VE TAKEN *GLOW*
IT'S JUST LIKE US TO STEAL THE SHOW

**I ROB AND STEAL, THAT'S HOW I LIVE
I TAKE AND TAKE AND NEVER GIVE
I'LL HURT YOU EVERY CHANCE I COULD
YOU JUST DON'T MESS WITH HOLLYWOOD

* Co-written with Steve Blance and Jeanne Basone
** Written by Steve Blance
All other raps written by Jeanne Basone

Chapter 20: Memorable Moments and Miscellany

Here are some other things from *GLOW* that, in addition to the matches and raps, are fondly remembered by a lot of fans. I often get asked about them.

1) *GLOW*'s Songs

GLOW's pilot included a song called "Raw Meat," which was shown before Matilda the Hun's match against Tammy Jones. The music was written by Hank Doing and the lyrics by Dee Booher. Dee sang the song, too. The accompanying video featured Matilda, Vine, and me strutting through the Riviera's casino and threatening a slot machine player.

Later on, Hank wrote the song "Nasty and Mean" for the bad girls and the vastly inferior "Good Girls Don't" for the good girls. Matilda said she contributed to these songs, too. The videos for both songs were shot in and around the Riviera Hotel. Lori "Ninotchka" Palmer did the choreography for both. If you look very closely at the video for "Nasty and Mean," you can see that the player who gets pulled away from a slot machine by the Soul Patrol's Envy is *GLOW*'s head writer, Steve Blance.

The only good part of "Good Girls Don't," which was shot at the Riviera's pool, was me and the other bad girls mocking the good girls' sappy song from up above!

2) The *GLOW* Games

By the summer of 1986, *GLOW* had finished shooting the first season and the show had already become a tourist attraction for the Riviera Hotel. The Riviera wanted to keep that momentum going, so *GLOW*'s team came up with the "*GLOW* Games of Summer," which pitted the good girls of Stallone's Sweethearts against the bad girls of Kitty's Killers.

The *GLOW* Games consisted of five events, which were shown in episodes 10 through 14 of season two.

Tug of War (Ep.10) - This involved the good girls and bad girls doing a tug of war with a tub of mud between us. The good girls, anchored by Mt. Fiji, weighed in at 1,527 lbs. The lineperson up front was Little Fiji. The bad girls, anchored by Matilda, weighed in at 1,533 lbs. The lineperson up front was Attaché. After some back-and-forth, Little Fiji stumbled and fell in the mud, giving the bad girls the victory and 25 points.

Escalator Races (Ep.11) - This involved the good girls and bad girls racing up a down escalator and then down another down escalator in the Riviera's Mardi Gras Plaza. Most of the races were worth 3 points, but the final race between Matilda and Mt. Fiji was worth 7 points. Vine and I were paired up against Tina and Ashley and should have won our race. But because of a BS call by a judge, we ended up getting disqualified. Fiji won the final race and the score for the event was Good Girls 13, Bad Girls 12.

Pizza Eating (Ep.12) - This involved Matilda and Mt. Fiji tried to be the first to finish five large pizzas weighing 3 lbs. each at Jacopo's Pizza in the Riviera Hotel. The winner would get 25 points. Fiji had pineapple pizzas and Matilda had meatball pizzas. After complaining that her pizzas had "dog food" on them, Matilda threw a slice at Fiji, starting a food fight involving all of the good girls and bad girls. Because of this, Matilda got disqualified and Fiji got the full 25 points. This made the total scores to this point 38 for the good girls and 37 for the bad girls.

Water Warfare (Ep.13) - This involved four races on rafts from one side of the Riviera's pool to the other. The first two races were 2 vs. 2, the third race 3 vs. 3, and the last race 8 vs. 8. The first three races were worth 5 points each, and the last was worth 10 points. In the very first race, Vine and I were paired up against Tina and Ashley in a close race that the good girls ended up winning. The last race with 8 vs. 8 included me and Vine again, and the bad girls ended up winning, making the final score for the event 15 for the good girls and 10 for the bad girls.

Arm Wrestling (Ep.14) - I didn't compete in this one, but Vine did and beat Tara the Southern Belle. Before the final match, the total score was tied at 64 points each. Unfortunately, the good girls ended up winning after Ashley Cartier beat Chainsaw, making the final score for the *GLOW*

Games 66-64. Mt. Fiji accepted the trophy on behalf of the good girls from the president of the Riviera Hotel, Arthur Waltzman.

Fans often ask if the *GLOW* Games were real or scripted. Believe it or not, everything in the *GLOW* Games was real except for the pizza eating. For that one, Matilda had been encouraged in advance to start the food fight. It made for good TV!

I'll also mention something that some fans don't know. The referee in the *GLOW* Games, Frank D'Amato, who was also our referee for the pilot and throughout the first season, was actually the husband of Tammy Jones, Debbie D'Amato.

3) *GLOW* Magazine

I'm often asked to sign copies of *GLOW* magazine or the posters that came with them. There were only six issues published between January and September 1988, but a lot of fans have good memories of the magazine.

It was published by Tempo Publishing Company, which had offices in New York City and Los Angeles. I've heard that the magazine and its writers had no connection to *GLOW*'s own writing team. In fact, *GLOW*'s writing team didn't even provide a "bible" (or writer's guide) to the magazine's writers.

Tempo Publishing was connected to a magazine publisher named David Zentner, who also handled adult magazines and rock music-related magazines. Vine and I ended up going to a magazine convention in Montreal and had dinner with David and his assistants. It was a very upscale restaurant, but I remember not being a fan of the kinds of meat we were served, which were exotic meats like reindeer and ostrich.

I'm on the cover of Issue #1 with Susie Spirit. There is a poster of me and Tara in the same issue. In Issue #2, there is a poster of me and Debbie Debutante as well as a poster of me, Susie Spirit, Ninotchka, and Tara the Southern Belle.

Issue #1 had a great feature article about me called "No Hoorays for this Hollywood." I also had a good feature article in Issue #4 called "Hollywood Does Hollywood" in which I went around to a couple of famous Hollywood clubs, the Rainbow and the Troubadour.

Today, all of the magazines can be found on eBay and similar websites. Scans of them are also available for free on the website www.archive.org.

4) *GLOW's* 1-900 Number

Even if they never actually called it, some fans remember seeing a 1-900 number for *GLOW* advertised in TV commercials, in *GLOW* magazine, and on banners and ads on the TV show.

I've heard that, like the magazine, the phone number did not have a connection to *GLOW* and its writing team. All the GLOW wrestlers recorded messages for it.

5) My Public Service Announcements (PSAs)

I appeared in two types of PSA for *GLOW*: one against drunk driving and the other against drugs. I was chosen because everyone thought the PSAs would work better if one of the popular and cool bad girls did them. Our head writer, Steve Blance, firmly believed I would be the person fans would respect and listen to the most.

Many fans have told me that they stayed away from drugs because of my PSAs.

6) *GLOW*: The Movie

If you watched any of the fourth season episodes of *GLOW*, you might remember a *GLOW* movie being advertised. Well, a movie was planned and a script was written, but it unfortunately never came to be. It involved the *GLOW* girls fighting terrorism in the Middle East (so '80s!) and even had a love scene between me and an Israeli soldier in a tank. At the "climactic moment," the tank's gun went off!

A great promo for the movie involving me and the Commissioner (Steve Blance) was shown on *GLOW* and went like this ...

C: "Hollywood?!"
H: "Hey, what's this rumor about a *GLOW* movie?"
C: "Where'd you hear this?"
H: "I picked it up on the street."
C: "That figures! That's where you get everything else."
H: "So what's the story, wimp?"
C: "The rumor is true."
H: "Great! Where do I sign up?"
C: "For what?! The foreign legion?"
H: "You can't do a *GLOW* movie without Hollywood!"
C: "But this film calls for experienced actresses."
H: "So what? I've been in front of the camera a million times!"
C: "Yeah ... for mug shots! HA-HA-HA-HA-HA-HA-HAAAAAA!!!"

I then proceed to pound on him!

7) "Life in the *GLOW* House"

The episodes of "Life in the *GLOW* House," which was a sketch that appeared in the fourth season, were scripted. But in some ways, it was almost like the first modern reality show. It preceded MTV's *The Real World* — which started in 1992 and also featured a group of diverse people living together — by a couple of years.

The episodes were mostly filmed at a house in Oxnard, California that *GLOW* rented for these sketches. All of them were written by Steve Blance, and Steve played most of the male characters. The episodes I appear in usually show me as a wannabe master thief, which was meant to build on my original season one character of a pickpocket.

It's interesting that one of the episodes, "A Date to Remember/Playing the Trump Card," featured us trying to trick Daisy into thinking she could get a date with Donald Trump. That episode was actually filmed at Trump Castle in Atlantic City. *GLOW* was doing an East Coast tour at the time and had stopped there.

Another interesting story is that, in the episode called "Ungrand Theft," Daisy says the line, "Aww, tell me more about the rabbits, Hollywood!" That line was a reference to John Steinbeck's novel *Of Mice and Men*. Steve Blance based the characters of Daisy and Gremlina on the characters of Lennie and George in that novel.

Chapter 21: GLOW Champions

To become a champion in any wrestling promotion is an honor. Yes, that champion is chosen by the promoter, but every champion is chosen for a reason. You need someone reliable as a champion — someone trustworthy. Someone who is not going to embarrass you. You want someone who consistently performs in great matches and does good promos. More than anything, you want someone who can carry the banner for your promotion — to be the face of WWE, AEW, WCW, and even *GLOW*.

Unlike many wrestling promotions, *GLOW* had a crown (a tiara, really) for the champion instead of a belt, and only seven women would wear the *GLOW* crown.

Tammy Jones, Pilot
In the pilot, Tammy Jones became the first woman to wear the *GLOW* crown by defeating Matilda the Hun. Her reign would last only 58 days and end in controversy.

Royal Hawaiian, Season One
Early on in the first season, Tammy's brief championship reign came to an end as she was defeated by the Royal Hawaiian. Royal Hawaiian cheated by putting her feet on the ropes for the pin. Of course, the referee missed it.

Americana, Season One
Americana defeated the Royal Hawaiian by pinfall to become the new *GLOW* champion. However, at the end of season one, the title was stripped from the champion when Americana faced her Russian rival, Ninotchka. Ninotchka officially defeated Americana through a double pin, but the *GLOW* crown was declared vacant pending a rematch in season two.

Tina Ferrari, Season Two
Ninotchka got a second shot at the crown, but it was Tina Ferrari, not Americana, who defeated her. Tina would reign as champion throughout the duration of season two.

Ninotchka, Season Three

Ninotchka became champion in season three, but her crown would be stripped when she defected from her tag team partner. With the title vacant, a decision was made to have a tournament called "The Run for the Rubies" in which everyone would get a chance to wrestle for the title.

Cheyenne Cher, Season Four

After defeating Godiva in the final of "The Run for the Rubies," Cheyenne Cher became the sixth *GLOW* champion.

Daisy, Season Four

The title changed hands just one more time, as Daisy defeated Cheyenne Cher to win the crown.

Daisy was the final *GLOW* champion before we went off the air. However, *GLOW*'s head writer, Steve Blance, told me if we went into season five, I would have become champion, beating Daisy for the crown. Unfortunately, we'll never know what a Hollywood title reign would have looked like.

Another Perspective: More GLOW Fans Speak Out

MIKE RAND: Someone that I am honored to know and be a part of her life is Jeanne Basone. Growing up, I was a huge fan of *GLOW* and, just like every other fan of the show, I loved Hollywood! *GLOW* pitted good girl vs. bad girl and, although I always rooted for good to conquer evil, that wasn't the case when you saw Hollywood! The character of Hollywood was a sexy, wild, bad girl from the streets, and there's a reason why fans were drawn to her. Jeanne has the "X-factor." Not only did Jeanne bring Hollywood to life; Jeanne herself is full of energy and life. When she walks into the room, she commands the audience's attention.

Never would I have imagined years ago that one day, with the invention of the Internet, I would not only get to know her, but also be proud to call her my friend. During my many conversations with her over the years, one thing is apparent: Jeanne is a very smart businesswoman. She works very hard to create her own brand and not only knows how to market herself, but also how to run a business. She's a very beautiful, kind, easily likable, gracious individual who loves her fans.

Sometimes in wrestling there are bad girls we love to hate, but it's hard to hate anything about the character Hollywood! Over the years, my favorite matches were her feuds against the Farmer's Daughters. One match in particular, against Sally the Farmer's Daughter, was so wild that it was the greatest match that never was! Hollywood attacked Sally as she was being introduced and entering the arena, and what ensued over the next few minutes was fast-paced action that would be a main event in any arena! Whether she was performing a rowboat with her tag team partner, Vine, giving a bulldog to Babe the Farmer's Daughter, or administering a flying head scissors to Tulsa, you knew a match with Hollywood would contain excitement!

There is no *GLOW* without Hollywood and there would be no Hollywood without Jeanne! Hollywood was the face of *GLOW*, bringing her character to such classic shows as *Married... with Children*, *Family Feud*, *The Sally Jessy Raphael Show*, and *Donahue*, to name a few. There's the one ... the only ... Hollywood. And there's the one ... the only ... Jeanne Basone!

SHAWN CAMPBELL: I think when you look at what impacts an entire culture, and generation after generation, it's fantasy fulfillment. It's how things connect with people on a personal level. *GLOW* was everyone's fantasy come to life. It was the classic good vs evil. It was every straight man's fantasy wrapped up in a hot costume. It was every woman's and bullied little kid's fantasy of total empowerment. As athletes and actresses, the ladies of *GLOW* brought the characters to life in a way that allowed people from any walk of life to find someone they could relate to, a fantasy that they could embody themselves.

I don't think there's really any other decade as identifiable as the 1980s – with its music and fashion, and political and technological advancements – so it was the perfect setting to lay down *GLOW* in a way that would continue to impact people as they remember a very memorable decade in pop culture. It was a perfect storm of 80s street culture becoming mainstream – wealth and over-the-top opulence becoming available to the everyday woman; neon and music and dance; in-your-face comedy; and the universal desire for good to prevail over evil, cast with the perfect "actresses" to make it come alive – that people just can't forget.

The Hollywood character hit every mark. She was mean and dangerous and strong. The bad girl every guy wanted as their own and every girl secretly wanted to be themselves. If you look a little deeper, she was cute as a button and Aunt Kitty's star girl – the kind that just maybe you could take home to mama if you covered her up and hid her weapons (or, in wrestling terms, her "foreign objects"). Behind that character, the real-life Jeanne, in the eyes of this fan, is just what you'd imagine: a straight shooter friend with a heart of gold and the life of the party. She's got a twinkle in her eye, and you can never quite tell if it's pure lust for life or her next mischievous "Hollywood" moment. As they say, Hooray for Hollywood.

STEPHEN FENNER: I became a *GLOW* wrestling fan from the first time I watched it, especially Hollywood. Whereas I live in Nova Scotia, Canada, I thought I would never get to meet or see her live. Then, a few years ago, low and behold she was the special guest for the Beauty Slammers tour in Nova Scotia. I bought VIP tickets to the show and finally got to meet Hollywood, get her autograph, and take a picture with her. All the women on the tour were super nice and friendly, but I felt like I had known Jeanne forever when chatting with her.

MANNY BRIANO: One of my favorite *GLOW* moments, in 1988, was when my mom took my brother and me to see the *GLOW* tour, twice, in San Diego. Meeting Hollywood was a dream come true because she was part of *GLOW* since the beginning, from season one. My favorite *GLOW* TV skits, including Hollywood, were when Aunt Kitty knocked on David McLane's door to try and set him up on a date with her. I loved the comedic elements that followed, from each of those skits, after David McLane opened the door. I've been able to meet Hollywood two decades later, after the *GLOW* series ended, and she's still as nice and beautiful as ever.

ADRIAN DUARTE: TV was a big deal for kids like me in the '70s and '80s. Pop culture showed us, the Gen Xers, that we could do whatever we wanted and be whoever we wanted. TV didn't just entertain us; it taught us stuff, showed us the world beyond our own, and fueled our imaginations. We copied our favorite singers we saw on MTV. Movies like *The Goonies, E.T.,* and *Stand by Me* made us want to ride our bikes around town looking for adventure. And then there was pro wrestling, a sport where everything was larger than life, with all sorts of characters you could connect with, even if you didn't want to wrestle yourself. I spent many a Saturday morning copying what we were watching on WCCW, WWF, and NWA with my sister and cousins in my granny's living room with no fear of getting hurt.

While guys wrestling was cool to see, I stumbled on a wrestling show that was more than just wrestling. It had a bunch of women with sparkly hair, bright makeup, in crazy outfits, and wrestling in a blue ring with neon pink ropes. I was instantly hooked and quickly found favorites among a group of over 40 Gorgeous Ladies of Wrestling. One in particular stood out to me: a badass chick named Hollywood.

Hollywood was everything I wished I could be if I were a wrestler. Hollywood's ring persona was everything I wanted to be in real life. Hollywood's ring gear was awesome; her moves were some of the best on the show; and her raps – which *GLOW* was known for – were iconic.

While my cousins and sister were representing the likes of Sting, Rick Rude, Hulk Hogan, and the "Macho Man" Randy Savage, there I was, the boy version of Hollywood from *GLOW* playing a part I now refer to as Wilshire from the streets of Los Angeles.

Most people have good memories of watching their favorite stars on TV when they were kids, but getting to meet them doesn't happen often. Besides running into Jackie Stallone at a psychic event and working with Beastie the Road Warrior on an idea for a TV show, I didn't think I'd ever meet any of the other *GLOW* girls. That changed when I talked my partner, Terry, into flying to Los Angeles for a few days before stepping onto the Carnival Imagination cruise ship with some of the original *GLOW* cast, including the *GLOW* girl I idolized as a kid. Meeting Jeanne was truly surreal. She was everything I thought Hollywood would be and then some. Among the *GLOW* girls, Hollywood stands out as the most welcoming to fans, radiating warmth and authenticity. Jeanne is genuine, cool, and just as beautiful on the inside as she is on the outside. As a kid, I never imagined I'd get to know the real person behind Hollywood's persona. Now that I do, I can't picture my life without her presence.

ANDREW ZERANICK: The year is 1987. I am 11 years old. The time is 11:00 p.m. on Saturday night. That means it is time to tune into channel 53, WPGH, because it is time for *GLOW*. I will be glued to the television for the next hour, enthralled by this women's wrestling show.

GLOW was a huge part of my childhood. There were many wrestlers that I admired, but two that stood out as favorites were the heel tag team of Hollywood and Vine. Even though they were "bad" girls, I found myself cheering for them any time they would wrestle. *GLOW* was such an amazing entertainment experience. The wrestling itself was great, but the stories of the wrestlers and the skits all combined to make an amazing show.

I am lucky enough to have had the pleasure of meeting Hollywood in person and keeping in touch with her. I am extremely grateful to have had the chance to grow up with *GLOW* and to now have the chance to revisit it by being a real-life friend of Hollywood and some of the other amazing women. I will always have a great affection for *GLOW* and the wonderful ladies that made it happen.

RAY DIVELBISS: In 1988 I attended a *GLOW* card with a few friends. I had been a huge fan since 1986 and finally had the chance to see them in person. Hollywood was my favorite, and when I saw that she would be in a tag team match that evening with Broadway Rose against the Farmer's Daughters, I knew I had to go. Needless to say, I was not disappointed.

Hollywood's wrestling skills were superior to her opponents, and she taught them a wrestling lesson on more than one occasion in that match. The match ended in a double count-out, but it was all action and was great. After that card, we were able to get some autographs and the only thing I was interested in was getting Hollywood to sign something for me. She was so nice and actually took the time to talk for a few minutes and thanked me for coming to see the matches.

It's a memory I'll never forget.

KEN DAVIS: Top 10 Things I Learned from *GLOW* ...

10) Toe sweat can induce catatonic states.
9) Lights off due to risqué action? Generators, baby!
8) The sexual tension between Ninotchka and Vladimir is palpable.
7) Demonic forces are powerless against a chicken foot.
6) The pillars holding up the Riviera Hotel sure are poorly constructed.
5) T&A > R&T
4) Fabergé shampoos have provitamin B5.
3) That farmer in Hog Hollow, Nebraska deserves a Nobel Prize for Hotties.
2) Anyone with "Little" in their name is gonna get their ass kicked.
1) Crown or no crown, Hollywood is the true queen of *GLOW*.

Chapter 22: The End of GLOW

When I was in Las Vegas for tapings, I would stay at "The *GLOW* House," a really big house we had off The Strip on Tropicana Avenue. I would come to Vegas on Wednesdays and leave on Saturdays after the shows were done. Godiva and I both had rooms there, and Matt, Tony (Matt's son), and Johnny C. all lived there.

I vividly remember the day we got the news that *GLOW* was finished. I was in Los Angeles, but Matt Cimber was back in Las Vegas with others at the *GLOW* House. I heard from Johnny C. that Matt was pacing back and forth, wearing his big white robe. He was waiting for a phone call from Riklis. "Nobody use the phone," he would yell out. "I'm waiting on a call." Again, this was back before everyone had cell phones, so they had to keep the line open.

Matt was walking back and forth with this nervous pacing until the phone finally rang. He ran over and picked up the receiver.

"Uh-huh," he said. And a pause. And, after a while, he said, "Okay," let out a little bit of a sigh, and hung up the phone.

"That's it," he said to Johnny. "No more *GLOW*."

Here's the story. A bit earlier, I mentioned that Meshulam Riklis, the money man behind *GLOW*, was married to the actress Pia Zadora. I don't think it's any secret, but Riklis had other women that he was seeing. One of them was Ursula Hayden, one of the Farmer's Daughter characters. Among the girls, it was pretty common knowledge that Ursula was friends with Riklis. She and I used to have little conversations about it. There was a car, a Mustang, that "someone" had bought for her, and it didn't take a rocket scientist to connect the dots. Pia found out about it, and she demanded that he pull the plug on the show. And that was it. Just like that, Gorgeous Ladies of Wrestling was finished, and we were all out of work.

Matt started calling some of the girls one by one to tell them the news. I know he told some of the girls that he "just got tired of doing the show" and that's why there wouldn't be a fifth season, but that simply wasn't true. Matt was making good money – $5,000 per week to direct *GLOW*. Johnny C. was making about $800 a week. Most of the third and fourth season girls were making between $150 and $250 per week. I was still on my season one contract and making $100 per day for both rehearsal days and match days. In addition to that, we got $50 per diem when we were on tour (but nothing from ticket or merch sales); got to eat at the Riviera's employee buffet (using a Riviera employee ID badge to get in); and, for insurance, we just got workers' comp. All in all, it was pretty shitty compensation for us, given what we went through, but Matt was doing well. He didn't "just get tired of the show." Pia Zadora killed *GLOW*.

I was shocked. We were all shocked. It was so sudden and there was no way to make an appeal; no way to say, "What if we did this?" or "How about if we do that?" The decision was made. If Matt said it was done, it was done. And it was done.

My first thought was, *Oh, my God, what am I going to do for a job now?* *GLOW* had been such a unique project, and it had just come to a dead stop. And the girls were spread out, all living in different places. It wasn't like we had a pow-wow to talk things over or consider the future. There was no opportunity for any kind of closure, really. That was it. No fanfare or series finale or anything. Just a phone call and our show became a thing of the past.

A few scans from my old *GLOW* notebook, tracking my matches.

HOLLYWOOD'S RAP

HOLLYWOOD IS BACK TO RULE THE RING
BEATIN' ON PEOPLE IS MY THING
ANOTHER YEAR OF HAVIN' FUN
AND MAKIN' MY OPPONENTS RUN.

I'm just too hot, I won't cool down
when you're with me you're goin' to town
You know that I'm up to no good,
That's what you get from Hollywood.

I rule the streets with my pal Vine
The two of us are real fine
And in three years we've taken GLOW
It's just like us to steal the show

I rob and steal that's how I live
I take and take and never give
I'll hurt you every chance I could
You just don't mess with Hollywood.

I'm hot strong Wild Strong & Slick
And I know every Dirty trick
I'll beat ya & I cold
You

Hollywood's *GLOW* rap.

164

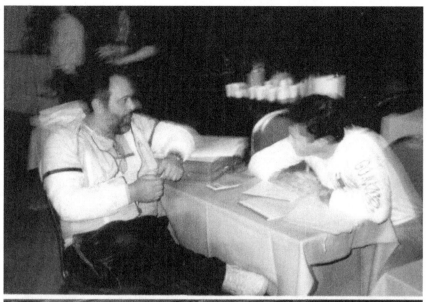

A couple of snaps with Matt Cimber above and David McLane.

Top: The *GLOW* girls from a Faberge commercial. **Bottom:** A later, larger *GLOW* family pic.

Top: The incredible Mando Guerrero. **Bottom:** Original *GLOW* girls promo pic from the pilot.

Top: Matilda with Hollywood and Vine. **Bottom:** Hollywood and Vine.

Top: My *GLOW* press pass and a ticket to *GLOW* at the Riviera.
Bottom: Hollywood and Vine.

Some famous - and infamous - encounters at the NATPE in New
Orleans, Louisiana.

A rare pic of *GLOW* writer Steve Blance with Hollywood and Vine.

Top: Hanging out. **Bottom:** Promo pic for the TV show *We've Got It Made* with Terry Copley.

Top: Aunt Kitty and Steve Blance. **Bottom:** *GLOW* girls in London!

On the cover and inside the magazine *Easyriders*. Photos by Reiko Hartman.

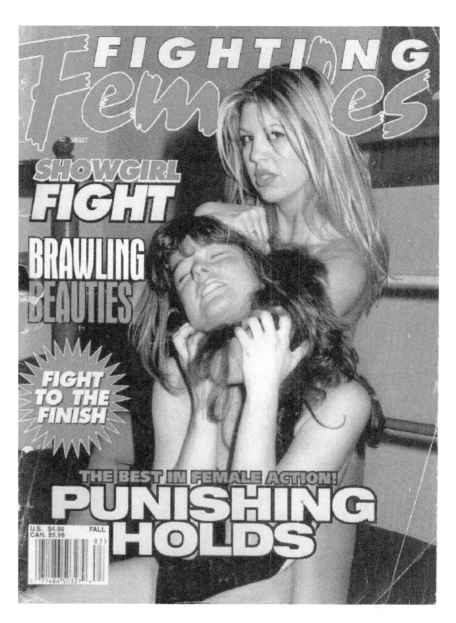

On the cover of *FIGHTING Females*.

Top: Hollywood promo pic. **Bottom:** Daisy & me heading to Hawaii.

Top: Did Hollywood steal Sly Stallone's son's heart? **Bottom:** *GLOW* ready to play *Family Feud*.

Top: Photo from a *GLOW* match. **Bottom:** Covers of the official **GLOW** magazine.

'Glamazon Queen Kong: My Life Of Glitter Guts & Glory,'
Autobiography of Deanna Booher, with Joshua Waldrop.

Deanna Booher, aka Matilda the Hun, wrote her autobiography as
well.

Top: Hollywood and Vine; a "Lost Classics" article from *Sports Illustrated*. **Bottom:** Santa and the *GLOW* girls.

GLOW girls in action.

Top: Behind the scenes: Rare pic of Chainsaw and Spike doing laundry.
Bottom: Me in a car headed to the Sunset Strip.

Top: Hanging out with Ursula. **Bottom:** The first original California Doll.

Top Left: An ad for *GLOW* on KDOC-TV. **Right:** *GLOW* girls backstage at *The Late Night Show* at NBC Studios. **Bottom:** Battling with Mt. Fiji.

TURN ON TO GLOW

GORGEOUS LADIES OF WRESTLING

AMERICA'S NEW SWEETHEARTS

Hey GLOW fans, the most exciting show on TV is right at your fingertips. That's right, it's your fabulous GLOW girls. Their spectacular show is taking the country by storm.

In most cities, you can catch America's Wrestling Sweethearts on TV every week. The thrills, the action, the beautiful girls and the fun—they're all yours at the flick of a switch. But you have to know where to turn, right?

No sweat. We've got you covered. Here are the latest local TV listings for GLOW: the city, station, channel and the time. The cheers and the boos you'll have to provide yourself.

"GLOW" STATION LINEUP

CITY/STATE	STN.	CH#	DAY	TIME	CITY/STATE	STN.	CH#	DAY	TIME	CITY/STATE	STN.	CH#	DAY	TIME
MIAMI, FL	WBFS	33	FRI	11:30 P	BALTIMORE, MD	WNUV	54	SAT	7:00 P	NEW YORK, NY	WPIX	11	SAT	12:00 P
MIAMI, FL	WBFS	33	SAT	11:00 A	ALBANY, GA	WTSG	31	SUN	2:00 P	GAINESVILLE, FL	TV69	69	SAT	7:00 P
ATLANTA, GA	WVEU	69	FRI	10:35 P	WEST PALM BEACH, FL	WFLX	29	SAT	8:00 P	WILMINGTON, NC	WJKA	26	SAT	11:00 A
ATLANTA, GA	WVEU	69	SAT	7:00 P	CHARLOTTE, NC	WPCQ	36	SAT	6:00 P	BIRMINGHAM, AL	XETV	6	SAT	12:00 N
MEMPHIS, TN	WPTY	24	SAT	9:00 A	MINNEAPOLIS, MN	KTMA	23	SAT	7:00 P	BIRMINGHAM, AL	WBMG	42	SAT	10:30 P
CANTON, OH	WOAC	67	SAT	8:00 P	GULFPORT, MS (BILOXI)	WXXV	25	SUN	6:00 P	SAN FRANCISCO, CA				
KNOXVILLE, TN	WKCH	43	WED	11:00 P	DAYTON, OH	WRGT	45	SAT	11:00 P	PITTSBURGH, PA	WPGH	53	SAT	11:00 P
LAFAYETTE, LA	KADN	15	SAT	2:00 P	LAKELAND, FL (TAMPA)	WTMV	32	SAT	8:00 P	OKLAHOMA CITY, OK				
CHATTANOOGA, TN	WDSI	61	SAT	12:00 P	(ST. PETE)					OK	KEMC	34	SAT	6:00 P
CLEVELAND, OH	WIXO	19	SAT	7:00 P	LOS ANGELES, CA	KCOP	13	SUN	12:00 N	ALBUQUERQUE, NM	KNMZ	2	SAT	10:00 P
INDIANAPOLIS, IN	WTHR	13	SUN	11:00 P	LOS ANGELES, CA	KCOP	13	SAT	10:00 A	(SANTA FE)				
INDIANAPOLIS, IN	WTHR	13	SAT	1:00 A	COLUMBIA, SC	WLTX	19	SAT	12:00 M	BOSTON, MA	WFXT	25	SAT	12:00 M
SAVANNAH, GA	WJCL	22	FRI	12:30 M	NEW ORLEANS, LA	WGSU	6	SUN	11:30 P	(NEEDHAM HTS)				
CHICAGO, IL	WPWR	50	SAT	6:00 P	HONOLULU, HI	KHNL	13	SAT	4:00 P	SEATTLE/				
CHICAGO, IL	WPWR	50	SUN	6:00 P	PHOENIX, AZ	KUTP	45	SAT	2:00 P	TACOMA, WA	KSTW	11	SAT	12:00 M
CHARLESTON, SC	WCBD	2	SAT	11:30 P	PHOENIX, AZ	KUTP	45	SUN	12:00 N	ROANOKE, VA	WJPR	21	SAT	11:00 P
PHILADELPHIA, PA	WGBS	57	SAT	11:00 A	BATON ROUGE, LA	WBRZ	2	D.O.B		(LYNCHBURG)				
PHILADELPHIA, PA	WGBS	57	SUN	11:00 A	SALT LAKE					HARTFORD, CT	WTXX	20	SAT	11:00 P
GREENSBORO, NC	WGGT	48	SAT	7:00 P	CITY, UT	KGBS	14	D.O.B		(WATERBURY)				
MELBOURNE, FL	WMOD	43	SUN	9:00 P	WESLACO, TX	KNGV	5	D.O.B		WICHITA, KS	KSAS	24	FRI	11:00 P
COLUMBUS, GA	W3TX	54	FRI	11:00 P	(BROWNSVILLE)					MILWAUKEE, WI	WVTV	18	SAT	10:50 P
FAYETTEVILLE, NY	WFCT	62	SAT	2:00 P	(HARLENGEN)					PORTLAND, OR	KPDX	49	SAT	11:00 P
MOBILE, AL	WPMI	15	SAT	5:00 P	ANDERSON, SC	WAXA	40	SAT	12:00 M	MADISON, WI	WMSN	47	SAT	12:00 N
SYRACUSE, NY	WSYT	68	SAT	11:00 P	(GREENVILLE/SPARTANVILLE)					DETROIT, MI	WXON	20	SAT	9:00 N
PUERTO RICO	WLUZ	7	SPANISH		MACON, GA	WXGA	24	SAT	11:00 P	(SOUTHFIELD)				
SACRAMENTO, CA	KSCH	58	SAT	8:00 P						DETROIT, MI	WXON	20	SAT	11:30 P
DALLAS, TX	KDFI	27	SUN	10:30 A						(SOUTHFIELD)				
DALLAS, TX	KDFI	27	MON	7:30 P										

Independent Network, Inc. 11150 Olympic Blvd. Penthouse, West Los Angeles, California 90064 (213)479-6755 Telex: 662612 INITELFVLSA
M.G. Perin, Inc. 124 E. 40th Street, New York, New York 10016 (212) 697-8587

What? Your hometown isn't listed above? Then use this handy coupon to write your local TV station's program director. Ask for GLOW to be broadcast in your area!

Dear Program Director:

I'm a loyal GLOW fan who frequently watches programs on your station. Only one question: Where's GLOW? It's my favorite TV show. Please air it on your station. Thank you.

Name_____

Address_____

City/State/Zip_____

GLOW's TV station lineup.

PART III

GLOW WAS GONE, IT WASN'T FAIR
BUT I JUST DREAM ON AND CLIMB THE STAIRS
I WALK THE TALK, CAN'T TEAR ME DOWN
HOLLYWOOD'S A QUEEN WITH MANY CROWNS

Chapter 23: WTF!

My *GLOW* career was over. But my wrestling career? Far from it! I was doing some local shows with "Stallone's Knockouts" with Hal Stone and several independent wrestling shows.

Hal Stone had a production company similar to *GLOW,* but his girls were mud and oil wrestlers and foxy boxers. Most of them lived in Los Angeles and worked at a famous club called The Hollywood Tropicana – not the casino in Las Vegas, but the old building in Hollywood at 1250 North Western Avenue. It was the world capital of female mud wrestling – the best in the world. The "Trop" was a place for celebrities of all types. You could run into rock stars, professional athletes, politicians, and more. It was a magnet for everyone who was anyone. I never worked there, but I knew lots of girls who did.

During *GLOW*'s first season in 1986, the Riviera Hotel and Casino had hired Hal's girls to put on an evening show for a few weeks through Dennis Morgan, the same guy that was helping with the first *GLOW* cattle call at the Hyatt on Sunset in Hollywood. They used our wrestling ring and put some kind of rubber pool in the middle, then added some mud or oil. Above it hung one pair of giant boxing gloves, and the show was called "Foxy Boxing".

These girls were the cream of the crop. All were drop dead gorgeous and came equipped with rad bodies, fake boobs, fake hair, fake noses, and tiny bikinis. They had names like Shelly The Burbank Bomber and Boom Easy riders Ashley. I remember running into some of the boxers at the pool one summer day. They told me that I should get breast implants and a nose job so I could be as perfect as they were. Their show consisted of the girls coming out in sexy outfits, dancing to a song, and stripping down to their bikinis until they received their bids. The highest bidder in the audience would get to help the girl with her match, like giving her water, rubbing her shoulders, and giving her a towel. This is how the girls made their money. This is when I started thinking about getting breast implants. I was getting body and image conscious. But I wasn't ready yet and wouldn't be for some time.

☆ ☆ ☆

Years later, Lightning, Tulsa, Babe, MTV, Stinky, and I would end up working for Hal with his next company called "Hollywood Hits." Hal had backers named Alan and Susan from Florida. The show consisted of female boxers and wrestlers. There was no mud or oil, but they still wanted us to come out in sexy outfits, dance to a song, and strip down to our wrestling gear. Babe never wrestled. Instead, she was our ring girl. The first tour we did, we went to Hong Kong and Malaysia. This was an extremely long flight. We went during the summer, so it was very hot and very humid. We didn't make very much for our weekly salary, but what we didn't make in salary, we made up in tips. They always planned day trips and touristy activities for us on our days off. Our hotel in Hong Kong was one of those high-rise hotels, and we stayed on the 20th floor overlooking the city and Kowloon Bay, as we were located on the Kowloon side of Hong Kong. I roomed with Tulsa a few times. She and I were always up for exploring.

After traveling to Malaysia, our first excursion with all the girls in Kuala Lumpur was a bus tour to a tropical rainforest, which included tours of pewter and batik factories. It was so damn hot and humid there it was hard to enjoy these tours. Thank God when we got to the rainforest, there was an area to go swimming. We took tons of pics there.

The tour began with a pickup from our central Kuala Lumpur hotel and a drive through the outskirts of Kuala Lumpur along "Ambassador Row," passing the Istana Sharif Ali Palace. Continuing into the countryside, we passed typical Malay villages on our way to our first stop, the Royal Selangor Pewter factory. Here, we had the opportunity to take a tour of the world's largest pewter factory, renowned for its craftsmanship and high-quality products. During the tour of the factory, we saw the different processes involved in working with pewter, including casting, filing, polishing, soldering, hammering, and engraving. I bought a pewter flask there. Then we climbed back onto the bus and our tour continued to a batik factory, where we were able to see how batik fabric is designed and printed. I had to buy some batik fabric as a nice souvenir. The next stop was the limestone hills of Batu Caves. There, a flight of 272 steps (trust me, we counted) lead up to a sacred Hindu temple cave that houses the shrine of the Hindu deity Lord Murugan, the god of war. The cave is filled with images of deities and murals depicting scenes from the Hindu scriptures.

Back in America, another juicy event we did with Hal Stone was at a local strip club on Raymer Street in Van Nuys, California. Inside, they had a small boxing ring set up where we would be doing an afternoon interview and promotion.

We were all dressed in our wrestling gear when we arrived and were introduced to everybody at the club. Hal Stone told us we would then come out to our music on the dancers' stage, where we would be tipped/auctioned to the customers who would be our trainers/water boys for our matches – kind of like Burgess Meredith as Mickey Goldmill in the *Rocky* movies.

I was very anxious about this. I had never danced/strutted in a strip club, so I looked at it more like being in a club on the dance floor – except I was being tipped for it. But we did not have to take off any clothes, thank goodness.

I wore a garter around my leg; high heels; a black leather, silver-studded bra; and black short-shorts. I came out to the song "Head Like a Hole" by Nine Inch Nails. It's a great song to strut to, and it gets the crowd's attention right away. Once the song started, I headed down the stage. I was a little scared, but … Holy Moley! My garter was being stuffed with so much money!

Damn, I thought, *I am in the wrong profession!*

I had a great big smile on my face. When I walked backstage to our changing room, I think some of the girls were envious. I made way more cash than any of the other girls that day.

I thought, *Hmmm, if I were topless, how much more money would I have made?* But I never took that path.

☆ ☆ ☆

I mentioned Debbie "The Killer Tomato" Pelletier and Jay "The Alaskan" York a bit earlier. They invited me and some of the other former *GLOW* girls (Lightning, Mt. Fiji, Beastie, and Tulsa), as well as professional wrestler Sue Sexton, to go on a tour of Panama. It was a week-long tour that paid $800 each, if I remember correctly, which was a nice payday. Unfortunately, the tour was in June, and we wrestled in this ancient arena with no air conditioning. It was hellishly hot and humid. This was also in the early 1990s and the country was still in turmoil following the U.S. invasion of Panama to oust Manuel Noriega. There were demonstrations and riots in the streets, and there were soldiers with machine guns everywhere.

We were there on Father's Day, and we had a little promotional press conference to hype the tour. Because I knew a tiny bit of Spanish, they had me go up to the podium and say a few words, so I wished all the fathers a Happy Father's Day and that got a nice reaction. Then they put all of us in a small white van to take us back to the hotel, but the streets were filled with people, and they could see us in the van. I think a lot of them recognized Mt. Fiji. People started crowding around the van, so we couldn't drive. They were pressing up against the van, pushing against the windows to try to see us. It must have been similar to how The Beatles felt when they were mobbed. It was pretty fascinating, yet scary at the same time.

When we got to the venue, we found out that we didn't have private changing rooms, so we'd have to get dressed in the stalls of the public restrooms. I finished my match against Tulsa and went to the bathroom to shower and change. I was a sweaty, exhausted mess. I still had to do a six-woman tag match, but I wanted to take a quick shower to cool off some, and I wanted to rush through it to finish up before any of the fans came in. No one else came in. *Awesome! It's my lucky day. Everyone must be watching the next match*, I figured. I finished up and got dressed. When I walked out of the restroom, I realized why no one else had come in. They had positioned a pair of armed guards at the door, standing there brandishing machine guns, to prevent anyone from getting close to us. It was pretty intense, and it really drove home

190

the point that we were in an area that could easily become extremely dangerous.

On that tour, we also made a point of visiting the Panama Canal. While we were there, we were waiting to see a big ship come through so we could see how the locks opened and closed and watch the whole process of a ship locking through. There were no ships on the horizon, though, and we were getting a little disappointed. I noticed a microphone and – being the smartass I am – I grabbed it and made an announcement: "Ladies and gentlemen, a ship is coming!" Mt. Fiji came running over in excitement.

"Did you hear that? A ship's coming!" She hurried to the railing to get a perfect viewing spot. I had to come clean and tell her it was just me playing around on the microphone. It was a funny moment, and it still makes me smile all these years later.

Chapter 24: True Crime After Hours

You meet all kinds of people in your lifetime and up to this point I must admit I've met some pretty nice people, and well...some shady ones. And I got a little reckless.

When *GLOW* ended, I had a lot of time on my hands. I could get into any club, any restaurant, and invited to any and every party I wanted to. Hey, I was a TV star, twenty-eight and looking good — *well, at least in my mind* — and I could do whatever I felt like. The world was my oyster.

One of my favorite hangs was the rock club FM Station in North Hollywood. A place where I could go with my friends — see bands play, go to parties after the gig — and then head over for breakfast at Denny's on Lankershim.

Every time I was at the club there was a guy — let's just call him Karl for now — who would buy me all the leftover red roses from the man or woman who was selling them at the end of the night. At first I was flattered, but then it was getting old and embarrassing. I looked like I had won The Miss America pageant.

Potential boyfriends and my girlfriends would ask me who that dude was.

I would reply, "Oh he's just a guy who likes me, but I'm not interested."

I know Karl was just trying to mark his territory. Throwing the flowers away at the club would be rude so I brought them home. I mean what girl doesn't want someone to give her flowers? And these were always red! To this day I do not like red roses. I'll take any color but please no red! *Cough, cough, wink, wink,* daisies are my favorite.

So Karl and I became friends. He was always trying to do nice things for me — ordering limousines to take me to the airport — fixing the deadman's car (see page 23) — leaving gourmet dinners and candy on my porch, and even leaving me more red roses.

One day he had the bright idea that he would buy a house, put the title in my name, and he would take care of the mortgage payments. I thought *Sure! Why not? This is really going to help enhance my credit score.* First red flag right there. Nothing in this world is free, but I thought what the hell, give it a shot!

Soon, I went to see the house that he was going to buy somewhere in the San Fernando Valley, and what a shit hole it was! No way in hell was I going to live there. Anyway, I figured Karl knew what he was doing, so I let him handle all the paperwork. Red flag number two.

Karl was always calling me: the bank needed this, the bank needed that, and now the bank needed my signature. I certainly didn't have time to go anywhere with him, especially to the bank. Why? Because I was out of town a lot, touring with *Hal Stone's Hollywood Hits* in Kuala Lumpur, Hong Kong, and Moscow.

The show was a mix of wrestling and foxy boxing. My gig was to wrestle Cheryl Lightning Rusa from *GLOW* and Ladies Professional Wrestling Association (LPWA). She had just returned from a Japanese tour and she was one tough little chick. If I had 10 bucks for every time she kicked me in the leg instead of my abs, I'd have a stack of cash for the casino. Every night she missed her mark, leaving me with a huge bruise that swelled and hurt. Finally I snapped — "Cheryl, I told you not to fucking do that!" *In my mind the problem was either our eight-inch height difference or she just didn't care.* I'm pretty sure it was the latter. Why? Because when the action is hot, sometimes wrestlers go blank and don't care. That was Cheryl on the Russia tour.

So when Karl eventually clued in that I was not around and I was not going to the bank, he told me to sign a blank piece of paper and he would take care of the rest. The third red flag, right? Well, that was that, until it wasn't.

When the tour ended and I was back in town, I continued to get on with my life doing my wrestling gigs, acting auditions, and hanging out with my friends. Things got busy again. Karl's house idea really wasn't on my mind.

One afternoon, I received a call from a casting agent to play the part of a mud wrestler for a TV show for the next day. It was going to be an incredibly early morning call at The World Famous Tropicana in Hollywood. I had never been there but knew it was where all the famous mud wrestling stars wrestled. It was also where Hal Stone recruited most of his roster.

The Trop gig turned out to be a 12-hour day. We wrapped around 4:30 P.M. and I drove through heavy traffic back to Burbank to mom and dad's. The day had been good but tedious and I was tired and slightly bitchy.

Mom was in the kitchen making dinner and dad was watching TV. Suddenly there was a very loud knock at the front door. I answered it. Standing before me was an FBI agent and a LAPD officer flashing their badges. I was dumb-struck. They identified themselves and asked if I was Jeanne Basone. I froze! Seconds turned into hours until I was able to spit out a horrified yes. My heart began to race.

I could sense from their tone of voice that this wasn't going to go well and I was about to face a good cop bad cop situation. The FBI guy was definitely the bad cop. The good cop asked if I knew Karl. I told him yes. Then my dad walked over and asked what was going on. The cops introduced themselves and said, "Well Mr. Basone, we're going to let you know what your daughter has been involved in". My heart red-lined. I thought, *what the hell are they talking about? What am I involved in?*

Was it drugs? I don't sell drugs. I mean, I had already seen what a brick of cocaine looked like — we called it krail, blow, yayo, coke — and I had seen bags of weed, tabs of acid and magic mushrooms. What do you expect? I hung out with the rockers and the bad boys. And Karl always had blow on him. He asked all the time if I wanted a bump. I never said no. What do you expect? I was a rock chick and a bad girl wrestler.

My mother went into the family room while my dad and me and the cops went into the dining room. My dad sat at the head of the table.

Across from him sat the LAPD good cop. I sat next to my dad. Across the table from me sat the FBI bad cop who held me under his gaze.

The good cop pulled out a thick mortgage loan agreement and thumbed through it. My signature was on each page. The bad cop said, "You are going to go to jail 10 years for each page you signed." That sent my heart skipping a beat and instantly a thought flashed out of somewhere. *Suck it up, GLOW girl.* I returned his gaze head on. *Think fast, Jeanne, very fast.* I held my gaze and everything became crystal clear: I had better play the dumb blonde and sing like a bird real quick.

The good cop asked me if I recognized the mortgage documents. I told him no. The bad cop interjected with, "Is that your signature?" I told him it was and that I'd never seen those papers and I'd never signed them.

The good cop asked me if I had worked at the Tropicana. I told him I didn't work at the Tropicana.

The bad cop said, "Are you sure?"

I told him yes and said I was a pro wrestler for a syndicated TV show called *GLOW: Gorgeous Ladies Of Wrestling*. I told him my casting agent had hired me as a day player actor for a TV filming at the Tropicana. The star was Martin Mull and my role was a mud wrestler.

So now it was my turn to flip one back to the bad cop. "Why are you asking me about the Tropicana?"

He fired back with, "We know you were there today."

I thought *oh my god! I was on surveillance.* I never ever saw anyone following me. My Tropicana call was super early and there weren't a lot of cars out at 4 A.M.

Surveillance? I had only seen "surveillance" on TV shows like *Starsky and Hutch, Adam 12,* and *Police Woman* starring Angie Dickinson. *How long had the cops been following me?* That thought totally freaked me out!

The good cop explained the reason they had me under surveillance was because they were looking to get information about Karl. The bad cop took over again and said, "Karl's got a storage unit with illegal guns and drugs. What do you know about it?"

At this point, I did not care about Karl — as the FBI cop had read out a list of alleged crimes that went on and on — and I just wanted to make sure that I was not going to jail. I was innocent. I didn't know about all that stuff. So I gave the cops all the information they asked for. An hour later they left our house and I never heard from them again.

Later, during dinner mom said, "Your dad was so nervous for you, the palms of his hands were wet, but he said, 'Jeanne was as cool as a cucumber.'"

I don't know whether Karl did any jail time or not. Several years later, he reached out and asked if I would work for his video production company. As usual he was persistent and to stop the pestering I finally agreed to work one match. Neither of us brought up the FBI/LAPD mess that he had created and I never saw him again.

Chapter 25: Hollywood the Jailbird

Shortly after I moved to my North Hollywood apartment, my mother called me to tell me someone had sent me a check for some kind of work. Obviously, that sounded good to me, so I drove over to her house to pick it up. On the way, however, I was pulled over by an unmarked squad car.

Uh oh, I thought. *This isn't going to end well.*

It hadn't exactly been a great year for me, driving-wise. I had received two speeding tickets, and while I had paid both, I hadn't paid the second one quite on time. Also, I had been pulled over twice in Burbank and had been warned that my registration tags had expired. Both times I had smiled as prettily as possible at the officers who pulled me over, and both times I got off with a warning.

"Yes, officer," I said each time. "I'll be sure to take care of it right away."

Only I didn't.

So, after pulling over to the side of the road, I checked my hair and makeup in the rearview mirror, preparing to schmooze/flirt with yet another cop. But when the officer arrived at the driver's side window, my heart sank. He was older than the other cops that had previously pulled me over, and no matter how prettily I smiled at him, his stone-faced expression didn't change.

"License and registration, please," he said.

I handed them over, and he turned to go back to his car. A few minutes later, he returned.

"According to our records, ma'am, you have an unpaid ticket."

"No," I argued. "I paid that, I swear. I just paid it late, that's all."

"We have no record of that, ma'am," he said. "Plus, your registration has expired. I'm afraid I'm going to have to ask you to step out of your car." Hearing that, I knew I was in trouble.

"Hands behind your back, please," he said. When I felt his handcuffs click into place, I *really* knew I was in trouble.

"Hold on, man! You're not going to tow my car, are you?"

Turned out, he didn't. But that didn't mean I wasn't going to jail. I'd seen enough cop shows and movies to know that they had to give you one phone call. So, as soon as we got to the North Hollywood jail, that's what I asked for. I used my one phone call to contact my mom, who was, of course, expecting me at her house.

"Hi, Mom," I said, trying not to sound like something was wrong. "Listen, I don't think I'm going to be able to pick up my check today. Something else, ummm, came up. I'll come by some other time, okay?"

Apparently, I did a fairly good job keeping the nervousness out of my voice, because my mom didn't seem too worried. Thirty minutes later, two different cops transported me to the Van Nuys jail, where I had to go through processing. It was an incredibly detailed process. They made notes of everything: the number of keys on my keychain, the contents of my purse, etc. They took just about all of my personal belongings, with the exception of my money. I thought that was a little weird. What was I going to spend my money on in jail?

In any case, after processing they put me in a holding cell all by myself. Not surprisingly, a lot of young male cops "conveniently" came by to check on me and see how I was doing. When they found out I got busted for expired tags, they shook their heads and said they would have let me off with a warning.

A lot of good that does me now, I thought. Why did that old cop have to make an example out of me?

Later that night, the female CO (Corrections Officer) gave me a duffel bag that contained a blanket, a toothbrush, and a small, black, cheap, plastic comb. She led me to a much smaller cell that contained one bunk bed, with a bottom bed that was already occupied by a sleeping prisoner. I immediately asked for another phone call, and since this was years before cell phones were invented, the CO had to wheel over a portable pay phone for me to use. I still didn't want to worry my mom, so I called my boyfriend to ask him to post the $750 bail and get me the hell out of there. As luck would have it, he wasn't home, so it looked like I was going to be stuck staying in jail overnight.

Needless to say, that night was a miserable experience. It was impossible to sleep, since the light in my cell stayed on the entire time and the other prisoners were making a terrible racket yelling – for food, for drugs, for the telephone, you name it. Finally, at about 4:30 a.m., they brought in our "breakfast," and it was one of the most disgusting things I had ever seen. It looked like eggs mashed into a piece of bread or hash browns. As awful as the meal looked, I ate it because I was hungry, and I didn't know if or when I would get the chance to eat again. Little did I know I would regret that decision later.

After breakfast, I was loaded onto a bus to be taken to see the jailhouse judge. The bus consisted of armed guards in the back plus all of us "jailbirds" in the front. On the ride over, I noticed the girl I was sharing a bench seat with (a short Hispanic woman) looking at me more closely than I would have liked. I assumed she was looking at my "rock and roll outfit": black leather jacket, black leggings, and cowboy boots with silver-tipped toes. Finally, she spoke.

"I know who you are," she said. "You're that wrestler Hollywood. From *GLOW*."

Normally, I would have been thrilled to be recognized by a fan, but in this particular situation, I was terrified. The *last* thing I wanted was for these real-life "tough chicks" on the bus to try to prove their toughness by taking on a professional wrestler and kicking her ass.

"Don't fucking tell *anybody* about this," I replied in a stern whisper. "You understand?" Luckily for me, she agreed not to say anything.

When the bus stopped, we were led into a building with multiple holding cells. One of my fellow prisoners must have been a "runner," because she had shackles on her legs. We were led into the third holding cell, where we joined a bunch of women from the Sybil Brand Institute for Women, a hard-core facility for hard-core prisoners that would eventually be shut down in 1997. One woman stood out: a hulking chick with a mustache, who I jokingly thought of as "Big Bad Betty." I walked as far away from her as I could and sat down on a hard concrete bench. It probably felt even harder than it actually was because of the miserable circumstances. I put my elbows on my knees and hunched over, looking at the ground. I wanted to look tough, but God knows I also wanted to avoid making eye contact with the "career criminals" in my cell. All of a sudden, I heard a husky, creepy, off-key voice singing, "I must have been through about a million girls; I love them; I leave them alone." – the old Elvin Bishop tune. I prayed that these lyrics weren't being sung by Betty.

Of course, they were. I made sure I didn't make eye contact with anyone at all, if I could help it.

I was sharing a cell with a pretty ragtag group of prisoners. There was Betty and her girlfriend, who had hideously dirty blonde hair. The two of them shared a blanket on the floor of the cell. There was a young Hispanic girl, who had just been busted for petty theft, so someone else was consoling her. I seemed to be one of the few girls in the cell who wasn't "paired up," and I wanted to keep it that way. With nothing to do and a lot of free time on our hands, the girls started going around the cell and saying what they had been busted for. When they came to me, I said, "Expired car registration."

"No way! You're lying!" several girls shouted. I guess their crimes were so much more serious that they couldn't even imagine something as minor as expired license plates. I had to think fast.

"Maybe I'm lying; maybe I'm not." I said, once again trying to sound tough. That was good enough. No one questioned me any further, thankfully.

At 9 a.m., I was called out of the cell. Thank God for alphabetical order! As I walked away, I heard the girl from the bus say, "That's Hollywood! From Gorgeous Ladies of Wrestling!" Apparently I hadn't scared her into keeping my secret. Oh, well … at least I was out of the cell.

When the judge saw how minor my "crime" was, he agreed to waive the $750 bail and released me. I was so relieved! There was only one problem: processing wouldn't take place until 3:00 p.m. that afternoon. Until then, I would have to wait in the same holding cell I had just left. Not exactly the news I had been wanting to hear!

When I got back to the cell, I returned to the same concrete bench where I had sat earlier. Betty looked at me and said, "You're on TV. How come you didn't get bailed out yet?"

"What?" I said, again trying to sound as tough as I could. I figured if she had to repeat the question, it would give me time to think.

"You're on TV. How come you didn't get bailed out yet?" she repeated.

"I didn't have the seven hundred and fifty bucks," I replied. Whether she believed me or not, that was thankfully the end of the conversation. However, I had more pressing concerns. It had been hours since I had used the bathroom, and I really had to go. The problem? There was only one toilet in the whole cell, and it wasn't exactly private. I shifted positions on the bench, trying to hold it in, but I knew eventually that nature was going to call. Finally, I got up to get in line for the toilet. On the way, I must have stepped on Betty's blanket.

"Hey! She stepped on our blanket!" the hideous blonde said.

"So what?" Betty replied. I breathed a sigh of relief.

Before long, I arrived at the front of the line. The girl in shackles from the bus was the only person in front of me, sitting on the toilet.

"Nice boots," she said to me. *Nicer than the shackles you're wearing*, I thought. But I didn't say it out loud. It was, to be sure, an awkward conversation.

When I was done using the bathroom, I returned to my bench. I used a quarter in my pocket to carve "Hollywood, 1991" in a nearby railing.

"You carve your name, you're coming back," a Hispanic woman snarled at me from a few feet away. *Hell no!* I thought. *There's no way I'm ever coming back here. I'll even pay for new license plates, if that's what it takes.* Once again, though, I bit my tongue and didn't say anything out loud.

For lunch, they brought us a brown bag with a bologna sandwich, an orange, and two cookies. After my cookies fell on the ground, I picked them up and threw them in the bag. No way was I eating something so filthy.

"Are you gonna eat those?" asked a woman who I could best describe as a crack whore.

"No," I said, handing them over. "Maybe you can tell me what they taste like." She ate them both, then turned back to me.

"They tasted like the first ones," she said.

Finally, at 3 p.m., I was released – with no ride and not enough cash on me for a cab. I called my friend, Joyce, who lived in my apartment complex, and thank God she came to pick me up. When I got home, I took the longest shower of my life, scrubbing myself clean like you would not believe. I didn't tell my parents about the incident until six years later. My mom was shocked, which was the reason I waited so long to tell her about it in the first place. Now that even more time has passed, I kind of feel bad that I didn't write about my experience sooner.

I mean, why couldn't I have been the one to come up with *Orange Is the New Black*?

Chapter 26: Custom Matches

One of the fourth season *GLOW* girls was a woman named Lee, who wrestled as Mexicali Red. In addition to hiring me to work some lingerie shows, she told me about a company called Triumph Studios. They filmed women's wrestling matches, then sold the VHS tapes through the mail. The style, obviously, was a lot different from what I was used to. In pro wrestling, there was a full-size ring, lots of spectators, and opponents with whom you had hours and hours of practice time. Triumph videos featured "apartment style" matches, filmed in a small setting with the cameraman and maybe a handful of other people in the room. Instead of the acrobatic, somersault-off-the-top-rope moves that were common with *GLOW,* we focused more on holds that could be applied – and suffered through – on the ground: lots of scissor holds, leg locks, and sleeper holds. Because the matches were filmed in a smaller space than *GLOW* matches, there were obviously a lot of close-ups. Luckily, I had a ton of experience "selling" the action from my babyface vs. heel days with *GLOW.*

Once I did a couple of matches for Triumph, I started to meet more people in the mail order business. This led to matches for other producers and companies, and the start of a lucrative career path for me. I shot several videos for DT which served as the beginning of a long-term, successful, professional relationship. DT had a pro ring, which obviously appealed to me, and they were great to work with. They were very professional, and the other girls they hired were great to wrestle with, which is important. In addition to Triumph and DT, I also shot matches for Les Femmes Fatales, owned by Robin, and Steel Kittens, owned by Belinda Belle. Over the years I've worked with many girls – too many to count probably! Some of the biggest names are:

Robin/Suzy Johnson – One of the best in the business. She started on the East Coast as a session wrestler, then moved to California and started Les Femmes Fatales.

Lisa Comshaw – A good friend and great actress, who unfortunately passed away in 2020. She and I had a lot of fun wrestling one another.

Onyx – Onyx, aka Bronco Billy, was one of the original WOW girls.

Candi – A cute little blonde with a "girl next door" look, but don't be fooled. Like Francesca Le, she was at her best in a "no rules" catfight. In her career she worked with a lot of different companies, and she was a sweet girl off the set as well. Sadly, she passed away in 2016. Like many of her fans, I miss Candi a lot.

Belinda Belle – Owner of Steel Kittens, a company I've shot several matches for. An excellent technical wrestler.

Stacy Burke – This curvy little spitfire was one of Hugh Hefner's girls. She is a good actress, but don't be fooled by her petite frame; she's a tough wrestler.

Christine Dupree – A former *Penthouse* Pet who can do boxing, wrestling, catfighting ... you name it.

Kristie Etzold – This girl got her start doing whipped cream and mud wrestling matches (separately, of course) in some of the clubs in Orange County. She liked it so much that she started doing videos. And she's the kind of girl that could hold her own in a barroom brawl.

Cheryl Rusa – Lightning from *GLOW*. A good friend of mine, perhaps because we have so much in common in terms of our backgrounds: pro wrestling, modeling, acting, and stunt work. She's a great girl and always a pleasure to work with.

Jennifer Thomas – One of the newer girls, but she's dived into the business head-first. She was a competitive fitness model. Gorgeous looks and a strong body. She's also a very dear friend.

Francesca Le – One of my favorite wrestlers from DT. And a really nice girl outside of the ring, and a hellcat.

One of the great things about filming videos is that there is so much variety in terms of the kind of matches we do. There is truly never a dull moment! Here are some of my favorite types of matches:

Pro style – My favorite type of match. Pro style matches aren't the most common type of video match because not all companies can afford to own a ring. (My company, Hollywould Productions, does, by the way.) However, I love to film them whenever I get the chance because I get to use the skills I learned way back in my *GLOW* days. There's no "live" audience, but I can still talk trash to the camera after I've clotheslined my hapless opponent and she's lying on her back in the middle of the ring.

Superheroine matches – Tied with pro style for my favorite type of match to film. If you've ever seen my Wonder Womyn (my spelling) matches, you know why. We get to wear great costumes and totally "ham it up" for the good vs. evil storylines. I LOVE turning the tables on a villain and making her pay for torturing "poor little old me."

Catfight (vs. another woman) – Remember the Miller Lite commercial from years ago when the two girls got in a catfight over the "Tastes Great" vs. "Less Filling" debate? For whatever reason, a lot of guys are turned on by the thought of two good-looking women slugging it out – no rules, no referee, the last woman standing wins. Maybe guys like it because it appeals to their primal "caveman instinct." These can be fun matches to film, but you've got to trust your opponent and know each other's limits.

"Mixed" matches (male vs. female) – Definitely the most straightforward matches to film. Why? Because 99 percent of the time, it's a "scripted" match where the guy loses! (Although in reality, the male actor gets to roll around on the floor with a hot, bikini-clad woman for a half-hour or more, so does the term "losing" really apply?)

100% competitive matches – These types of matches I could never do well in. Once I tried doing one of these matches for Femme Fatales. I got this blonde girl in a full nelson-leg lock combo right away, but I had to keep it on her or I would have lost the match. I held the hold for what felt like an eternity, which was actually about 20 minutes. Finally, the producer called "time," and I won. Another reason I won't even attempt competitive matches today is that I have seven screws and two plates in my right leg from a match that went wrong. But I'll get to that story soon enough.

Today I offer all of the above through my website, which I launched in 1998: HollywouldProductions.com. Want to write the script for your own personal wrestling video? Then get to it and let me know what you'd like to include. Of course, nudity and anything sexual aren't options. Other details are on the website.

Professional Independent Wrestling Promotions I Worked For

AIWA
NWA
WWA
MLW
PPCW
GLOW
G.L.O.R.Y. Wrestling

Another Perspective: Jeff Urband (Photographer and Videographer)

From the '90s on, I expanded my interests and portfolio as a part-time photographer and videographer. I found myself photographing athletic women, bodybuilders, dancers, fashion models, actors, stuntwomen, wrestlers, and athletes engaged in sports and competition – all requiring strength, balance, technique, and skill!

In the early '90s, I met a fighter, stuntwoman, and wrestler from the TV show *Gorgeous Ladies of Wrestling*. On *GLOW*, she had wrestled under the name Hollywood, sometimes joined by her tag team partner, Vine. Jeanne was already well known, achieving an international following and reputation.

I met Jeanne outside a dojo in Marina Del Rey, California. Seeing her for the first time, I was a bit starstruck! Here she was in person: tall, slender, athletic, sexy, blonde, beautiful, skilled, and strong! I was scheduled to film a wrestling match that day with Robin, another skilled wrestler who also had an international following and reputation.

Hollywood applied her pro wrestling skills acquired on the TV show against Robin, who had a variety of skills and techniques herself! Needless to say, it was quite a match! I was fortunate to witness and film it.

Both athletes developed companies producing and distributing videotapes that exhibited their skills. And all of this was before the Internet got big!

Jeanne and Robin were both acrobatic, flexible, and strong for their sizes, taking on opponents much larger and heavier. Jeanne was fierce and could pick up and throw both men and women to the mat. She had an amazing skill set!

I still work for Jeanne and Robin. Jeanne travels to autograph sessions and conventions, still produces videos, and is an astute businessperson. I am still privileged to photograph and film her matches. We remain friends, and she can still throw me to the mat! Believe it!

☆ ☆ ☆

Another Perspective: Jennifer Thomas (Mixed Wrestler, Owner of SessionGirls.com)

"Jeanne *please* don't body slam me so hard the ring breaks – But I was too busy chasing boys around the neighborhood. I never watched *GLOW* growing up or WWF. Wrestling came much later in my life. I watched part of NETFLIX *GLOW* but that's not the same."

Mixed wrestling is an underground sport that is considered a treasure by the men and women who participate in it. Women feel empowered, as they are able to athletically dominate a male in a fun and professional manner. The men feel euphoric as they experience the overwhelming sense of power, talent, and skill.

Yes, it's taboo, as most of these sessions take place privately in a hotel room. Most men travel for business, and training centers don't offer private rental to those not registered in their training program. Mixed Wrestling is just one open door to a thrilling experience, but there is so much more, such as performing in wrestling videos and live events.

The mixed wrestling industry changes lives by creating memories and allows you the freedom to go on the path less traveled, which is extremely rewarding for those who have a genuine passion for wrestling and are willing to think outside the box (or ring).

☆ ☆ ☆

Another Perspective: Kim Krieger (Longtime Women's Wrestling Fan)

I started buying wrestling magazines in the late '70s. They always had an apartment house wrestling match in each issue. In the back were advertisements for different studios that produced female wrestling matches. So I purchased matches from many different studios. One of them was DT. They would produce custom matches – which could be spy stories, superheroine stories, etc. – that starred their wrestlers. So I picked a favorite wrestler and had her starring in different scenarios.

After a few years, Gina, the producer at DT, said she was no longer available. She sent me an envelope with several girls' pictures. One of the girls was Jeanne Basone. Of course, I recognized her as a *GLOW* girl – I watched the show every week – and immediately asked if she was really available for custom videos. The answer was yes, and I quickly wrote a script with her in a strongman competition with another wrestler named Robin. She did a terrific job. She did five more custom videos for me. Then, when I turned 50, I asked for a special video with her playing a gunslinger. DT had the girls wish me a happy birthday. When I saw that, I knew I had to meet her in person.

By then, everyone had email and I was able to get in touch with Jeanne. She said she had her own production company and sent me a list of the wrestling videos she had for sale. I couldn't wait to order as many as she had! She said she would be happy to produce and star in any video I wanted her to do. So I had her make a few custom videos for me.

Now I HAD to meet her.

I met Jeanne in person for the first time in Strongsville, Ohio. She was so nice. I was breathless. She said come on in, just sit down and relax, and I will get you some water. She was SOOO beautiful and SOOO nice. I couldn't believe it. She signed several magazines she had appeared in. It was a perfect day.

Chapter 27: Israel: The Shortest "Tour" Ever

I had a rule of thumb when it came to international tours: Don't be the first to arrive. You see, you never know what's going to happen with these tours. A lot of times, things just get fucked up and the tour doesn't come off as planned. I'd rather let the first group arrive and get settled in, make sure the shows were actually happening and that everyone was getting paid, and then arrive later, once I knew everything was on the up-and-up.

On this one occasion, I didn't follow my own advice.

It was around 1995, and I was living in West Hollywood. I had just broken up with a guy and I wanted to get out of town to take my mind off things. A wrestling promoter named Herb Abrams had booked me for a tour of Israel that he was putting together. Now, if you're a wrestling fan, the name Herb Abrams probably already sets off alarm bells in your head. Herb was an eccentric wrestling promoter from Queens, New York. He had a vision of competing with the World Wrestling Federation and held a few pay-per-view events to showcase his upstart promotion, the Universal Wrestling Federation, which featured a lot of respected veterans and some up-and-coming young wrestlers. Herb even managed to book appearances by Andre the Giant, Bruno Sammartino, and Captain Lou Albano. He was known to throw money around, live the rock-and-roll lifestyle, and make a lot of big promises that didn't always come true.

According to sources Herb died of a heart attack in 1996 after police found him naked and covered in baby oil, reportedly after a cocaine-fueled tryst with some escorts. He had a high-octane personality, to put it lightly.

Anyway, Herb had booked a women's wrestling tour of Israel. They had these posters plastered all over, advertising us as "Chippendolls," using our sexiest promo pictures. I wanted to see Israel, and the timing was right for me personally, so another girl and I went over with the first crew. It took two days to get there because they booked us the cheapest flights possible. We were scheduled for a weeklong tour, and I was thrilled when we landed and got to the hotel. It was gorgeous and overlooked the ocean. The rooms were lovely. There were these nice, comfy, beautiful bathrobes in there that I never wanted to take off.

They shuttled us down to a TV studio where we were set to be interviewed to promote the wrestling shows, but when we got to the studio, things seemed a bit off. It seemed like they didn't know why we were there. We were there in front of a live TV audience, and it went well, but that little confusion in the beginning should have been a big old red flag.

We got back to the hotel and had dinner at the hotel restaurant. It was wonderful and I was looking forward to a week of wrestling, sightseeing, and more delicious food.

That night, Herb's assistant, wrestler "Mr. Outrageous" Al Burke, called my hotel room. "Hollywood, you and the other girl are leaving. We're flying you home," he said. *What?!* I thought. *What do you mean we're going home? We just got here. Heck, it took us two days to get here.* "When are we going home," I asked. "Your flight leaves tonight," he said.

I had about five dollars in my pocket. "What about our money?" I asked. We were supposed to be paid five hundred dollars each.

"There is no money," Al said. Apparently something had gone sour and the tour had been canceled, just like that. Who knows what kind of deal Herb had worked? All we knew was that it had fallen apart and apparently Herb had no way to salvage it.

"Where is Herb?" I asked. I wanted some answers. Al said that Herb was in the hotel, but he had gone radio silent. He wasn't returning any calls.

I was told, many years later, that the organizers told Herb that they wanted a sexier product and that Herb wasn't going for it. Herb had booked a pro wrestling tour and wasn't going to turn it into a wrestling sex show, so he shut down the deal and sent us back home. If that's the case, then I respect Herb for standing up for his crew, but I wish I had known that at the time.

This was the 1990s, before we had cell phones. I had to get in touch with Cheryl Rusa, who was scheduled to join us in Israel, and tell her not to get on the flight and that the tour had gone downhill. I didn't have enough money to make a long-distance hotel phone call (remember, I had expected to be paid for the tour, but that wasn't going to happen now), so I had to fax her a note from the hotel's business office: "Cheryl, don't come to Israel. The tour has been canceled. We're coming back tonight." I may have used some more colorful language, to be honest.

I met with the other girl and, since we still had a few hours before our flight, we decided to do whatever sightseeing we could do on short notice and basically for free. We walked and checked out the local Hard Rock Cafe, but it was still a tense time. Not only did we have a long and unexpected flight home ahead of us, but Israel could be a dangerous place. Bombs were occasionally planted in outdoor marketplaces. We didn't really know what to expect, and I know I was a bit jumpy. I really wanted to see all of the historic sites that Israel had to offer, but that just wasn't going to happen this time around.

When we got to the airport, security pulled us aside and interrogated us. This was before 9/11, and I wasn't used to such a thorough search and questioning. They separated me and the other girl. They wanted to know why we were there; why we were going home so quickly; what we did for a living. After they questioned us, security switched up; the guy who had questioned me went and questioned her, and vice versa. They wanted to make sure our stories matched exactly. It was intense. I mean, here were two women wrestlers who had traveled all this way with barely any cash in their pockets, did a TV interview, and were now flying back home on tickets that had just been purchased. It must have seemed awfully shady. Though, if they had known of Herb Abrams' reputation, maybe they would have just waved us through.

I was thrilled to get home and be back on American soil. The entire experience was one of the most stressful and frightening experiences of my career. My takeaway from that trip – and my new rule of thumb – was to make sure you get half your money or all upfront before every booking. And remember those nice bathrobes at the hotel? We took those home as souvenirs. How's that for a unique payout?

Chapter 28: The Internet

As the 1980s ended and the 1990s began, I began to make the transition from *GLOW* girl to an established performer on the wrestling video circuit. To date, I have filmed over 1,000 matches for several different companies, and after a couple of years, I felt like I had a pretty good toehold in the industry. Little did I know that my career was about to take a drastic turn for the better. You could call it karma, fate, or just plain old good luck.

Or you could call it the Internet.

A computer? The Internet? What the hell is a website? This was all very new to me, just like it was to everyone else in the mid-1990s.

While I was working for Hal Stone's "Hollywood Knockouts," I met another wrestler named Christine. From what I remember, she and I were there to do a boxing match. While we were on a break, her webmaster told me that I should have my own website. I asked him to tell me a little more about it and decided to follow his advice. He agreed to help me set one up. I had no clue what I was doing so I came up with www.webkitten.com as the name of my first website.

Now that I had a name, I had to come up with a plan for what it would look like. I bought an eMachine personal computer so I would be able to figure out how to do this "Internet thing." Honestly, I think I still had my old Prodigy.net email address at the time.

With help from my new webmaster, I started putting up glamour photos of myself that were taken by Jon Abeyta, my favorite photographer from L.A. I then added some wrestling photos as well to try and attract as many people as I could. Next, I opened a members only area that I think I updated once a month. I charged $19.99 a month, which is what all the other sites were charging at the time.

Now that my site was ready, I had to advertise. I made up 4x6 postcards with photos of me and the website information on them. I used these postcards at conventions and at GlamourCon in Los Angeles and Chicago to help get my website information out to my fans. In addition to the postcards, I would have Bob Harris, a contributing member to *FIGHTING Females* magazine, mention my website whenever he could.

Before I knew it, business was booming. I started working constantly on videos, photo shoots, sessions, and my website. The harder I worked, the more people I seemed to attract to my site. Before the days of MySpace, Facebook, X (Twitter), and Instagram, we had a place called Yahoo! Groups. In the early 2000s, in addition to sending a newsletter to my fans, I would post there almost daily.

The newer social media outlets have all but killed off these groups. That's a shame because I really enjoyed posting and interacting with my fans on those groups. I love social media, and I hate social media at the same time. The plus is that it's a great way to interact with my friends and family and post about all my events. I still post on my Instagram, X, and Facebook almost every day. But the downside is all the bullying that people do when they hide behind a screen.

Another Perspective: Steve (Longtime Women's Wrestling Fan)

This is the true story of just one guy who was a teen in the 1980s. I was born in 1970 and perhaps a little bit of a late bloomer. Many of us guys don't control what turns us on. When we see, hear, or smell a certain stimulus, it immediately affects us, whether we want it to or not – especially for those of us who were awkward teens way before the Internet existed.

By the time *GLOW* came on, I already knew that the '80s trends of girls in heavy makeup, highly teased hair, neon colors, skin-tight jeans, leather jackets and skirts, and smoking cigarettes all turned me on immensely. I was a jock, but I was attracted to the "bad girls."

I was an occasional fan of the WWF, back when we had only a few TV channels to choose from and Bob Backlund, Jimmy Snuka, and Roddy Piper were big stars. Then I stumbled upon *GLOW*. Girls fighting each other definitely stirred something in me that guys fighting did not.

The same involuntary physical reaction that I had to seeing a sexy girl in the mall in painted-on jeans, boots, and a leather jacket lighting up a cigarette happened to me when I saw the young ladies of *GLOW* in their tight, shiny outfits and boots entering the ring to battle other women. Hollywood definitely stood out. To my thinking, the only other *GLOW* girls who were in her class as far as pure beauty and sexiness go were Americana and Tara the Southern Belle.

But Hollywood added some things very important to this horny young guy: the black leather skirt, her wrestling gear, and her makeup and hair.

Another involuntary reaction I had was that I was drawn to the "jobbers," the girls on the losing end. So I was incredibly turned on when Tara the Southern Belle was demolished and humiliated by the bad girls, as when the Heavy Metal Sisters made her jump through a flaming hoop like a circus animal, or when Mana the Headhunter dislocated Susie Spirits arm. And when Americana was "hung" in a noose by the Heavy Metal Sisters, and Ninotchka ended Americana's career by ruining her knee. I'm not sure, but it may have been the beginnings of a "damsel in distress/male rescuer" fetish that caused me to fantasize about being their boyfriend and taking care of them.

But Hollywood never met such fates. She was far more athletic than the jobber girls, and she was a heel, so she was always on the winning, tormenting end. She still looked amazing! I confess that each time she was on, I was secretly hoping that Vine would turn on her, and maybe some of the other heels would jump in to put a beat down on her, and she'd be stretchered out of the ring and later return as a "good girl" – but still in her leather.

Eventually, *GLOW* ended, but my fantasies and memories did not. When the Internet was born, in 1995 or so, I quickly found that there were thousands, perhaps millions, of guys who shared all of my interests. I cannot explain how ecstatic I was when I first found Steel Kittens' "Harley's Little Angels," with Hollywood back in her leather and taking many more bumps than she had in *GLOW*. I think she even took a break from that battle royale in her leather bikini, climbing through the ropes and saying, "I need a cigarette!"

Then, of course, as the Internet grew, Jeanne created Webkitten / HollywouldProductions / WrestlingBabe and continued to make awesome videos, often featuring her in her leather or superheroine cosplay outfits. I've purchased plenty of videos starring her.

Hollywood was an important part of my maturation from a boy to a man. Olivia Newton-John smoking a cigarette in a leather jacket and spandex in the last scene of *Grease*; Rebecca De Mornay as the heavy smoking hooker in skin-tight designer jeans in *Risky Business*; Jeanne Basone as Hollywood in leather and boots and neon colors, entering a wrestling ring to battle other women. All of these played a big role in forming, and allowing me to understand, my special interests.

Thank you, Jeanne!

Another Perspective: Dave "Jackpin" Jackson (WWC Organizer and Promoter)

My first recollection of Jeanne "Hollywood" Basone, like many people who know her today, was in the late '80s on the TV show *Gorgeous Ladies of Wrestling*. I loved to tune in every week in hopes of seeing her go up against the "good girls" and be the heel and bad girl that she portrayed so well. I was very bummed when the show was canceled and believed I would never see her again.

However, in late '96/early '97, along came the Internet, and I came across an ad to have a mixed session wrestling match with her. I contacted her first by email, then by phone, and set a date and time in Hollywood, California for our match.

Now, I was not in the habit of wrestling women, but this was Hollywood (I didn't know her real name at the time), and I thought it would be fun to meet her and see how well she could do against me. When I arrived, I was met at the door of this dance studio by Hollywood herself. Compared to the Hollywood on TV years before, this new Hollywood was even a more beautiful woman: strong, toned, and ready. I was truly impressed.

She showed me where I could change into my wrestling shorts, and I returned to find her in a black bikini, which was so amazing and made her look even stronger and more daunting. I walked onto this big mat and stood across from her.

She said, "Ready?"

I responded with a nod, and that beautiful smile of hers turned into a very focused "this is a real match" expression.

We wrestled, and even though, at first, she took control and had me tapping very quickly, I soon was able to snap out of my shock and awe at what she was doing to me. After a few rounds, I was even with her on submissions, but no matter how many I got, she never wore down. Each round she kept coming at me more strongly with everything she had. This was a turning point in my life, and I wanted to become a part of the women's wrestling industry.

Fast forward two years. I decided that, since women were always second to men in terms of wrestling shows and events since *GLOW*, I wanted to promote an event for and about women called the Women's Wrestling Convention (WWC) in 1998.

The first woman I contacted to be at the WWC was, of course, Jeanne Basone. When I told her about the concept, she was onboard immediately and gave me some great advice, since she herself covered the entire spectrum of the event. From live matches in the ring (women vs. women, pro style, and mixed pro style), she also had her company booth, which either she or Cheryl "Lightning" Rusa, also from *GLOW*, would attend to when not in the ring.

No one I have ever seen has utilized the WWC for all its worth more than Jeanne. She was always on the go, doing one thing or another: signing autographs, selling her CDs, taking photos with the fans, in the ring showing off her great pro talent, or in session matches.

We held a semi-formal banquet on the Friday night before the matches on Saturday and Sunday, and she was, of course, the belle of the ball. All eyes were on her. During the happy hour icebreaker, fans would come up to me and ask me to introduce them to her, as they were too intimidated to approach her. Once I did, they found her to be gracious, smart, and she could speak their language about women's wrestling. They all soon were put at ease, and many set up session matches with her for the weekend.

That evening Jeanne and Cheryl went to the podium and spoke to everyone who attended the banquet (150 people). They gave a wonderful speech about the current state of the women's wrestling industry and the potential it had to become so much more than it was at the time. Jeanne had a realistic vision where women would own companies like she did and put on events like today's Women On Fire events by Jennifer Thomas and, of course, all of the *GLOW* events that were to come in the future. Then she turned to me, "Jackpin," and thanked me for doing this event and continuing to help progress the women's wrestling industry with events like the WWC. The next conventions were in 1999, 2000, and 2008, and Jeanne attended them all.

In 2008, I promoted my last WWC event. Jeanne had always set the example for the women who attended to follow, as it is a business and she treated it that way. She has mentored many newcomers on how to conduct themselves and how to treat the business and industry. No woman or man tried to tell her how to do it, and that is true to this day.

One last of many memories was at the 2008 convention, when Jeanne was in a mixed tag team match in a ring. We were holding the event in a ballroom, and the hotel manager just happened to come by to take a look when he saw Jeanne climb to the top rope, then turn and soar into the arms of her male opponent. I thought the manager was going to have a coronary.

He said, "Does she do that often?"

My answer was, "Yes, pretty much." He just shook his head and left.

Throughout all the WWCs, it seemed that Jeanne and I would see each other at the "pre-event" meeting, the banquet, and then just before she departed on Sunday. We both were always so busy doing the business at hand. But on the final day before she departed, she would always take the time to seek me out to share a warm hug and tell me how much fun she had and what a great event it was. She always thanked me and encouraged me to keep going forward.

Throughout the years we have remained great friends, and I know if we ever needed one another, the other would be there. Jeanne and so many other women have brought us to where we are today with the hope of a better future for women's wrestling in all forms. I always say, "Let's make Herstory again."

Jeanne and I have been friends for over twenty-five years, and I am so blessed that she is in my life as a great friend and buddy. My only complaint is that we don't get the chance to see each other often enough, but we do keep in touch, and I do love her new business of making the very best and unique soaps you will find anywhere.

I will always have a very special place in my heart for Jeanne, not just as a fan of her talent and accomplishments, but more so as her friend.

Chapter 29: Stunt Work, "Lingerie Lunches," and Plumbers Don't Wear Ties

In 1998, Cheryl Rusa came to me with an idea. She had been doing some stunt work and she wanted me to do the same. We went over to the set of *V.I.P.*, a campy Pamela Anderson comedy-drama about a voluptuous blonde who just happens to be the star employee of a private bodyguard agency. We "hustled" the set – an industry term for introducing yourself to the stunt coordinator and letting him or her know your availability – but never wound up working on that particular show.

At the time, I was pretty ambivalent about stunt work. If a job offer happened to come through, that was fine. If not, that was okay, too. After all, I had plenty of part-time work that allowed me the freedom to travel and to wrestle.

And some of the work I was finding was pretty easy – basically, working at bars in the Los Angeles area. I was doing some promotional work for Jägermeister at Barney's Beanery, a famous chain of sports bars in Los Angeles, when the manager asked me if I'd be interested in working on something called "Lingerie Lunch." Essentially, the job entailed dressing up in a sexy outfit, walking around the bar, and selling raffle tickets to customers – a dollar apiece or eight for five bucks. The girls got to keep all of the ticket sales money, so obviously we were motivated to work the room pretty hard. It was an easy way to make a little extra money. They actually required us to wear nylons, so it was still a bit conservative, all things considered.

In addition to being a good side hustle, the lingerie gig also allowed me to rub elbows with some celebrities from time to time. On one occasion, Quentin Tarantino came into the bar with another guy and two stuffy-looking, suit-wearing businesswomen. Tarantino was very excited by the whole scene, asking things like, "Hey, what's going on? What are we doing today?" in the high-pitched, hyper voice that his fans could recognize in an instant. I explained the raffle ticket deal to him, and it seemed like he was totally on board. But then he looked over at the two women sitting next to him, each of whom had a sour, disapproving look on her face.

"Sorry," he said to me, shrugging his shoulders. I thought it was pretty interesting that a guy whose movies include hardcore, graphic scenes – think "Stuck in the Middle with You" from *Reservoir Dogs* – would hang around with such stuffy people.

Another celebrity who came into Barney's while I was working there was the late Anna Nicole Smith. She came into the bar after a night that I suspect had been filled with all sorts of debauchery. Despite the late hour and lack of sleep, though, she looked amazingly beautiful. Like Tarantino, Anna seemed pretty excited to be there when she walked in. When I told her about the raffle tickets, she said, "You've got nice boobs – I'll take five tickets!" I'll always have fond memories of that day, and I was sad to hear about Anna's untimely death a few years later.

Considering the fact that I'm such a big music fan, I also thought it was cool when Tom Petty, Jason Bonham (son of Led Zeppelin drummer John Bonham), and Reb Beach (guitarist for Whitesnake and Winger) came into the bar. It's not that anything out of the ordinary happened; it's just that it was fun to be around such heavy hitters in the music industry. That was pretty typical of my fifteen-year career working at local bars. (But I had to take some time off in 1998 when I broke my leg. More on that later.) And it wasn't just Barney's Beanery, either. I also worked at Texas Loosey's in Torrance, Slam Dunk in Whittier, and Chuy's in Glendale.

It didn't happen at Barney's, but the first and only time I ever met Jimmy Page was at the Rainbow Bar & Grill. It was around 1:30 a.m. on the night before Thanksgiving in 1994. Jimmy was sitting at a table with an acquaintance of mine named Rick, who sold rock concert T-shirts for a living. I went over to the table, Rick introduced me, and I sat down.

Jimmy had a "to go" soup cup sitting on the table in front of him, so I asked him what kind of soup he was drinking.

"I am drinking gin," he replied.

We both smiled.

☆ ☆ ☆

It was at Chuy's in 1993 that I met Michael Anderson, who asked me to star in a 3DO video game called *Plumbers Don't Wear Ties*. I didn't know much about video games, and didn't know a thing about 3DO, but I learned that 3DO was a unique console that was designed to work with a variety of games from different companies. I would be playing a character named Jane, and I would be one of the stars of the game. It would be an adult-oriented, romantic comedy "visual novel" – a sort of interactive video. We would film scenes, and the player could somewhat control what would happen next. At least, that's how it was described to me.

Michael said the project wouldn't involve any pornography or anything like that. Basically, it wasn't much different from what I was doing with the lingerie lunches. It was a cool concept, and it sounded like an interesting opportunity, so I agreed to do it.

I would be the first narrator and introduce the player to the objective of the game. The basic plot is that two characters, Jane and John, are both being pressured by their parents to find a partner and get married. John is a plumber (and now you know how the game got its name). John meets Jane in a parking lot and falls in love, so he decides to skip work and wait in the lot for her, as she has a job interview inside. When Jane is at the interview, the boss (played by Paul Bokor) tells her the position has been filled, but maybe "something can be worked out after all." He then tries to get Jane to take off her clothes and attempts to attack her, which leads to a series of chase scenes throughout Los Angeles, where I'm running around in my underwear and high heels.

OK, it's not exactly a classic. In fact, the game got some pretty terrible reviews when it came out, but it also attracted something of a cult following. A review of the game posted on YouTube by Angry Video Game Nerd has amassed 9.5 million views to date. That's some pretty remarkable publicity for our little game. That's more views than most *GLOW* content!

The shoot was pretty fun. We filmed all the scenes in one month, shooting on weekends. The game used a little bit of video and a lot of still photos. I shot a lot of scenes in a bra and mini skirt, but I had no problems with it. I thought everything was filmed in good taste. There was a little shower scene, but I was behind a towel. I figured maybe you could see the side of my breast and one shot of my butt, but that was it, so I didn't mind. There wasn't anyone there to do hair or makeup, but I wasn't thinking about what I looked like. I just rolled with it. The makers did, however, pay for my transportation, meals, hotel, and fees, so I have to give credit where credit is due for that.

We shot a bunch of scenes outdoors around L.A., including scenes in Chinatown, Griffith Park, and the Griffith Observatory. Those were some of my favorite places in town, and they allowed me some input on where we shot, so I made sure to work them in. Did we have a permit to be filming? Of course not! I'm sure we turned plenty of heads as I got chased around Los Angeles in my lingerie.

Again, it was a silly little one-off project. But years later, once the Internet had gotten established, I began receiving emails from people who had played *Plumbers Don't Wear Ties*. Some loved it; some hated it. But *a lot* of people had opinions about it.

Fast forward to 2020 during the COVID-19 pandemic. Limited Run Games bought the rights to the game and asked me to shoot some scenes and provide some commentary and narration for the new version. I went to their studio in North Carolina. They played the game on a big monitor and had me record some commentary. The next day, they gave me a little script and had me record a new introduction. I wore a black outfit that showed off a bit of my chest – just to capture the spirit of the original, I guess. This time, they had hair and makeup on set, which was nice. It was really a great shoot.

Limited Run re-released *Plumbers* on Xbox, PlayStation 4 and 5, Nintendo Switch, 3DO interactive multiplayer systems, and other consoles in 2023. I've been doing a lot of conventions and fan fests to promote it, and I'm looking forward to meeting more of the *Plumbers* fans in the future. Shout-outs to some of the people at Limited Run connected to all of this: CEO Josh Fairhurst, VP of Marketing & Digital Publishing Alena Alambeigi, Producer Audi Sorlie, and Brian Adams.

From 1993, I also worked at various bars on Monday nights; the *Monday Night Football* crowd was good to me. There is something about a bunch of red-blooded, American men drinking cold beer and watching football that makes them willing to buy raffle tickets from a girl dressed in skimpy lingerie.

One of the great things about working part-time at local bars was the freedom it gave me. I could accept or decline a job depending on my schedule, and declining allowed me to pursue other opportunities, such as shooting videos for Hollywould Productions or traveling to other parts of the country to shoot videos for other companies.

The more I talked to Cheryl, though, the more I wondered if I shouldn't pursue stunt work a little more aggressively. After all, she had made out quite well for herself in residuals for all of her stunt jobs. "Residuals" is industry slang for "residual income" – once a unionized actor plays a part in a movie or television show, he or she gets a check every single time that movie or television show is shown, either domestically or abroad. In other words, you do one job and collect checks for decades to come. Not a bad deal!

It wasn't like I hadn't acted on TV shows before. I had previously had roles on *Married... with Children*, *Saved by the Bell*, and *The Larry Sanders Show*, among others. (After shooting *Larry Sanders*, the cast went out to a Thai restaurant on Ventura Boulevard. Did Jeremy Piven hit on me? I'll give you three guesses ... and the first two don't count!) I'd acted in movies like *Son-in-Law* (starring Pauly Shore), in which I mud-wrestled with Cheryl about a half-hour into the film. I even had a role as "Wrestling Coordinator" on VH1's *Real Chance of Love,* where I coached the girls about how to wrestle as part of their competition to win the affection of one of the two hosts ("Real" and "Chance," two brothers who formed a rap group called The Stallionaires).

But I had never really done any stunt work after hustling the *V.I.P.* set in 1998. In addition to my friend Cheryl, I was also encouraged by my friends Marijane Cole and Joni Podesta, a fellow wrestler and *American Gladiators* contestant who had done stunt work on feature films like *Million Dollar Baby* and *Marley and Me*. Joni and I were registered with the same agency, Missy's Action Services, which helps stunt men and women connect with various stunt coordinators.

My first job as a stuntwoman came in a movie called *Beneath Loch Ness* in 2002, in which I allowed the famous Loch Ness monster to knock me out of a boat and into the water. It might not have won any Academy Awards, but it was a lot of fun. Thank you, Cheryl Rusa and stunt coordinator Chris Doyle!

In 2005, good friend Marijane Cole introduced me to stunt coordinator Diamond Farnsworth, who hired me to play a professional wrestler named Anaconda Angie on the CBS drama *JAG*. He also gave me the title of wrestling coordinator. In 2008. I had another stunt job on a movie called *Legacy* (starring Hilary Duff's sister Haylie), and once again I played a wrestler.

In 2009, I worked on the iconic and long-running soap opera *Days of Our Lives*. It was my first stunt work in which I didn't play a wrestler or take a bump from a sea serpent. Instead, I was a stunt double for actress Nadia Bjorlin. My scene involved walking up to a door that – due to a gas leak behind it – exploded violently when I opened it, causing me to fly through the air backwards and land on my you-know-what. Not only did I do the scene without padding on the floor (pretty sure my *GLOW* background helped me in that respect), but I did it in one take. This was kind of a big deal, since it saved the network the time and money of having to shoot multiple takes. Carl Ciarfalio coordinated the stunts on *Days*, including the one I did.

In 2010, I worked on the NBC action comedy *Chuck* with the late, great stunt coordinator Merritt Yohnka. I played a Moroccan guard – definitely one of the "bad guys" – who was the last out of four girls shot and killed in a fast-paced action scene. Incidentally, one of the guest stars on that show was five-time Emmy Award-winning actor John Larroquette. Immediately before shooting the scene, Merritt gave us three pieces of advice: "1. Don't hit your head on the floor – it's hard. 2. The gun is heavy, so don't hit yourself in the face with it and don't point it at the actor's eyes. 3. Make sure not to fall on the girl to your right or your left." Then, just like that, the director called, "Action" and we shot the scene. I was amazed at how fast everything went down, and I quickly learned that when you work stunts, you have to pay attention and have your act together.

In March 2023, I worked on the movie *Holland, Michigan* that was filmed – where else? – in Nashville, Tennessee. They needed some stunt drivers for the movie, and I was hired by Hiro Koda. Hiro hired me on the recommendation of Chavo Guerrero, who was also doing stunts and working as a stunt coordinator.

Part of me wishes I'd pursued stunt work more aggressively back in the late 1990s. But as they say, hindsight is 20/20, and at least I'm actively working in the field today.

I've hustled stunts for *CSI*, *Castle*, *Sons of Anarchy*, *The Walking Dead*, and *Nashville*. While I haven't worked for any shows like that yet, there's always a chance that I will sometime soon. So tune in and keep your eyes peeled … maybe you'll see me.

Chapter 30: Get Your Wings and Fly

In the late '90s – around 1996 – I was living with my two friends Lisa and Linda Moore. They were sisters – twins actually. We met through my good friend Kay Walsh, who did makeup for my boyfriend and his band. I moved from my West Hollywood apartment on Martel into their home on Laurel Canyon, just up from the Mt. Olympus neighborhood.

There's a lot of history in Laurel Canyon, which was a nexus of counterculture activity and attitudes in the mid to late '60s and early '70s. The community became famous as home to many of L.A.'s rock musicians: Cass Elliot of the Mamas & the Papas; Joni Mitchell; Frank Zappa; Jim Morrison of The Doors; Carole King; The Byrds; Gram Parsons; Buffalo Springfield.

My street was a one-way road lined with large trees, small cottages, and older homes. Right up the street was the Canyon Country Store, and to the right side of that, above the cleaners, was an apartment Jim Morrison once lived in. The person who owned the apartment at that time held huge Fourth of July parties, in part to celebrate when Jim died on July 3, 1971. I am a huge Doors fan, so that was right up my alley.

The owner hired a band to play outdoors, and party goers could walk around Jim's old apartment. Just being inside the space where Jim used to live was so exciting. The owner showed me one area that he wanted to keep as it was in Jim's memory. It was a little area of a remodeled bathroom where he kept the original shower intact. It was pretty cool to see that. I've always thought that Love Street was surely written there.

Before that, in December 1996, Lisa had asked if I wanted to go to her company's Christmas party in Century City. I was always up for a cool party! On the way I had this weird feeling inside and said to Lisa, "Somebody is going to offer me a job tonight."

We ate, drank, and chit chatted with her coworkers all night. As we were getting ready to leave, this brunette girl came up and introduced herself as Sahar and asked if I had any experience as a flight attendant. I told her my uncle was a pilot and my aunt had been a stewardess many years ago, but not me.

Sahar said she worked for International Lease Finance Corp. (ILFC), a company responsible for leasing and selling planes to airlines all over the world. She was looking for someone to work their corporate flights while one of their girls was going to school. She gave me her business card and said, "Call me tomorrow so we can talk more about it."

Wow! See? My ESP had really kicked in!

I called the next day. They scheduled a meeting for me with their CEO, James Hazy (pronounced "Haw-zee"). The company did a background check, and once that cleared, I met with their main girl at Van Nuys Airport. She went over all the particulars, like what meals the CEO and pilots liked and how to order from their catering company. I had to give the plane number, the company name, and what to order for flights.

"You better order everything on the menu," she advised. "The CEO will most likely just want cornflakes and milk, but you better have fresh fruit, eggs, bacon, and pancakes because you never know."

She also instructed me on how the stoves worked, how the bed worked, where seats were, and where the china was kept. It was a lot to learn in six hours, and believe it or not, there was no emergency training whatsoever. We didn't have cell phones like today, so I had to write everything down by hand.

On my first few flights, I felt like I was in an episode of *I Love Lucy*. Remember the one where Lucy is trying to put all the chocolates in the boxes? You get the idea. The galley was a mess, and all of the dishes had to be put away before we landed. I didn't even know how to make coffee because I wasn't a coffee drinker.

The pilots turned out to be very nice. The only particular thing that they wanted was the espresso I learned to make.

We took off from Van Nuys Airport, where most of the jets flew out of, refueled in Maine, and flew across the ocean to Europe.

Our first stop was Sweden, where our CEO had a meeting scheduled with Swissair. We flew to Stockholm Bromma Airport, and the crew stayed at a Hilton while the boss stayed at a higher-end hotel. I remember the beds in the Swedish hotel were Tempur-Pedic. They were so warm and comfortable, and it was snowy and freezing outside.

Typically, we would go three or four days to Europe. I barely had any time to rest during flights because I had to check on the pilot every so often. I figured I would just get a lot of sleep when I got back home.

Our second trip was pretty fun. We flew into Zürich, Switzerland. On this trip the boss, James, brought his son, who was probably around twelve years old. When we landed in Zürich, James had arranged for his son, one of the pilots, and me to take the train through the Swiss Alps and meet up with them in Malpensa, Italy. I had never been to Zürich or the Swiss Alps. It was a beautiful ride.

While on the train, I had to use the restroom. Since I hadn't been on a train in this European country, I didn't realize that when you went to the restroom, you were literally peeing on the railroad tracks!

We stayed at a beautiful place in Malpensa while our CEO attended his meetings. I think we got a half a day of rest before we were back on the plane.

Another trip took us to Paris, which was so much fun. Before we landed, James asked if I had been to Paris before. "No," I replied. He wrote down some places for me to see and gave me $300 cash. He actually was pretty cool that way. I tried to see as many places as I could, but I really needed rest. I felt guilty, but was tired as hell.

On the second day in the city, James wanted to go shopping. I went with him and one of his friends. He bought me a piece of china from a very prestigious dealer, which I gave to my mother. She still has this in her china hutch. That evening we all met for a really nice dinner with fresh oysters. I remember the pilots smoking cigars and drinking brandy. That was one of my favorite trips.

The gig didn't last long. I got sick with a serious sinus infection, so I went to a doctor. He told me not to fly. ILFC did not take no for an answer, or accept the doctor's note, so they never called me back.

Now, if I were smart, I would've called them back another day. But young me wanted to play around and have fun and have no responsibilities at all. Live and learn.

Another Perspective: Michael Strider (Rock Music Photographer)

Jeanne "Hollywood" Basone was THE original *GLOW* girl. Like all the other teenagers from my generation, I loved the show and found myself glued to the television set every time it aired on Saturday night.

In the late '90s, Jeanne and I were both going to be in NYC for our separate gigs, and we decided to do a photo shoot while we were there. I brought two "spotters" (friends that watched for cops and bad guys) to ensure everything ran smoothly. We traveled all over the city that day, starting in Central Park. A large church in Harlem was another location. Around sunset, we stopped in Little Italy. We arrived just in time for their street festival, and after a full day of shooting, we were all starving. Jeanne was wearing a long black trench coat over nothing more than her American flag thong bikini. Damn near every head turned as we walked through the streets on our quest for delicious food. I vividly remember one man getting slapped by his girlfriend for the crime of daring to look at Jeanne. Not since Sophia Loren and Gina Lollobrigida had Italians in that neighborhood been so awestruck over a woman!

After leaving our mark on the good people of Little Italy, we were off to Times Square for our most audacious shoot of the trip. Originally, we had planned to do a nude shot in the center of Times Square, but common sense prevailed, and we went with the American flag bikini instead. Jeanne and I talked about the details. We instructed the taxi driver to wait for us. As soon as he stopped, we jumped out, Jeanne dropped the coat, and we successfully pulled off the fastest photo shoot I had done to that point in my life. Although we had only shot for less than 40 seconds, hundreds of people began to rush the scene. I made sure Jeanne was safely in the taxi, and I jumped in just as the driver sped back to the hotel.

Throughout the years, Jeanne and I have done countless shoots from coast to coast, most of which involve her female wrestling compadres and range in venue from wrestling rings to penthouse suites. One thing's for sure: regardless of the environment, there's never a dull moment. Without Jeanne, my life would be very boring. I respect and appreciate her.

Chapter 31: A Brutal Broad, Broken Bones, and a WWE Opportunity

In late 1998, I had an encounter with "Sam" and "Mary" (not their real names). Sam emailed me for months, asking me to wrestle his wife in a competitive match. They did not live in California, but somewhere in another state. Sam was incredibly persistent about this request. He would email me three or four times a week, and he also called me many times. Clearly, he was not going to take no for an answer.

I didn't think too much about what "competitive" actually meant like I do today. Because he was so pushy, I naively accepted his challenge. Sam and Mary wanted to know what hotels were in the area so that they could stay near my studio in North Hollywood. The day we met, both of them were very kind. She was shorter than me, but much more muscular. She was trained in BJJ (Brazilian Jiu-Jitsu, a popular martial art), but not pro wrestling. I know this because she had trained in BJJ with a very well-known competitive wrestler in Northern California just before her arrival in Los Angeles.

When we began our match on the mats, she immediately took control, sitting on the mat behind me and putting me in a tight body scissors. She squeezed my ribs so tight I thought they would break right then and there, so I tapped out immediately. On our second go, I noticed how large and strong her quads really were. She got me in another tight scissors, with her back on the ground and her legs up in the air and around my waist. I tapped again very quickly. On the third time —about fifteen minutes into a one-hour match — I stopped and looked at Sam and said, "Your wife is much stronger than I could ever be. I should run out that door right now!" We all started laughing and then continued the competitive match.

I could tell that Mary meant business. She wanted to show her husband who would be taking charge of this challenge; but then again, so did I. I am Hollywood, after all, so did I want to lose to somebody I didn't even know? Hell, no!

By this time, I had finally figured out exactly what "competitive" meant to them, so I put her in a very tight headlock. However, she was quick to put her left leg around my right leg and hook my ankle. In my head I was thinking, *I've only done pro style wrestling. This is not The Farmer's Daughter or Mt. Fiji, nor is this pro style wrestling. This chick is way stronger than I am, and she wants me to look like a fool in front of her husband.*

I tried desperately to get out of that joint lock she had put on me. All I can remember is I heard three sounds in rapid succession – crack, crack, crack! – and the word "FUCK!" came rushing out of my mouth as I crumpled to the floor. I instinctively knew my leg was broken, even though I had never broken my leg before.

"What happened?" Sam asked, staring at me, dumbfounded. Mary looked surprised but said nothing.

"Hand me the phone," I managed to say, through gritted teeth and in excruciating pain. They were both so surprised that, despite my pain, I had to repeat it again. "I think I broke my leg. Get me the phone!" Finally, Sam gave me the phone and I called 911.

About ten minutes later, the ambulance arrived, and of course the paramedics asked us what was going on. When I replied that we were wrestling, their eyes got wide and excited. But I had no time for their wide-eyed fantasies. I was in agony.

"Get me to the hospital, please! I am in so much pain."

My friend, Cheryl, lived next door, but she wasn't at home at the time. My mom and dad were at work, but I didn't want to get them involved because I didn't want an "I told you one day something would happen" lecture from my mom. Mary never apologized to me, and Sam simply gave me my wrestling fee and left. I never saw either of them again.

When I got to the E.R., they stuck me in a room where I waited, as one usually does at the hospital. Regulations, I guess. Finally, they wheeled me into the X-ray room. At this point I thought the doctor would come in and tell me I needed a cast, but no, they came back in again and needed more X-rays to look at the other side of my lower leg.

I'm telling you, they gave me no pain pills whatsoever, so lifting me up onto the gurney and then back onto the X-ray machine was beyond excruciating. I don't think I've ever felt that much pain in all my life. It took me over four months to rehab my leg, and even that was not long enough. I needed to work; no money was coming in.

The timing of the broken leg couldn't have been worse. I was still recovering from the injury when I landed an interview with the WWF. The company had been looking to build up its women's division and was in California scouting talent in February 1999, about three months after I broke my leg. I landed an interview and met with Jim Ross, who was the vice president of talent relations at the time. He and several other executives interviewed me, and I could tell they were interested because they were taking copious notes and were very positive regarding my responses. They were quite pleased to learn that I had been trained by Mando Guerrero, and since fellow *GLOW* girl Lisa Moretti (Tina Ferrari) had just been signed as "Ivory," I thought things were looking good for me.

Then it was time to get into the ring. I was wearing sweatpants to try to hide the atrophy in my right leg. They put me in the ring with a male wrestler I didn't recognize, and we began to go through some lock-ups, holds, and exchanges. We weren't clicking very well together, so once we were finished with my ring time, I came clean. I mentioned that I was working through a broken leg and not at my best. My agent was a little irritated that I had been so forthcoming, but I felt I had to explain the circumstances. Needless to say, I didn't get signed by the WWF. And maybe I sabotaged myself. See, by that point, I had been on the road for so many years and was tired of it. I wanted to be a twenty-year-old again. I wanted to not have curfews and not be back on the road – especially with the grueling WWF schedule of that era. I wanted to be free and spend time with my boyfriend. I wanted a break.

Chapter 32: JB + RC 4 Ever

When I meet people at events or signings, I am often asked whether I'm married or single, or what the deal is. Well, I fell in love with a very special man more than twenty years ago, and I can't imagine life without him.

I met Ryan Cook at a rock club in North Hollywood in 2001. I was there with a group of my friends. We had five or six people sitting together at a table, when this guy came walking in and said hello. He had long, flowing brown hair, piercing blue eyes, and this confidence like he owned the place. Everybody else in the group knew him and I'm thinking, *Who in the world is this incredibly good-looking guy? And why does everybody know him except for me? Why have you jerks not introduced us?*

One of my friends told me that his name was Ryan Cook and that he was the lead singer of a band called Hair of the dog, which I knew nothing about. We were all at the club to see another band and we all traveled in the same circles, but this was the first time I had bumped into him. Ryan chatted briefly with us and headed off, five minutes later, our friend JJ Garcia came up to me and said he had a friend that wanted to meet me. I just knew it had to be Ryan. I followed JJ over to his friend and, sure enough, it was him.

Ryan and I immediately hit it off. We spent time at the club together, talking and getting to know each other. He was born and raised in Topeka, Kansas and grew up just like I did. He had a loving family and was raised on conservative values. He was Catholic and went to church. But he always knew that he would leave Kansas and not live there the rest of his life. He got his first guitar at age six and managed to convince his mom to take him to KISS concerts when he was just thirteen. I had never asked my parents to take me to concerts; I wish I had. He had formed a band while he was in school, and he idolized KISS. I impressed him when I was able to name every song on KISS's *Alive II*, which is a double album with twenty songs on it. One of my favorites.

At that time, Ryan had a full-time job working for Disney in publishing. He had left Kansas to go to college in Florida. After a couple years in Florida, he found work in Nashville, Tennessee. He was still playing in bands and doing well. One day, a famous songwriter and producer named Desmond Child said he liked Ryan's voice and wanted him to be the lead singer of a new band in Los Angeles called Hair of the Dog. They moved him to Granada Hills, and he started touring with Hair of the Dog. He opened up for Alice Cooper and Ted Nugent, and also went on the road with Winger, Warrant, and Skid Row. I didn't know any of this at the time. He didn't have any idea that I had been a Gorgeous Lady of Wrestling; in fact, he didn't know anything about *GLOW* or really anything about pro wrestling at all before he met me. I don't even know if *GLOW* aired in Topeka. I just found him to be a kind, passionate, sweet, and respectful man. But he also had the bad boy vibe, and I like the bad boys.

I immediately felt compatible with him. It was almost like we had known each other for years, even though we had just met. Conversation was easy and flowing, even though I felt nervous talking to him (but having a couple of drinks probably helped me with that). He is a Sagittarius, and they love life. He can be the life of the party, but he's not a bigmouth. He was – and is – very reserved, smart and funny, and we spent that night talking and laughing. I honestly remember thinking to myself, *Oh, my God, this is a person I could marry.* I knew right away.

We eventually left the club and went to a party at a friend's house. Ryan and I continued talking. At the end of the night, he gave me a little kiss on the cheek. It was so sweet and charming that I later wondered whether it had actually happened or if I had somehow just imagined/fantasized that it happened.

It wasn't until after he had left that I realized I had never gotten his phone number. But he had also told me that he was still living with a woman. They were at the end of a relationship and trying to figure out which one was going to move out and which one was going to stay. So I let it go. If I ran into him again, and if his situation had changed, we'd see how things went. I'm not the type to go for guys who are in a relationship, even if that relationship might be ending. Still, I found myself thinking about him all the time.

About a month later, that band I had gone to see was playing again. I wondered if Ryan might go to the show. I got so worked up and nervous, wondering whether I would see him again, that I dropped my hot curling iron and it landed on me! I still have a pink scar on my right shoulder to remind me of that night. I had gone to this particular club plenty of times, even to see that same band, and had never seen Ryan there. I figured if he showed up that night, I would know he was there to see me.

I walked into that club with my head on a swivel. I was trying to look cool and collected, but I was scanning the room and watching the door to see if he showed up. Then suddenly there he was. He had come in through the back door and had found me before I had seen him. My first thought was, *I am getting this guy's number and I am taking him home with me tonight.* It turned out that he was still living with the other woman, and that put a damper on that. But I still found him to be funny and charming, and I was just as interested in him as I was the night we first met. He took my number and told me he would call me when he was not with her anymore.

A month went by. Then a second and a third. But I wasn't quite pining away by the phone, waiting for a call. During that time, I had actually closed on my first home. It was a dream to own my own place. I had been busy moving things into the new place and getting everything set up exactly as I wanted.

It was March 2002 when he finally called me and said that everything was officially over with his ex-girlfriend, and he wanted to know if I still wanted to see him. I did. We went out to a Mexican restaurant for dinner that night and talked over margaritas. We have been together ever since.

Now, it hasn't always been easy. Ryan and I would meet at different venues to see bands and there were always other girls around, trying to get his attention. Then there were times when he was on the road, or I was traveling for conventions or signings or wrestling/acting bookings. We had to develop trust and mutual respect to keep us together, even when we were physically apart.

We also experienced heartbreak.

One day, we were having lunch together and I suddenly became violently ill and began vomiting. I went out to CVS Pharmacy and bought a pregnancy test. It turned positive immediately. I found out I was already at sixteen weeks. That's a long time in. I had an upcoming wrestling booking with a promotion in the Midwest called CRUSH that Johnny Cafarella and Jimmy Hart were involved with. I wondered if I could still wrestle this far along. I wondered how having a baby would change my life, and how it would change Ryan's life. I was just about to turn forty years old. People have kids at forty all the time. I knew I was up for the challenge, but it obviously would change our lives. I sat down with Ryan and told him, and he promised his love and support. He would be there for us.

Then I got a phone call from the doctor's office. They had done an ultrasound and said they could see a lot of water on the baby's body and brain. They asked me to come in for an amniocentesis, which is a test to determine whether a baby will have a genetic or chromosomal condition, like Down syndrome or spina bifida. I did the test, and they determined that there were significant issues. In fact, it seems weird that they would say this, but they actually recommended I not go the full term since there were issues and I was so far along in the pregnancy. I ended up having to abort a baby boy.

It was very sad. I could have had a baby at forty, but I just wasn't ready to have a child that wasn't healthy. It was a painful choice to make, but it was the decision that had to be made.

Shortly after that experience, Ryan got an offer to open up a company in Nashville. It was a great opportunity for him, and he came to me and asked me what I thought – should he take the job or not? I had just bought my house, and I wasn't about to move across the country. But I also didn't want to stand in the way of his career. I wouldn't want someone to tell me that I couldn't take a job, so I wasn't going to stand in his way. In 2004, he moved to Nashville, and we continued with a long-distance relationship. We made that work for eight years. I would visit him, he would visit me, and we would go on trips together: New York, Cozumel, Maui.

Nothing is perfect in this world. Things were not going the way they should. You just cannot do that back-and-forth thing for too long, and after eight years, it just wasn't working. I had a cat at the time, a nineteen-year-old cat named Keekster, and Keekster had issues. I needed to be with her all the time. If I took a wrestling booking, I felt like I could only leave her for a day or two. But when Keekster passed, I realized that there was nothing really keeping me in California except for work and family. I could always travel back to California for work. I discussed it with Mom and Dad. "How would you feel if I moved away?" I asked. They said I should do what I had to do and that I didn't need to stay there for their sake. Ryan wanted me with him in Nashville and I was ready for a change. So, with my parents' blessing, I left Los Angeles and moved to Music City in 2012.

We built a life together in Nashville, and any issues that had developed during our long-distance phase faded away. After a while, he started playing gigs again. In 2016, he caught the attention of Gene Simmons (my former water-happy cornerman), and Gene asked him to go on tour with him as part of his solo band. Ryan did a bunch of dates with Gene. Then, while they were touring Australia, Ace Frehley (KISS's original lead guitarist) told Gene that he loved his band and asked if he could borrow them for his own solo tours. Ryan, who grew up idolizing KISS, played alongside both Gene Simmons and Ace Frehley, and he's still actively touring with Ace today. In 2023, Ryan formed the band RCMC (Rock City Machine Co.) with two other members of those bands, Jeremy Asbrock and Philip Shouse. As of this writing, they've released one album, *RCMC*, which was produced by Marti Frederiksen. Their music is currently available on Spotify and Apple Music, so please check them out.

One thing I love about Ryan is he taught me to be kinder. He is the type of person who is genuinely grateful for the jobs that come his way and is genuinely kind to everyone he meets. He makes time to talk to fans after shows. And all the times he's been with me for my signings or events, he has never said, "Come on, you're spending too much time with this fan." or anything like that. He is patient, compassionate, and grounded, and he makes me a more patient, compassionate, and grounded person, too.

I travel with my work and Ryan travels with his work. I don't have issues and he doesn't have issues. You have to have trust. If you don't have trust, you don't have anything. I've done about twenty tours with Ryan: the KISS Kruise tours, Monsters of Rock, and other tours. For two music lovers, it is an awesome life. But if we hadn't built up the trust we have for each other, it never could have worked.

People ask how we have managed to keep the relationship alive for more than twenty years, between living in different cities and being separated so often by tours and work. We're both on the road a lot, and I think that actually is good for us. I don't think we're the kind of people who could be together 24/7. We're both very independent and sometimes we each need a little space. And because we're both wired that way, we understand it and encourage it. For example, Ryan will go out for his morning coffee instead of having it here. He'll take his laptop and go down to Starbucks and hang out there for an hour or two, and I'll be doing my stuff at home. We have learned to cherish the time we have together and still carve out any time we need for ourselves. I really think that's the key to a healthy, long-lasting relationship. At least, it is for us.

Chapter 33: Back To School

In 2003, I decided that I would try college. I talked Cheryl Rusa into taking the classes with me, and she was game. I took several courses at L.A. Valley College to get my website software specialist occupational certificate. I thought since I have a computer and a website, I should know how to update it and learn about the Internet as much as I could. The courses I completed were: Microsoft Windows Application, Microcomputer Software Survey in Microsoft Office, Introduction to the Internet for Microsoft Office, Web Page Design, Web Applications for Microsoft Office, and Professional and Image Creation for Microsoft Office. I completed the coursework in August 2007.

I enjoyed college so much that I decided I would take another class the next semester, but this time the subject would be much different. Film.

The college offered a class in low budget filmmaking, which was right up my alley. It was one of my favorite classes. The students were required to come up with an idea for a low budget movie. The wheels in my head started turning! I knew this was going to be some kind of horror flick. Now this was way before *The Walking Dead* series, but I had always wanted to make a movie about wrestlers getting attacked by zombies.

I talked to Steve Blance, our writer from *GLOW*, and had him help me with the synopsis. We ended up calling this little film *Death Match at Diablo*. The beginning of the film shows an atomic bomb blast! It then transitions into the late '90s, showing two men shoveling some kind of radioactive material into steel cans in some abandoned town. The next scene is a wrestling event, where the ladies are finishing up their wrestling gig for the evening. They get into their bus and head off to the next town. Lo and behold, somewhere out in the dark of night, the bus breaks down. The director and a few other girls decide that they are going to walk to a town they had seen a few miles back to get help.

The rest of the girls and the crew stay on the bus. The greedy director gets to this quiet, vacant place they had passed and decides to head straight into a bank; the first thing on his mind is money, not help.

He opens up the money vault and is attacked by the first zombie. Little by little, talent and crew go missing. I think you get the picture.

A few years later, I got together with my friend Brian Hopson — who had read the synopsis — and wrote me a 78-page script for *Death Match at Diablo*. I then registered it with the Writers Guild.

The next semester I took broadcasting, and that was quite interesting.

I really enjoyed going back to school, especially because I was ready for school at that time. I made As in all the classes I took.

Whenever I'm speaking at a convention, a guest on a podcast, or doing an interview, my words of advice for young people are: Go to school; learn something; and have a Plan B and a Plan C.

Chapter 34: Inked – Not

Do you remember the show *Miami Ink*? It was an American reality show that ran on TLC from 2005 to 2008 and followed the events that took place at a tattoo shop in Miami, Florida. The show had several spinoffs, including *LA Ink*, *London Ink*, *NY Ink*, and *Madrid Ink*, most of which were also shown on TLC.

During one season – probably 2005 or possibly 2006 – I heard the show was searching for people around the country who wanted to appear on the show and get a tattoo. I needed to make an audition reel of what tattoo I wanted and what part of my body I wanted it on. If they liked it, they would call you to come down to Miami and shoot an episode.

I was pretty down to get this tat. Many of my friends had tattoos. I was one of the very few that did not. My good friend Laura had a tattoo. Some of the *GLOW* girls had tattoos. My dates had tattoos.

One guy I dated took a photo of me to Gill "The Drill" Montie, who had a shop on Sunset Boulevard called Tattoo Mania. He wanted the tattoo on his left shoulder. I was standing there when Gill looked at him and said, "Are you sure you want a picture of your chick on your arm?" Gill's face was like, *Don't do it dude.* But the guy said yes. I was pretty surprised that someone I dated would even think about putting a tattoo of his girlfriend on his arm. But unfortunately, everywhere we went, people thought the girl on his arm was Heather Locklear.

Anyway, back to *Miami Ink* …

I made an audition reel and told them I wanted some cherry blossoms on the back of my shoulder – maybe about an inch or two, but nothing more. I mailed it in, and about two weeks later, the phone rang. It was *Miami Ink*. They wanted me on the show, but the stipulation was they wanted the tattoo to go all the way down my back.

I tried to barter with them, but it was a no-go. If I was going to get it done on the show, it was going to have to be big and bold. I was too chicken to do it. I kept remembering my Grandma Carney saying, "If you ever get a tattoo, I'm going to cut it off your skin!"

As much as I love tattoos on my friends and on Ryan, I looked in the mirror and thought, *Where would I put it?* I looked myself up and down and turned around and said, "I have no idea where I would want it." Ryan advised me, "If you haven't gotten one already, don't do it."

I mean there's always time to do one. I guess I am a virgin in that department.

As for the boyfriend that had my photo tattooed on his arm, he got married. His chick said, "If I have to look at that girl on your arm every day, I'm going to divorce you." Then he went and turned my picture into an ugly looking skull!

I guess Gill was right.

Years later, I ran into Gill again. I had hung out that night at the Rainbow on Sunset Boulevard with my friends Vinni Stiletto and Peter D. Peter who was from Sweden and still had his accent. He always asked a lot of questions.

Just after 2:00 a.m., we decided to go to Rock 'N' Roll Denny's on Sunset for some breakfast. We sat down, and all of a sudden, we heard a very loud noise. It was the sound of Harley riders parking their bikes. They were the Vagos, an outlaw motorcycle club like the Hells Angels. I recognized them by their green colors.

The Vagos did not have a great reputation. You don't wanna screw with them – ever.

Gill the Drill was riding with them that evening. I said hello to Gill since I recognized him. The bikers sat around me and my friends.

Now, when there's a pack of hardcore-looking bikers around, you should mind your own business and keep your mouth shut. Everybody knows that. But no, not Peter. He decided to open his trap and ask them why they were wearing the color green on their leather vests.

My heart started beating so fast.

The bikers got really quiet. One of them dropped his fork from his mouth down to the plate and looked at Peter like he was going to kill him. Gill looked at me and did not crack a smile or say a word.

Vinni quickly apologized for Peter and said he doesn't speak English very well. Peter was lucky he made it out of there in one piece.

Speaking of tattoos, Ryan has a tattoo of the ring that he and I both wear as a couple. The rings combine a cross and a heart, and we got them in 2005 at a flea market on Melrose Avenue in West Hollywood. We often ate at a famous Mexican restaurant called Antonio's that was close to there, which unfortunately closed in 2022.

The tattoo goes from the inside of his elbow to the wrist on both arms.

I love 'em!

Chapter 35: CRUSH

It was February 2003, a little over a year after Ry and I had met. I was asked by Johnny Cafarella to perform on a new pro wrestling show he and Steve Blance, Jimmy Hart, and Eddy Sharky (who had trained The Road Warriors, Rick Rude, and many other famous wrestlers) were producing. I was super, super excited. I had done a lot of indie shows and matches for my company and others, but nothing like this since *GLOW*.

His promotion was called CRUSH. It was being commissioned by Comedy Central, and they shot it in Minneapolis. Cheryl Rusa was also asked to join. We were the only two *GLOW* girls who were invited. We were both in great shape and still very active in the wrestling biz, but we were starting to push forty. In my mind, as long as we could keep up with the younger ones, do our job, and look great, we would have no problem. And of course, we could still do a live show ... and do it well!

At first, Johnny had been a little hesitant to hire us. But when the money people saw us, Mr. Tom Jones (not the singer from Wales) wanted us there. This was the first time I had met the legendary Jimmy Hart, whose job was to warm up the crowd. Jimmy started out in the music business, singing with a group called The Gentrys. He produced a record with Jerry "The King" Lawler in Memphis, Tennessee, and through Jerry, he became a wrestling manager. He went on to manage the Hart Foundation, The Honky Tonk Man, and The Nasty Boys, among others. Jimmy is such a very nice man, and he has never said a bad word about anyone ever. He is always positive and so energetic!

Like in *GLOW*, we did some comedy sketches to go along with the wrestling. At CRUSH, one of the cook sketches I did was with the famous comedian Chris Farley's brothers, Kevin and John. Now let me back up a little bit. Right before I traveled to Minneapolis, I found out I was three months pregnant. I did not want to cancel on Johnny, so this was weighing heavily on my mind. I was super scared, wondering if I would harm the baby or myself. Cheryl and I were the only ones who knew. I could always trust Cheryl to keep a secret.

I wrestled in a six-woman tag team match, which I knew would be much easier on my body and safer than a singles match. I did not tell anybody involved with the show about my pregnancy.

While at CRUSH, I met up again with WOW Women of Wrestling sensation Lana Star. We had met before in Los Angeles at interviews, auditions, and rock clubs. We both loved the live rock scene in Hollywood. Johnny hired a lot of the WOW girls because the original WOW had just gone off the air. Another lady I met was Melina Perez. Steve Blance discovered her when he flew out to L.A. and went to Jesse Hernandez's gym to find talent. But the budget was tight, and CRUSH didn't have enough money to hire her. Steve liked her so much, though, he said, "I'll pay out of my pocket. She is perfect for the show!" They got rid of one WOW girl and hired Melina. Melina had only been wrestling a couple of months. She played the Native American character, Little Deer, complete with a beautiful headdress. She was a shy, beautiful, demure girl. I remember teaching her how to do the Sunset Flip. Every time I see her, she reminds me of that move I taught her. WWE saw Melina on the CRUSH web page and hired her for a Thanksgiving sketch as an Indian with John Cena. And the rest, as they say, is history. Unfortunately, CRUSH didn't have the same success as Melina. And as far as the pregnancy … as I mentioned before, that would end in tragedy as well.

Another Perspective: Lana Star (WOW Wrestler)

As a kid, I had a very strict mom, but I was lucky enough to have a TV in my room. The catch was that it had to be turned off at a fairly early hour, which really interfered with my favorite show at the time: *GLOW*. It aired quite late at night, so I would turn the volume down as low as possible, hoping my mom wouldn't catch me before the episode ended.

I thought Hollywood and Vine were the coolest! I loved Hollywood's crimped hair and outfits, and I wished I was a *GLOW* wrestler. I actually thought I should be Hollywood's tag partner, LOL! I also watched WWF (now WWE), but at that time, the women's division wasn't prominent. Still, I knew I wanted to be involved in wrestling, and looking back, I realize *GLOW* was my inspiration.

Years later, I got an audition for a wrestling show through my agent, and to my amazement, it was for WOW, run by David McLane – the same man behind *GLOW*. I'm blessed to still be happily working for WOW today.

In between, I had other opportunities in wrestling, and I remember the excitement of working a show in Minnesota where I found out Jeanne would be there. She was incredibly kind and helpful. Over the years, we've crossed paths at various events, and it's surreal to now have the chance to contribute something to her book. Jeanne, you are a legend, and I'm honored to know you. Thank you for everything.

Chapter 36: New York and 9/11

When most people hear "professional wrestling," they think about body slams and backbreakers. They think about the small space inside the roped-off wrestling ring, and about the arenas and convention centers where pay-per-view events are held. But one of the other major parts of every pro wrestler's life is travel. You're always on the road, or in the air. *GLOW* was filmed in Las Vegas, less than an hour by plane from Los Angeles. But, since then, I've worked in lots of cities across the country – and the world – that I might never have gotten the chance to see if it hadn't been for wrestling.

I continued to travel after *GLOW* ended, of course. I still get the chance to go to conventions, shoot videos for independent companies, and sometimes I travel just for the fun of it. One of my favorite places to visit is London, England. There is so much history, so much tradition. I'm lucky to have a lot of fans there. Who knew that a former *GLOW* wrestler would be so big in the city of Big Ben and Buckingham Palace? But I do enough business that I'm usually able to travel there twice a year for a week at a time. Once I'm there, I enjoy the city. But like a lot of other travelers, I also use London as a "hub" for traveling to other great places in Europe.

It was one week after returning from a trip to London that everything changed. I was trying to sleep off the jet lag when my phone rang around 6:00 a.m. Pacific Standard Time. Dead-tired, I ignored it. It rang again and again, then finally stopped. A bit irritated at the early wake-up, I got up and checked my voicemail. There was a message from Cheryl Rusa telling me to turn on the TV immediately. "You're not going to believe it."

As groggy as I was, I turned on the TV. And, of course, Cheryl was right. Every news channel was showing video clips of a plane crashing into the World Trade Center.

As it turned out, I was scheduled to travel to New York City three months after the terrorist attacks. I suppose I could have canceled, but people all over the country were pulling together in such an incredible way to support the people affected by the attacks. There was such a push to "get back to normal" and "not to let the terrorists win" by succumbing to fear and paranoia. It just would have seemed wrong to miss the trip.

In early December 2001, I flew to New York. The first thing I noticed was that airport security was a lot tighter. Unfortunately for people who travel as much as I do, this is a trend that continues to this very day, with TSA's "delightful" full-body pat-downs. Anyway, I eventually made it to New York and took care of my wrestling obligations as planned. The minute I finished, I went directly to Ground Zero with my bodyguard, Big Brian. As much as I had seen pictures and videos of the site on the evening news, it was *nothing* compared to being there in person. Even though the attacks had taken place months earlier, there were still tons of people paying tribute – leaving flowers, signing banners, and crying. I did all of those things, too. And then I became aware of a smell in the air unlike anything I had ever experienced. It smelled like smoldering glass, metal, and human bodies.

"Let's get out of here," I said to Brian. "It smells like death."

I've been back to New York many times since then. I usually stay in the city. There are grocery stores and bars on every corner. The subway is incredible and makes it easy to travel through the city. (Hello L.A., did you hear me? The SUBWAY!) Anyway, The Beekman Tower or Milburn aren't exactly the most luxurious of hotels, but they are clean, have big rooms, and their staff are nice. Pizza is always yummy there, too – try Grimaldi's, a coal brick-oven pizzeria at 1 Front Street in Brooklyn. Of course, shopping is always fantastic in the city.

If I have time while in New York City, I always try to see my old friend from *GLOW*, Steve Blance. We usually head out to a deli for lunch or dinner.

But one of my favorite things to do is to look at the old buildings and take photos of them. I bet they could tell some great stories. I also like to visit the Metropolitan Museum of Art. I try to see a different wing every time I go, and usually get a hotdog and sit on the steps in front of The Met to eat it. I usually don't have a lot of time, but walking through Central Park is a nice walk. I don't mind taking the subway, either. Quick, cheap, and fast! I still have not checked out some of the speakeasies that are around the city, but I definitely want to do that sometime.

Everyone says that life in New York is so fast-paced, and it's true. It seems like there's a deli or a market on every street corner; you never have to travel very far to get something to eat. It used to be home to the world-famous Carnegie Deli, which has since closed. I liked Carnegie, but to be honest, I think that Katz's Deli on the Lower East Side might be even better.

A few years ago, I went to Ellis Island with my parents, and we looked up our ancestors. We already knew a lot about our family history, but it was still really neat to see Ellis Island live in person – a place that is so important in terms of making our country the "melting pot" it is today. I've never been to a Yankees home game – either in the old stadium or the new one – but that might be a neat experience. When I was in high school, as a matter of fact, my grandfather (God bless his soul) took me to a Yankees-Dodgers World Series game in L.A. It seemed like the Dodgers and the Yankees were playing every year back then. This was in 1978 or 1981. He actually had tickets for all three games. He took my grandmother first, then my dad, and I got to go to the third game. When we got to the ballpark, I asked him, "Grandpa, where are our seats?" and he said, "They're right behind home plate!" As we walked into Dodger Stadium, we kept climbing the stairs higher and higher and higher. We were right above home plate all right, but two rows from the back wall! But all that really matters is I went to a game with Grandpa. He even bought me one of those souvenir pennants – for the Yankees! I wanted one for the Dodgers, though, because what kind of hometown girl would I be if I cheered for the other team? Fortunately, later Grandpa told me to go look in the car because he had a Dodgers pennant in there for me as well.

Today, I am actually partial to the Yankees. Grandpa would be proud.

Another Perspective: Todd A. Kaylor
(Producer, Director, Writer, Visionary, and Hellspawn of ATAK Productions)

The first 'fan' letter I ever wrote was to Lynda Carter. The second? A hastily scribed submission for a contest posted within the pages of *GLOW* magazine, which encouraged readers to share their love affair with the Gorgeous Ladies of Wrestling, with the winner granted an opportunity to meet their favorite wrestler. Of course, the feisty vixen Hollywood was my first choice (Tina Ferrari and Little Fiji followed suit). I didn't win. But, if it's any consolation, I've yet to receive a reply from Ms. Carter (and I'm still waiting).

It's been said that "fortune favors the bold." And as an avid celebrity hound, my dogged persistence is a testament to that. So, when the curtain fell for *GLOW* in 1990, I shadowed Hollywood (within the court-levied distance) through her many pursuits and ventures as an independent wrestler, stuntwoman, and actress. But it wasn't until 2004, and the G.L.O.R.Y. Wrestling Convention in West Patterson, New Jersey, that the stars properly aligned, and I finally basked in Hollywood's glow. It was worth the wait.

Jeanne is the epitome of "Hollywood" – glitzy and glamorous, minus the vanity – a perfect pairing of beauty and class. When the Beach Boys crooned, "I wish they all could be California Girls," they had Hollywood in mind. The consummate professional, her personality (and smile) shines inside and outside the ring. She is fierce and competitive, constantly defying convention in the squared-circle, while beyond the ropes and the spectacle, she is generous and gracious, almost to a fault – ever-mindful, attentive, and appreciative of the entourage of fans that have supported her, and continue to support her, to this day.

It was purely happenstance that, at that time, I was dabbling with photography and video as a burgeoning micro-micro-budget filmmaker, focusing on fantasy peril and "damsel in distress" themes, and broached the possibilities of her serving as a subject for any number of creative (and perilous!) undertakings. She was very receptive to the collabora-tive invitation, and the rest, as they say, is history. The official "ATAK Productions" moniker and branding became ingrained in my work only after Jeanne and I had a few photo sessions and "Motion Picture" slideshows under our proverbial belts. Thus, in a sense, she was its matriarch.

From our initial photo shoot in a NYC hotel (where she tussled with a monstrous prop snake I affectionately christened "Anna") and our joint video ventures with Scream Queen icons Brinke Stevens (*Curse of the Kijoka Talisman* - can you say "Rubber Snakes on a Plane"?) and Suzi Lorraine (*Girlfriendsssss*), to her titular roles as *Holly Croft: Monster Huntress* and *D.Y.N.A.M.O.* ("Trail of the Toymaster" series), there isn't a persona or challenge she wouldn't willingly take on! Utterly fearless in the face of serpentine nemeses, tentacled monstrosities, mutant octopuses, giant spiders, pernicious plants, cursed totems, demon-haunted Tiki Dolls, and possessed plush killer bunnies, Hollywood leaps into the perilous fray with almost sinister glee and wild, reckless abandon! She is, by all accounts and purposes, the ultimate "Fantasy Girl."

I'm a bit older now, maybe even wiser, but my affinity for Hollywood hasn't waned. Not a wink. And with over fifty collaborative video shorts and vignettes under the ATAK Productions banner as of this writing – not to mention my ardent assistance and support behind and in front of the camera as videographer, editor, and occasional antagonist, as well as spontaneous script developer, synopses scribe, and proofreader – I continue to tap into her seemingly fathomless wellspring of inspiration and creativity. Yes, I envision the seeds of great and wonderful things yet to be planted, take root, sprout, and blossom, then to be plucked at the peak of ripeness and harvested for her long and storied career. So, even though my hopes were dashed as a wide-eyed fanboy almost thirty years ago, I've been "winning" ever since.

Chapter 37: Hollywood Nationwide

Most of the travels I have enjoyed take place right here in the States. There's so much to see and do, so many historical and beautiful places to visit. There are little things that make each city unique. Unfortunately, I never seem to be able to stay in any one place as long as I'd like.

In May 1993, my boyfriend wanted to surprise me with a trip. He told me to pack a bag and get in the car and did not tell me where we were going. We headed down the 110 Freeway and started heading towards San Pedro.

"Are we going to Catalina Island?" I asked, remembering my trip there with the Girl Scouts.

"Maybe," he said enigmatically.

We pulled into the lot of the Catalina Express, but we weren't taking the boat over. He arranged for a helicopter ride over to the island. It only took us fifteen minutes to get there. It was a very cool birthday surprise. I was wined and dined!

Unfortunately, after dinner I realized I had lost the key to my rental locker holding all my stuff. I had to call a second cousin, Danny, who lived on the island, and he helped us crack open the locker. But we lost so much time trying to get my stuff that we were in a mad dash to catch the ferry to get back. The helicopter ride had been a one-way trip. We barely made the last boat out for the night. Later that evening, I found the key to the locker in my purse. Oops. I blame all that wining and dining ... well, the wining, at least.

On one of my trips to Boston, I got to visit Salem, Massachusetts, the site of the infamous witch trials of the 1600s and home to some fascinating history. It is still one of my favorite places. I try to visit there whenever I can. And, of course, I always try to have some of Boston's clam chowder or their crab cakes. Those things are *epic* – local specialties like Pollo Loco in Southern California, In-N-Out Burger in Burbank, or deep dish pizza in Chicago, which is a great "stopover city" when I'm traveling from the East Coast back to L.A. I don't do as much work there as I do in other cities, but I try to get to Navy Pier when I'm there during the summer. It's kind of like Santa Monica Pier, only it's located on the shore of Lake Michigan instead of the Pacific Ocean.

Speaking of Boston, I had one of my most embarrassing in-ring moments happen when I was there on a tour. If you're a female wrestler, you always want to make sure that nothing "falls out." I didn't really have boobs per se during my early *GLOW* days, but once I got implants, keeping the girls in check became a bigger concern. (Ha!) I was in the middle of a match when one of the straps broke on my top and I had what's come to be known as a "wardrobe malfunction." Wrestling is a live, semi-competitive performance, so it's not like somebody can call "cut" and shoot the scene over. I covered up as best I could until someone came into the ring and brought me a T-shirt. Man, did he get heat from the audience! You should have heard the Boston crowd boo that guy for covering up the goods!

An even more embarrassing moment happened at Big Bear Lake in California – though thankfully, not in front of an audience! It was the year 2000, and I wanted to try snowboarding. This was just two years after breaking my leg, so I still had seven screws and two plates inside my right leg. But hey, snowboarding looked like fun!

I called an ex-boyfriend in Hollywood, and he loaned my boyfriend and me some snow chains in case we needed them for the drive up. (You never know when an ex might come in handy!)

The drive from Los Angeles up the mountain took about two hours. We made it up and found our cabin. It was pretty chilly and there was snow blanketing the ground. The cold actually made the metal in my leg ache, so we went down to the lodge and had a drink or two, then made our way out to the local bar for a nightcap.

The next morning, my boyfriend was in the shower, and I was feeling a bit playful. I got some cold water and splashed it over him as he was showering. We had a laugh. When it was my turn in the shower, he decided to get me back.

When I came out, wrapped in a towel, he grabbed me in a tight bear hug (Mt. Fiji had nothing on him!), tore off my towel, hoisted me up off my feet, opened the door, and threw me – butt-naked – out into the snow. Ever go from a steamy hot shower directly into a snowbank? It's an experience you won't forget!

I leapt up and tried the door. Locked. "Open up," I muttered. I didn't want to raise my voice because I didn't want to attract attention and have everyone looking out the windows of the other cabins at the naked *GLOW* girl outside. I knocked lightly but with urgency. "Come on," I pleaded. Finally, he opened the door, and I rushed into warmth and privacy.

I learned my lesson. I won't be throwing cold water on anyone anymore. I think that was my only display of public nudity since my mom had me out sunbathing as a baby.

Even with all of the great travel experiences I've had, I'm still a Los Angeles girl at heart. I was born there, I grew up there, and with the exception of short stints in Las Vegas and Tokyo during my *GLOW* years, I lived there my whole life until moving to Nashville. Where else can you live forty-five minutes from the beach and two hours from snow-boarding?

When I was a kid, we used to go camping at Leo Carrillo State Park; hiking was a cheap and fun form of entertainment in those days. We'd also go to Refugio State Beach in Santa Barbara with some of the families on our block. My dad, who loves to fish, would wake me up before dawn for some father-daughter bonding time. With memories like that, why would I ever want to leave Los Angeles? As I mentioned before, it was only for true love.

Chapter 38: A Hollywood Haunting

Do you believe in ghosts? You know, supernatural phenomena? I remember my grandmother talking about such things once in a blue moon with my mother. But I was a kid. What did I know? I was skeptical at first. But then … well, here is my story …

It was November 2015. I flew to Portland, Oregon to visit my best friend, Laura Bennett, who lives in Keizer, Oregon. It was cold, and especially so on the coast. She picked me up at the airport and we went to a nearby hotel.

I did a shoot the next day, and right after, we headed on a journey down the Oregon coast.

As we drove down the coast, the first city we stopped in was Astoria. We actually went to the shore first and took some photos at a very windy cold beach, where a famous shipwreck still stood on the sand. The ship, named the *Peter Iredale*, was a four-masted steel bark built in Maryport, England in 1890 and was owned by British shipping firm P. Iredale & Porter. On September 26, 1906, the *Iredale* left Salina Cruz, Mexico bound for Portland, where it was to pick up a cargo of wheat for the United Kingdom. Despite encountering heavy fog, they managed to safely reach the mouth of the Columbia River early on the morning of October 25.

The captain of the ship, H. Lawrence, later recalled that, as they waited for a pilot, "A heavy, southeastern wind blew, and a strong current prevailed. Before the vessel could be veered around, she was in the Breakers, and all efforts to keep her off were unavailing."

The *Peter Iredale* ran aground at Clatsop Beach, hitting so hard that three of her masts snapped from the impact. Fortunately, none of the crew were seriously injured. Captain Lawrence ordered the ship to be abandoned, and rockets were launched to signal for help.

The stranded vessel became an immediate tourist attraction. The day after the ship ran ashore, *The Oregon Journal* reported that the wreck proved to be a strong attraction. Despite the gale that was raging, scores of onlookers flocked to the scene of the disaster. The *Journal* noted that the Astoria and Columbia River Railroad was already planning to run excursion trains to the site.

Although the ship has been broken up by waves, wind, and sand over the years, the wreck of the *Peter Iredale* continues to be a popular tourist attraction. The wooden beams of the ship are still attached, but there's nothing inside – just an empty image of the outside of a ship. It was quite beautiful. We took photos with our iPhones, even though we were so cold. The high wind was blowing really hard, and the ocean was rough and dark looking.

It was an eerie sight, but nothing like what we'd encounter in the days to come!

☆ Day 1 ☆

In the morning, Laura and I headed south on the 101, stopping at beautiful sites to take photos.

One of them was the beautiful area of Cannon Beach, which is a small coastal city known for its long, sandy shore. We climbed Haystack Rock, which stands tall in the ocean, and took many pictures there. It was so picturesque, with azure skies and crystal clear deep blue wind-driven waves. I could not get enough of this place. Nature is just so organic. So perfect.

We stopped at Rockaway Beach and visited Arcadia Beach, with its tide pools and a picnic area. We explored some sea caves, boutiques, and galleries before eating lunch.

Around 4 p.m., we made it to Heceta Head Lighthouse, where you can stay the night at the lightkeeper's cottage. Built around 1894, it is a working lighthouse still staffed by lightkeepers. We arrived just in time for some stunning views of the Pacific Ocean and a beautiful orange and pink sunset. The lighthouse light sits 200 feet above the ocean. We walked down the path that leads from the lightkeeper's home to the lighthouse and the beach, taking several photos.

Laura had told me weeks before that the lighthouse was supposed to be haunted, so I did some due diligence and read about it. It is rumored that one special woman who resided in the lightkeeper's house never left, even after she died. They say her name was Rue. She is thought to have been the lightkeeper's wife, but no one has been able to confirm it because no list was ever kept of the women and children who stayed in the cottage. People say that one of Rue's daughters drowned, and after Rue died, she returned to the lighthouse and stayed forever, looking for her daughter. There is an unmarked grave on the hillside by the lighthouse that has remained undisturbed for decades. No one knows who is buried there.

☆ Night 1 ☆

After Laura and I did some exploring through the house and grounds, we got hungry and decided to drive south to a small town called Yachats. We ate our meal and then drove back to the lightkeeper's house, hung out in the living room area, and enjoyed some wine. We also met a few other patrons walking around the bed and breakfast.

It had been a long day, so we went up to our room. I showered first, then Laura. We got ready for bed. Our room was small. The colors were pink and white with one queen size bed, a dresser with a mirror to my left, and a dresser to Laura's right. There was no TV. The bathroom was to the left inside the room.

I fell asleep first. Laura was always up later than me, reading.

Around midnight, something loud woke me up. Laura looked at me and started laughing.

"Why are you laughing at me?" I asked.

She said, "Your face. You look startled!"

I said, "Well, I heard something. Did you hear it?"

She said, "I heard nothing."

I replied, "It sounded like something hit the floor or the wall." She swore she heard absolutely nothing.

I went back to sleep. When I woke up in the morning, I used the bathroom that was inside our room. I noticed that the door would not close. I thought, *That's the weirdest thing. It closed perfectly when I took my shower last night.*

As I started looking around the door and floor, I noticed that one of the bolts from the door hinge was on the floor and concluded that was the noise that had woken me up. I grabbed my iPhone and took a photo of it. I was curious how the bolt had come out of its hinge. I thought maybe it was loose.

Hmmm …

In the back of my mind, I wondered if it could have been Rue.

☆ Day 2 ☆

The next day, Laura and I drove up the coast to see some other beautiful landscapes: tide pools, shops, and beach areas. We took some beautiful shots of the sunset that evening down below the Airbnb. The later it got. the darker the colors became: gray, dark blue, orange, red, and pink. It was beautiful.

☆ Night 2 ☆

When we got hungry, we decided to drive south to Yachats. We enjoyed another nice meal and drove back up to the house, where we mingled with some of the guests and, of course, our host, who was a very kind, sweet, middle-aged woman. She showed us this tiny little kitten that was so cute; I took some pictures with it. I was getting tired. I knew we were going to have to be up early for breakfast and hit the road.

I went upstairs to take a shower and get ready for bed. This time I couldn't help but think about the bolt that fell onto the wooden floor. I decided to take a towel and hang it on the mirror that was next to my bed. I was thinking, *I don't want to see what Rue looks like, especially if I get up during the night and look in the mirror and see her staring at me!*

I fell asleep, and once again, something woke me up. It felt like when your cat or dog jumps up on the bed, but when I sat up, there was no cat or dog on the bed. As I looked to see what it was, I saw an indentation in the bed form slowly near my feet, like somebody just sat down on the edge. In my mind, I was not scared at all. I did not feel threatened or spooked. I thought, *Well, there she is! That's Rue.* I was not dreaming. I pinched myself and looked over at Laura, who was fast asleep.

When I woke up that morning. I told Laura about it. But she had felt nothing.

We went down for breakfast. The host said, "Good morning, girls. How was your night?"

I said, "Fine, thank you."

Laura said, "Ahaaa. Well, Jeanne had an interesting experience last night." She told our host the story I had told her. Our host didn't bat an eyelash or stop what she was doing as she heard the tale. She simply said, "Ah, yes, that's what people say."

I know that it was Rue who came to visit me that night. I will never forget the experience as long as I live.

Will I ever go back to that place again? Yes! Absolutely.

If you'd like to check out the place for yourself, she resides at Heceta Lighthouse Bed & Breakfast in the lightkeeper's home, located at 92072 US 101 South, Yachats, Oregon 97498. They have free parking, Wi-Fi, a beach, outdoor furniture, free breakfast, and of course … Rue.

Chapter 39: Hollywood Worldwide

I have already mentioned my trip to Japan and my visits to the United Kingdom. I have also worked in plenty of cities throughout the United States and been able to travel to several other countries. Wrestling has been my passport to the world.

Sometimes you plan your travel for a vacation. Sometimes you plan your travel for work.

Sometimes (switching to my best Rod Roddy "Price is Right" game show announcer impersonation:) You just won a fantastic trip to Jamaica on a game show!

Twice!

Yes, I won two trips to Jamaica on game shows. Back in 1990, I won a trip to Hawaii after appearing on *The Dating Game*. I guess I either made a good impression with that appearance or all the game shows just shared mailing lists, because I kept getting to appear on various dating shows for several years.

I figured, why not? Do a TV show, have fun, then maybe win a nice little trip. You only live once, right?

I won one trip on a show called *Studs* and the other on *Change of Heart* during the mid-1990s. One of the trips was to the infamous Hedonism resort. Thank goodness there were two sides to the resort: the nude side and the clothed side. The clothed side was more to my liking. It didn't seem like there were too many people that were open-minded enough to be running around stark naked, but the ones who were willing to bare all were the ones who really shouldn't have been.

The second time, I took my friend Laura Bennett with me. My biggest memory of that trip was that we shared a bus to the hotel with former Los Angeles homicide detective Mark Fuhrman, who had become a famous face during the O.J. Simpson trial in 1995. His face seemed to be everywhere back in those days. You can imagine how surreal it was boarding a bus in Jamaica and seeing that face looking back at you.

Laura was a natural redhead with pale white skin, so she had to slather on the heavy-duty, take-no-prisoners, ultra-high SPF sunscreen every time she stepped outdoors. We used the beautiful surroundings of that crystal blue water to take photos of ourselves for our websites. We had a fabulous time.

One of my favorite spots to visit is the Mayan ruins in the Yucatán. My boyfriend and I went down to Mexico in August 1996. Naturally, it was super hot in Cozumel. We decided to take the ferry and go over to the Yucatán side. We rented a car and stayed the night near the ruins. On our way, we got a flat tire and had to change it in the excruciating heat. Nobody was on that road ... and I mean nobody. On the way, we found a cenote, which is a natural swimming hole that's formed when limestone collapses, revealing a hidden pool of water. Perfect place to cool off with an unforgettable little swim!

In the evening, we got to the hotel. They gave us flashlights because a big storm was coming and there was a good chance the hotel was going to lose power. That's exactly what happened, so we navigated the hotel and restaurant by flashlight as the storm raged outside.

I got up early in the morning to start the tour and was amazed at the beautiful Mayan ruins. They were from a large pre-Columbian city built by the Maya people of the Terminal Classic Period (600-900 AD). The temple is the most famous of the buildings. I walked up the stairs, which were pretty steep. It took a while, but I made it to the top. We walked inside the old structures and through the grand ball court. I kept imagining all kinds of fighting and sacrifices going on, trying to envision the things that had happened there more than a thousand years ago. The experience truly made the history of the region come alive for me.

One of my most memorable international tours was in the early 1990s when promoter Hal Stone booked a group of us for a wrestling and boxing promotion at a casino in Moscow under the *"Hal Stone's Hollywood Hits"* banner. We were all excited to be going to Russia, especially in that era of perestroika and glasnost when the Soviet Union was beginning to open up to the West. But as we were going through customs, I couldn't help but notice that Hal, the promoter, was a nervous mess, just sweating bullets. Cheryl Rusa asked him what was wrong, and he revealed that he was smuggling computers in with our wrestling ring. Apparently computers could have caused delays, so he figured he'd just pack them in with the ring equipment and play dumb if questioned about it. Fortunately for him – and for us – everything went through without an issue, but it definitely put a damper on our mood. You did not want to mess around with the Russian authorities, even during the "Era of Glasnost."

The shows in Moscow were fine, but the weather in November was freezing cold, and if you wanted some McDonald's food, you had to stand in a massive line and wait for more than an hour just to get into the restaurant. Plus, we didn't get the per diem we were promised, so money was tight. As soon as I finished my wrestling gigs, I would run downstairs to the casino and start playing roulette to try to make the money I had been told I would be earning. I did that for five days and managed to make up some of the money, but none of the other girls would risk the meager amount they were making, so I was the only one pressing my luck on the casino floor.

The language barrier was another major problem. We didn't speak their language, and they didn't speak ours, so it was almost impossible to communicate certain things. Ursula Hayden, the Farmer's Daughter, developed a bad case of "the runs," shall we say. We went to a pharmacy to try to get her medicine because we were due to fly back to America, and she really needed something for the flight. We were unable to get the pharmacist to understand what we needed, so Cheryl grabbed a pen and a piece of paper and drew a picture of a person seated on a toilet with little droppings falling all over the floor. Once she handed that to the pharmacist, she knew exactly what we needed. To this day, that memory makes me laugh so hard it brings tears to my eyes. We teased Ursula the entire flight home and started singing,

"When you're sliding into home and your pants are full of foam … Diarrhea! Diarrhea!" She was laughing just as hard as we were. I think we were all just giddy about heading back to the U.S. of A.

I had an opportunity to do some wrestling in South America not once, but twice! Liz L. and I flew down to Santiago, Chile in 2013, all expenses paid plus our fees. We were paid half upfront and the remaining thousand when we left.

I think it was their summertime, and it was lovely. The hotel was nice. The pool was beautiful, and the food was amazing. Every morning, they had a huge bowl of fresh guacamole.

When I went back in 2014 with Jennifer Thomas and Liz, we were in town the same time as Metallica. I just had to go. It was in a soccer stadium called Estudio Monumental David Arellano. I'd never seen so many people at a concert!

I was on a special floor they had laid on the field, and I stood in front of the soundboard where it would be safer. I had heard that once Metallica started to play, fans would go nuts and start climbing over seats and the metal barriers to get onto the floor. And yes, they did in droves. They didn't have enough security people to keep the fans back, so they just let them through. The concert was badass.

I really wanted to take a trip to the coast, but I did not have enough time to do so. We had tickets to fly to Rio de Janeiro in Brazil, but right before we boarded the plane, they decided they couldn't let us get on. I didn't know the language and couldn't understand what they were saying. Basically, we did not have a visa to go into the country. I'm not sure why we needed one. We were just going to visit for a few days.

Things got kind of weird because we left early. I had to change my flight, so we went downtown to get our tickets. It seems like it took forever to get it figured out with the language barrier, but we got it sorted out. I had two stops on the way home, one in Panama and another in Miami. It was a long day, but I was glad to be home safe.

Chapter 40: Hollywood Worldwide: European Edition

On one trip to London, I decided that since the UK was so close (relatively speaking) to so many other countries, I should try to visit a different country every time I made it to London. In September 1999, I decided I would visit Amsterdam and see if it really was what people say it was.

The first cafe I went to, I asked if I could see a menu and they looked at me very strangely.

"You wanna go to the 'coffee shop' over there," they said, pointing. I guess they could tell that I wanted to check out the places where you could smoke soft drugs like marijuana or hash. I ordered some hash that was not too potent. They had a system ranking the potency from 1 (the lowest) to 10 (prepare to be carried home). I chose a four; I figured it was strong enough to experience it, but gentle enough to keep me from getting knocked on my ass.

They let you rent a pipe, and I toked up right there in the coffee shop like everybody else. I was only there for a day and a half. On that trip, I almost came home with a tattoo. As I mentioned in a previous chapter, I do not have any tats. I love them, but not on me.

I did see the marketplaces where the tulips were. The Dutch have a clear affinity for plants and flowers, as evidenced by the many markets in Amsterdam bursting with flowers in the spring. There were lots of bicycles everywhere, but I never saw the prostitutes showcasing their wares in the windows. I guess I never made it down to the red light district.

On another visit to London in 2004, I took the Channel Tunnel (or "Chunnel") into Paris. People warned me that the French were rude, but that wasn't my experience at all. The people were lovely. I stayed in the Saint Germain area and visited the famous Notre Dame Cathedral, which was absolutely beautiful. I had lunch at a nice cafe called Central Pompidou and visited two major department stores, Gallerie Lafayette and Printemps. I also went to visit the Louvre so I could see the Mona Lisa. It was much smaller than I had expected it to be. It was encased in bulletproof glass and drew a huge crowd of people.

In 2006, I went from London to Berlin. I wanted to check out East Berlin and see the difference between west and east and, yes, there was a difference. As I took the subway, I noticed that West Berlin had more brightly colored walls than East Berlin. I was told that after World War II, when they destroyed all the buildings, they used those materials to build the subway in East Berlin. I saw Checkpoint Charlie, the best-known border crossing between East Berlin and West Berlin during the Cold War. At the height of the Berlin Crisis of 1961, American and Soviet tanks faced each other there. It attracts huge crowds of tourists from Germany and abroad. I saw the graffitied remains of the Berlin Wall in East Berlin, and I went to the Wall Museum, where visitors can learn about the numerous escape attempts from east to west and view various escape objects. I also saw the remains of Hitler's bunker, which was a small grassy area surrounded by many apartments. It was nothing special. If not for a small sign there indicating that it was a historic site, you would never know anything had happened there.

As a city, Berlin had a different vibe from the other major European cities I've visited. Serious, solemn … almost depressing. But I would still go back, as I have heard it really rocks there. I must have stayed in the wrong area, or maybe I went to bed too early because, as they say, everything happens after midnight. When I do get back to Germany, I will try to visit Berlin again and another city.

I went to Prague after a 2007 trip to London, but I arrived in Prague with a cold! My hotel had a spa with an indoor pool and steam rooms, so I immediately went into one of those and later found some medicine so I could breathe. I had maybe two days to see everything while I was feeling under the weather.

I took a train to Karlštejn Castle, which is about ten miles southwest of Prague. It sits up on a hill, so you have to walk up to the castle. The large Gothic castle was founded in 1348 by King Charles IV and served as a place for safekeeping the Imperial Regalia as well as the Bohemian Crown Jewels, holy relics, and other royal treasures. Karlštejn is among the most famous castles in the country. They say that it gets more than 200,000 visitors per year.[1]

It was October, and since it was pretty cold, I stopped at one of the little restaurants to warm up and have lunch on my walk back to the train. Unfortunately, I wasn't impressed because they only had pork and gravy, potato pancakes, and roasted duck-type options. What I really wanted was a McDonald's hamburger! I did a little shopping through the old town square with the Prague astronomical clock and walked over the beautiful Charles Bridge.

The next morning, I went to the airport, still not feeling well at all. My flight was delayed, so I took another flight that went into Washington, D.C. The wait for customs was almost two hours! I literally had to run to the gate and was the last person to board the flight. Thank goodness I brought an extra change of clothes because I was not feeling well at all, and I had perspired more than I ever had right through the back of my shirt, but I made my flight into LAX safely and could rest up.

It was chilly again when I returned to London in November of 2008. This time I took Ryanair from London Heathrow to Dublin, Ireland. I rented a car at Dublin Airport and headed west to Clifden. Clifden is a coastal town in County Galway, in the region of Connemara, located on the Owenglin River where it flows into Clifden Bay. Along the way I stopped at a beautiful graveyard with Celtic headstones to take photos. The gray skies that day and the old tombstones against the bright green grass were just amazing![2]

I was hungry, so I stopped at a place to eat that was inside what looked like a castle. I thought it would be cool to go inside. Who knows how old that place was? All I know is I was still freezing inside the stone building because the only heat was from a fireplace by my table. The people in the 19th century and earlier had to be way tougher than me. Maybe that's why their fireplaces were much bigger ... to heat the entire home. All I know is I was very, very cold.

After lunch, I headed towards Clifden for Abbeyglen Castle Hotel. The historic castle rooms were built in 1832, and each room had a classic feel with a fireplace. I remember going down to the bar and ordering a Guinness. When the bartender gave it to me, I asked him, "Can I have a straw?" I thought he was going to faint! He was probably pissed that I was drinking Guinness with a straw. But, hey ... gotta keep my lipstick looking good!

I walked outside and up the hill. Over the hill was the ocean, and the winds were blowing hard. It was pretty cold.

The next day I drove to Galway and had some lunch before I had to head to the airport. I thought Ireland was a beautiful place, and I'd like to do a complete tour of Ireland where you rent a car and drive to several different Irish castles. Waterford Castle would be my first stop, and then Dromoland Castle, the Cliffs of Moher, and Ashford Castle.

Because of my family background, Italy is one of my favorite places to visit. In fact, if I had to live in a place other than Southern California or Nashville, it would probably be in Italy. I do tons of work in Milan, which is such a great city. Wrestling, like show business in general, has its share of shady characters, but the people in Milan are punctual and polite. Best of all, they respect me as a wrestler and an actress.

After a March 2010 visit to London, I flew to Milan and then took the train to Florence, one of the most beautiful places I have ever been. The food there is incredible – so fresh! No Jack-in-the-Box or Carl's Jr. Everything is home-grown, homemade, local, farm-to-table. The food in Italy is so good that I always worry about gaining weight while I'm there. But unlike L.A., where people drive everywhere, you do a lot more walking in Italy, especially in smaller towns. I guess that's how everyone stays in shape, even with all of the delicious, carb-filled breads and pastas.

It was still a bit chilly in March when I took a bus from Florence to the ancient town of San Gimignano. San Gimignano, named after St. Geminianus, is a small, walled, medieval hill town in the province of Siena, Tuscany and is known as the "Town of Fine Towers."[3] Encircled by 13th century walls, its old town centers on Piazza della Cisterna, a triangular square lined with medieval houses. It also has the Duomo di San Gimignano, a 12th century church.

The town was established in the third century BC and flourished until 1348, when it was struck by the Black Death that affected all of Europe and about half the townsfolk died.[4] Today, though, it is a beautiful, thriving town with interesting architecture and delicious white wine. It is one of my favorite places in the world.

GLOW girl Americana, Cindy Maranne (Ferda), had been to San Gimignano with her husband. They said I definitely needed to go there and gave me some excellent tips. Cindy told me to take the bread from the table that you hadn't finished eating, and when you're in the piazzas, to throw the bread to the birds! Boy, did that make for some beautiful photos!

I highly recommend visiting this artistic and touristic place. The town is awesome for spectacular photos, with Bougainvillea growing where it overlooks the vineyards. I had lunch sitting in the sun to stay warm.

I took the train back to Florence and visited the Cathedral of Santa Maria del Fiore/Duomo di Firenze, a Gothic masterpiece built in the 13th century. It is decorated with statues by Michelangelo and Donatello. I also visited the museum Gallerie Degli Uffizi, which was established in the 1500s. I saw the painting *Birth of Venus* by Sandro Botticelli, *The Woman with the Veil* by Raphael, *Adoration of the Magi* by Leonardo da Vinci, and many others.

There are many replicas of Michelangelo's David in Florence, the most prominent being the one in the original's position in the Piazza Della Signoria, which was placed there in 1910. The original sculpture was moved indoors in 1873 to the Accademia gallery. It weighs 12,500 pounds and is seventeen feet high.

I returned to London and Italy in September of 2010. On this trip I flew to Milan and then took the train to Venice. I must say I love taking the train through Europe. It's very peaceful. You can go into the pastry shops, get yourself a sandwich, maybe some wine, and have lunch on the train. Or if you are in first class, you will be able to get drinks and other items from the cart.

I arrived in Venice by Vaporetto, or water taxi, just when it was getting dark. I walked around and took a few photos of Rialto Bridge. I also took some really cool photos of the narrow alleys. You never know what hidden places you might find.

I got up early the next morning and had breakfast in my hotel. It was a little chilly in September, but I just had to take a gondola ride. I then walked around to the little shops in the area. I remembered Cindy's advice and took some bread to St. Mark's Square, also called Piazza San Marco, Venice's main public square. I fed the pigeons and got some more amazing photos. I also took photos of St. Mark's Basilica, the most famous of Venice's churches, and bought a Venetian carnival mask. I took the water taxi back to the train station, went into Milan, and flew back to Los Angeles.

A year later, I flew to Milan from London and took the train to Rome. This was my second trip to Rome, and I wanted to see the catacombs.

I went by bus to the Catacombs of San Callisto, which is outside Rome.

Before I took the tour, I stopped at the gift shop and saw all these beautiful silver medals of Catholic saints. I picked one of Saint Cecilia, who is the patron saint of music. I started on the tour, and as we walked through the catacombs, we came to a statue of a woman. The tour guide told us it was Saint Cecilia! I thought about how ironic it was that

I had just bought her medal. I asked if I could touch my medal to the statue, and he said of course.

On my second day, I wanted to go to the coast, so I took a train to one of the beaches at Ostia. I wasn't very impressed with this beach. It looked more like mud than sand, but it was very refreshing. I was happy to be visiting a beach on a different continent!

In August 2015, I skipped over London and flew from the United States to Copenhagen. I arrived at Kastrup Airport and stayed two nights in the Nyhavn, or "New Harbor," district of Copenhagen, which has a 17th century waterfront canal and entertainment district. It is currently lined by brightly colored 17th and 18th century townhouses, bars, cafes, and restaurants, and was originally constructed by King Christian V from 1670 to 1675 and dug by Danish soldier and Swedish prisoners of war.[5] It is a gateway from the sea to the old inner city at King's Square, where ships handled cargo and fishermen's catches. It was notorious for beer, sailors, and prostitution. The Danish author Hans Christian Andersen lived at Nyhavn for eighteen years. I took very beautiful photos here.

I also went to visit the infamous Freetown district of Christiania in Copenhagen. I took a walk on "Pusher Street," which was famous for its open trade of cannabis, but I didn't see any cannabis there.

I then went via the majestic Öresundsbron bridge to beautiful Skanör, a beach in southern Sweden. I enjoyed some great food and fresh local fish. Then I headed to London for work.

Chapter 41: F Cancer

Right after my grandma Ofelia passed away at 79 on November 2, 2005, my mother went to the doctor and found out she had breast cancer.

She had been at the hospital every single day while my grandmother was slowly dying. It was a lot of stress on her. I was on my way to work when my mother called me and said, "If you want to say goodbye to your grandmother, you'd better get to the hospital quickly." So I canceled work and turned around and got to St. Joseph's in Burbank as soon as I could.

I had never seen anybody die before.

They had my grandmother hooked up to morphine. Once they took her off the machine, I saw her take her very last breath and, when it flatlined, I heard a sound out of my mother that I've never heard before. It hurt my heart so much I began to cry.

It was right after that that my mother was diagnosed with breast cancer. That was another huge shot to our family.

No one in our family had had cancer before, so seeing my mother and our family going through that disease was very scary. I kept thinking, *Am I gonna lose my mother now?*

The doctors suggested that she have a double mastectomy – which she did – and go through a series of medications, but no chemotherapy. A year later, she decided to get breast implants. I remember talking to her about them and telling her I thought it would be a good thing for her to do.

As time went on, she would have her yearly tests, and fortunately they went very well.

She is still cancer-free today. Thank the good Lord for that!

☆ ☆ ☆

It's important to remember that cancer affects not only humans, but also animals and the people who care about them as well.

While I was working on this book, both of my cats, Lala and Zsa Zsa, would always come into my office and watch mama while I was talking on the phone, scanning photos, sending text messages, etc. They would lie down by my feet or lounge on the back of the chair. Zsa Zsa had to sit on the printer or in the window, watching my every move. She and I bonded strongly. In the evening, she would run up to me in bed like a dog and "make biscuits" on my chest. Then she would fall asleep on my chest or my stomach and sleep there all night long.

On September 4, 2024, I noticed she wasn't feeling good, so I made an appointment and took her to the vet. That would be the last time that I would see my four-year-old, beautiful, blue Russian kitty. I tried to prepare myself because I've been through it quite a few times, but it doesn't get any easier. Her lungs were raspy; she was having a hard time breathing; X-rays showed dark masses on her lungs; her gums were really pale; blood test results showed she was severely anemic; and her heart was beating fast. All of these indications were not positive. They gave us three options, and I was not going to put my cat through any more suffering, so we made the very painful decision and let her go off to the Rainbow Bridge, where she will join Elvis, Purrcilla, Keekster, Marris, and Lilith.

This always does a number on my heart, and it takes me time to recover. Our fur babies are like our family. My heart aches as I'm writing this, but I know one day I will see all my kitties, and we will be reunited again somewhere, someplace.

FIGHTING Females and the Quest for a GLOW Revival
(Contributed by Bob Harris)

On a Saturday morning in April 2008, I sat with Jeanne "Hollywood" Basone in her exhibit booth at the Women's Wrestling Convention in San Diego, California. A female fighting enthusiast strolled over, greeted Jeanne, and then asked me, "What happened to that magazine you were a contributing editor of?"

Before I could explain that the magazine had ceased publication after releasing its Winter 2000 issue, Jeanne interjected with a loud, "I loved that magazine!" She was referring to *FIGHTING Females*, which had been published in New York City by Opal Inc. as part of the Tribeca Publishing Inc. roster. The 84-page glossy magazine was an offshoot of *Wrestling Eye*, one of the biggest and most popular professional wrestling monthly magazines on worldwide newsstands. It was under the managing editorship of a wonderful woman named Helene Bleich.

FIGHTING Females' premiere issue launched in 1994. It was positioned as a quarterly magazine with Spring, Summer, Fall, and Winter editions. It possessed a large circulation and had major market distribution in the USA, Canada, the United Kingdom, Europe, Australia, and a host of smaller international markets. Its content covered the female fighting genre, ranging from professional wrestling, boxing, amateur and competitive grappling, to nightclub mud and oil wrestling, apartment wrestling, and catfights.

By 1998, I had been on the *FIGHTING Females* magazine columnist line-up for two years, authoring a three-page news column under the moniker of K. Harris. That came about after I managed to make a successful debut as a writer for the magazine in the 1996 Winter issue with a front cover, feature story, and centerfold spread on a blonde wrestler/boxer I had been grooming in Vancouver. The photography and editorial feature made a favorable impression with Helene Bleich's staff. She told me it also made a splash in the female fighting community. It caught the attention of several video producers, numerous females who fought, and the fans who loved them.

By November 1998, I was ready to create another splash and was digging around for a hot-looking girl to do a front cover and feature spread with. I found a contact in Las Vegas, and she led me to Jeanne Basone.

I was attending COMDEX, the massive computer technology show in the Las Vegas Convention Center. After three days, I was ready for a break. The adult entertainment expo at the Sands Hotel seemed like a good place to scout around for a possible front cover model. The Sands expo was what I had expected – an enticing menu of superbly stacked California blondes and raven-haired Vegas showstoppers sitting at exhibit booths huckstering video product, adult toys, and apparel, as well as signing publicity photos and snapping Polaroid pictures for smitten fans at ten bucks a pop.

A pretty redhead caught my eye. She didn't strike me as being a porn star, as I watched her happily dealing autographed Laura Kimberly and Hollywood glamour photo postcards to eager conventioneers. I struck up a conversation and discovered she was a glamour model and aspiring Internet website entrepreneur whose best friend was Jeanne "Hollywood" Basone. Bingo! I had struck paydirt.

"Where's Jeanne?" I asked.

"She was supposed to be here with me this weekend, but she just broke her leg and had to stay in L.A.," Laura replied.

Laura Kimberly was Laura Bennett. She was at the Sands expo to promote the new Planet Model websites she and Jeanne had recently launched. She had worked at A&M Records in Los Angeles for eight years and was currently working weekly lingerie shows with Jeanne at Barney's Beanery in the city. Laura wasn't a wrestler, but she had been a Corona beer ring girl at a Reseda Country Club event and had experienced a few wrestling hold lessons with Jeanne. That was enough for me to start thinking about an angle for *FIGHTING Females*.

I thought, *Why not pair an L.A. glamour model whose best friend is wrestling's blonde bombshell, Jeanne "Hollywood" Basone, for a front cover, feature article, and centerfold spread using the Internet glamour siren angle?* I pitched it to my managing editor in New York, Helene Bleich, and she gave me the go-ahead.

Laura hooked me up on a telephone conference call with Jeanne, and within minutes we had laid out a plan for the photo content. Jeanne directed the studio shoot in Los Angeles with Samantha Glover doing makeup and the notable L.A. photographer Tony Weltzin behind the camera.

Jeanne delivered an eye-catching series of action and posed hotshots. She had an excellent eye for creating sell shots. They blended perfectly with my article and some outstanding glamour photos by Jon Abeyta that Laura supplied. The *FIGHTING Females* editorial and production team in New York loved the content. They gave the Summer 1999 magazine front cover to a wrestling action shot of Laura and Hollywood, accompanying it with a colorful centerfold layout of the two girls as part of K. Harris' feature article titled "Laura Kimberly ... Internet Glamour Siren!"

Jeanne scored big points with the magazine and with me by directing and producing some terrific photographs for the Laura Kimberly feature on short notice. Her efforts were duly noted for future projects. My working relationship and friendship with Jeanne led me to another one of her close friends: her *GLOW* co-star Cheryl "Lightning" Rusa. In April of 1999, the three of us met in San Diego at the Women's Wrestling Convention produced by Dave Jackson of Jackpin Productions.

My Vancouver pal, J.P. Erickson, a writer/photographer of women's fitness/bodybuilding and contributing editor to *FIGHTING Females*, joined me at WWC '99 to cover the weekend's action for the Fall issue of the magazine. The event attracted competitors, vendors, writers, photographers, and videographers from North America and Europe. Jeanne had her Webkitten.com exhibit booth set up with her and Cheryl's merchandise. The two of them were extremely busy – autographing photos, posters, and personalized postcards, as well as selling videos, networking with vendors, and wrestling at designated times – but they always found time for chatting and posing for their fans. True professionals!

After a hectic day at the convention, Jeanne went the extra mile for J.P. and me on Saturday night by rallying Cheryl and bodybuilder/wrestler Kasie Cavanaugh for a location photoshoot at the newly opened L. Scott Sales video store in San Diego. Her energy was remarkable. Clearly, she loved her profession. Headquartered in New York City, L. Scott Sales was the largest retailer of female fighting merchandise. Under the helm of the very personable Larry Druss, L. Scott Sales distributed products to more than 30 associated retail outlets in the USA and maintained a booming mail order business worldwide.

Cheryl organized a glamour shoot with photographer/makeup artist Veronica Simms. The photos were absolutely gorgeous; so much so that the FIGHTING Females production team in New York gave my entire submission a thumbs up. Cheryl was featured on the front cover of the Winter 1999 magazine.

The art director spread three of her glamour shots over a two-page centerfold, complementing my article, which my managing editor titled "Cheryl Rusa – From Body Cast to Bodacious!" They gave us an exceptional four pages. The popularity of my regular three-page news column and Cheryl's feature boosted me up to contributing editor status. Jeanne played a significant role in making that happen.

One day in early 2000, during a conversation about content for FIGHTING Females, Jeanne casually mentioned that she was grateful for the exposure the magazine had given her, but when it came to front covers, she was always profiled in an action shot shared with another girl. She had never had a solo cover. That would soon change.

In one of my submissions for my regular column, I included a hotshot Jeanne had sent me. It was a Tony Weltzin 3/4 length color photo of Jeanne posed against a medium pink textured backdrop. Her makeup and hairstyling were beautifully done, and she wore a modest black halter-top bikini outfit. Her expression was serene and she struck a confident pose, leaning slightly to her right with both arms tight to her side, and hands balled into two white-knuckle fists. Her almond eyes bored straight through the camera lens. She hooked you with a "try me" magnetism that drew you in to wonder, Who is this amazing woman?

The shot was smokin' hot. So hot in fact that during my weekly phone call to New York, Helene informed me that her art director lifted the photo from my column and told her, "Bob can't have it. It's a front cover shot." Jeanne "Hollywood" Basone finally got her solo *FIGHTING Females* cover in the Fall 2000 issue. The magazine also featured her fighting with attractive redhead Lisa Comshaw in the centerfold as part of a three-page layout titled "Mean Jeans" for California's Les Femmes Fatales Productions.

Jeanne was a writer and publisher's dream. Her image and popularity attracted readership and sold magazines. It's interesting to note that in the seven years the magazine was in publication, spanning 1994 to 2000 and producing 31 issues, Jeanne appeared on four front covers. No other girl got that many. Belinda Belle – wrestler, video producer, and founder of Steel Kittens – had two covers and the WWF/WWE star Chyna had two covers (one photographed by J.P. Erickson during a coliseum show in Vancouver).

When Jeanne's Fall 2000 front cover was racked on newsstands, her image against the pink photographic backdrop just bounced out at you. She owned the shelf! Without a doubt, it was one of the best covers the magazine's art department produced.

Many of the girls on the independent wrestling circuit or the private studio video wrestling scene that I met over the years missed opportunities for self-promotion and increased visibility in print media. Jeanne was clued into the value of self-promotion, and I was happy to give her image, websites, and mail order business a plug in my regular *FIGHTING Females* column. I would insert one of the posed glamour or action hotshot photos Jeanne would send me and write a couple of paragraphs such as:

"Southern California's best-rated wrestling babe, Hollywood, is back in action and has launched a terrific new website. This statuesque, sunkissed blonde has really gone the extra mile to develop a first-class site. She loads it up regularly with sizzling news about her career, her personal appearance itinerary, and offers fans an excellent catalog of merchandise. The feature attraction is an outstanding gallery of wrestling & glamour photography and a V.I.P Members club!" – Excerpt from K. Harris' column "Surf's Up for the Female Fighting Internet," *FIGHTING Females* Summer 1999, (Laura Kimberly & Hollywood front cover).

In the summer of 2004, Jeanne traveled to Vancouver for a business meeting with her webmaster. She also visited with me in the city's historic Gastown district. During the evening of laughs and storytelling, we got around to discussing the movie and television business. Our conversation drifted to Jeanne's GLOW days and her current stunt work. We talked about whether there was any hope of a television revival of the series.

Jeanne mentioned she was still in touch with Ursula "Babe the Farmer's Daughter" Hayden, who had ownership of the GLOW copyright/ trademark. Ursula also had some of the GLOW master tapes in her possession. We discussed the idea of re-releasing the series, and Jeanne said she would talk with Ursula. I mentioned I was acquainted with a multi award-winning writer, director, and producer of numerous feature film and television productions. I would run the idea by him and also talk to my business colleague about it. Both individuals were based in Vancouver, the city deemed "Hollywood North" by the movie and television industry.

Within days, Jeanne was back to me with word that Ursula was interested. I replied that I had received positive responses from my side, and I explained to her that my film and TV acquaintance would lead the project if we moved forward. Jeanne agreed to participate and take on the additional workload while maintaining her website, modeling and acting commitments, personal appearances, and road travel. And so began a year-and-a-half waltz with Ursula Hayden.

The project required a considerable amount of due diligence, culminating in assembly, inspection, and safe storage of 104 television episode master tapes. It also required Ursula Hayden to sign a Product Representation agreement granting rights to explore interest within the television industry with the objective of acquiring distribution deals. The concept was to repackage the series, re-introduce the brand, and generate an expanded, new audience. The immediate strategy was to attend two of the largest television and film content markets: The 2005 National Association of Television Program Executives (NATPE) Conference & Exhibition in Las Vegas and the 2005 Marché International des Programmes de Télévision (MIPTV) in Cannes, France.

Jeanne worked her butt off. Time was of the essence. Her role was to communicate and work with Ursula and keep me up to date on progress. Mine was to work with the two Vancouver team members and keep her abreast of developments and requirements. Jeanne did not have an easy job. My perception was that Ursula needed friendly guidance and resources toward making this deal a reality. Jeanne was that person. She and I communicated almost daily.

One afternoon, when negotiations with Ursula were at a critical point, I had a call from Jeanne. Within seconds she was in tears. It was the first time I'd ever heard her break down. Her tears were those of frustration. She had poured her heart and soul into trying to make things work for all of us. She had even offered to put up $10,000 of her own money to help Ursula recover the *GLOW* master tapes from storage in Las Vegas. We were on a tight timeline and Ursula's response, or lack thereof, had finally gotten to Jeanne that day.

It was during that phone call when I experienced and really felt Jeanne's passion for good business and ethics – her desire to do a good job, get it done promptly, and not let anyone down. The girl had heart.

As the project progressed through 2005, it became clear there were some major hurdles related to accessing the 104 *GLOW* episode master tapes. Ursula had possession of only nine masters. The remaining masters were in the possession of Tony Cimber, Matt Cimber's son and one of *GLOW's* assistant directors.

The Vancouver team continued to build interest from the television and Internet sectors, and, by December 2005, there were two offers on the table. They involved using the nine masters Ursula could deliver. Both deals were time-sensitive and needed to be signed. They would serve as building blocks toward the redevelopment of the *GLOW* brand and moving along negotiations toward usage of the remaining 95 masters in the possession of Tony Cimber.

But the project came to an abrupt end during a conference call between the Vancouver team and Ursula and her attorney in Los Angeles. Midway through the call, my film and TV acquaintance sensed that delays and more posturing for concessions from our side were in the wind from L.A. He suddenly stood up and quietly said, "I think I'll pass." And that shut down the project immediately.

It's interesting to note that, on May 31, 2016, an article in *Variety* magazine online announced Netflix, the California-based provider of streaming films and television series worldwide, had ordered a 10-episode fictional comedy series based on *GLOW*. To my mind, that announcement gave credibility to the idea Jeanne had participated in years ago (repackaging the series, rejuvenating the brand, and expanding its audience) and clearly illustrates the validity of her forward-thinking and entrepreneurial vision at that time.

A Canadian writer and women's professional wrestling archivist specializing in the 1940s – 1970s era, Bob Harris co-promoted All-Star Wrestling shows in the British Columbia Interior during the mid-1970s with former wrestler and Vancouver promoter legend Sandor Kovacs. Harris also wrote for New York-based *FIGHTING Females* magazine from 1996 to 2000. He has been a production associate and close friend of Vancouver's fight promoter Gerry Gionco since 1986. Harris worked in the music and recording industry for twenty-seven years. Jeanne Basone is his best friend in America. For over twenty six years, Bob has enjoyed mentoring and sharing his business and promotion expertise with Jeanne. He currently resides in Vancouver.

Chapter 42: GLOW: The Story of the Gorgeous Ladies of Wrestling

Has it really been over 20 years?

That was the first thought that ran through my mind when I heard that some independent filmmakers were planning on making a documentary about the whole Gorgeous Ladies of Wrestling experience. As of this writing, it has now been over thirty years since *GLOW* ended in 1990. But at the time I heard about the documentary, only two decades had passed.

My second thought?

Sign me up!

Brett Whitcomb and Bradford Thomason are two guys from Texas who loved *GLOW* as kids and wondered what ever became of their favorite *GLOW* girls. Their documentary, *GLOW: The Story of the Gorgeous Ladies of Wrestling*, came out in 2012. At that time, I was asked to travel to Las Vegas to do a commentary track on the DVD with Billy Corgan from The Smashing Pumpkins, who is now the owner and president of the National Wrestling Alliance (NWA). *GLOW*'s Matilda the Hun and Little Egypt also participated in the commentary.

The first time I saw the film, it was a little bit overwhelming. Part of that is because I was busy working on the DVD's commentary track while I was watching it. But more than that, it was also because the documentary's main point was to record a cultural event that I not only participated in but was also a big part of my life. I did the voiceover work and went back home, but I suspected that I would be seeing the film at least one more time.

The second time I saw the film was actually the first time I saw it on a movie screen. The screen was *huge*, and the film was shown as part of the Newport Beach Film Festival. Without a doubt, though, the third time I saw the movie was the charm. Why? Lots of reasons. Mostly because the third time I saw the movie, it was in Hollywood. Besides the obvious connection to my *GLOW* wrestling name, the sold-out theaters in Hollywood – The Los Feliz Theatre on Vermont Avenue and The Silent Movie Theatre on Fairfax – were jam-packed with family, friends, and fans. Some of those fans had followed me since the beginning of *GLOW*, but others had jumped on the Hollywood bandwagon more recently through Facebook or X. Either way was fine by me. I signed tons of autographs, many on wrestling paraphernalia. One of the fans even gave me a Wonder Woman belt buckle.

Upon those later viewings of the movie, I noticed some things that I had missed the first time around. I noticed that some girls got more screen time than others, which was interesting because some didn't play as big of roles in the original *GLOW* as some of the other girls. I guess the filmmakers had their favorites, or those girls just had better information to share in the interviews.

There were other surprises as well. For example, I had forgotten that the Heavy Metal Sisters, Sharon and Donna Willinsky, by their own admission, couldn't actually wrestle! They didn't have the kind of professional training that I had (from the legendary Mando Guerrero), but they were great actresses who provided a unique flavor to the show, so the producers kept them around. It makes sense when you think about it. Professional wrestling in general is as much about theater (heroes, villains, storylines, etc.) as it is about the physical act of wrestling. David McLane originally wanted *GLOW* to be purely wrestling, but Matt Cimber envisioned a campy variety show. What viewers saw on *GLOW* during the 1980s, and continue to see years later, was really a combination of those two visions. We were also lucky that head writer Steve Blance had answered an ad in the back of *Variety* magazine, since he wrote all of the sketches. Would the show have been as big of a hit as it was without that collaboration? Honestly, I'm not sure. I'm just glad it worked out the way it did.

I was also surprised at how many girls got injured during the filming of *GLOW*. Maybe that surprised me because during the time I was on the show, I never suffered a major injury myself (thank God). I was already pretty athletic going into the show, having played softball and volleyball in high school, and the training with Mando gave me enough technical knowledge that I suppose the risk of me getting hurt was maybe lower than it was for the other girls. After the pilot, *GLOW* didn't hire Mando to train any of the newbies; after that, it was a matter of "girls training girls." As hard as we tried, I'm sure it wasn't the same as the training we had with Mando. He was so very serious about the art of professional wrestling.

"Respect the craft," he used to tell us all the time. When some of us were giving him a hard time early on during training, he put one of the girls in a sleeper hold and almost knocked her out.

"Now do you believe it's real?" he asked. We did. And believe me, we "respected the craft" from that point on.

One of the sad things I noticed about the movie was the way Mt. Fiji (Emily Dole) had to deal with so many issues, both physical and emotional, since *GLOW* first aired. Physically, she had to endure a lot of wear-and-tear on her body (her knees, especially) because she was such a big-boned woman. Her size was great for the show (hence, the ring name "Mt. Fiji"), but not so great for her body. This is the "darker" side of show business. What looks good on-screen doesn't always look good in real life. I never knew that Emily struggled with some mental/anxiety disorders until I watched the documentary. I remember on a flight somewhere Matt was trying to calm Emily down; she wanted to get off the plane while we were in mid-air, and we were trying to keep her from opening or slamming into the exit doors. Poor Fiji. Emily Dole was the heart and soul of our show. Sadly, Emily passed on January 2, 2018.

What were my "final thoughts" after seeing *GLOW: The Story of the Gorgeous Ladies of Wrestling*? First of all, I thought it was pretty authentic. Whenever someone makes a documentary about real-life events, there's always a chance that the finished product will look totally different from what actually happened. (Remember Mark Zuckerberg's complaints about *The Social Network*?) But the guys who made this documentary were huge *GLOW* fans, and I could tell that they really wanted to "get it right."

My second thought was, *How about a sequel?* Because as good as the documentary was, it also raised some questions I'd like to see answered … questions like, "What about Zelda?" and, "Why did Vine really leave *GLOW*?" (To this day, I still don't have an answer to that question.) Some people might think these questions can't or shouldn't be answered. But I wouldn't think twice about fighting those people for the right to learn the truth.

We are, after all, Gorgeous Ladies of Wrestling.

Chapter 43: A Trip Down Memory Lane

In 2015 I attended the annual Cauliflower Alley Club professional wrestling reunion with some of my fellow *GLOW* wrestlers. It was also a month before the Riviera Hotel was set to close and be imploded in the name of "progress" for the expansion of the Las Vegas Convention Center. I knew that I had to go visit one last time before it was gone forever. *GLOW* wrestlers Lightning, Tulsa and MTV also went.

As I walked inside, I was very happy and sad at the same time — remembering all the places that we had filmed our sketches and wrestled.

Jacopo's pizza stood out first. It was there where Mountain Fiji and Matilda the Hun had their pizza food fight.

In another area next to the slot machines, I had recalled the time where Vine, Matilda and myself were dancing and singing to our music video Raw Meat. The Riviera Hotel gave *GLOW* free will inside their casino to film to our hearts content! I guess it doesn't hurt when your boss owns the place.

We then went over to the long staircase, near Jacopo's pizza where season one bad girls were sliding down the rails of that staircase. It took me a minute to get my balance — something I hadn't done for over 25 years but I did it.

I then went through the casino, one last time to look at the cashier window where we once cashed our *GLOW* checks — the bar that we would always get our Poland waters from after practice and the fast food place that was not there anymore.

I decided to try my luck gambling — playing the slot machines — I was on a roll for a minute. I saved my winning ticket that evening which had a dollar on it for a souvenir.

Outside was a famous bronze statue of the derrieres from the Crazy Girls burlesque show. On the wall above their heads it read *Crazy Girls*

No "IFs" "ANDS" OR... Riviera Hotel and Casino. The show ran for over 30 years. It's considered America's longest running burlesque show. Tulsa, MTV, Lightning, and myself tried to imitate that pose.

It would be the last time that I would ever step inside or see the Riviera Hotel. What great memories I had there.

Chapter 44: The First Original GLOW Cruises

In 2019, I organized the first Original *GLOW* Cruise pretty much by myself. I had some help from Don Goodlin, who had worked on the AfterGLOW cruises that came before ours, but he wasn't able to come on board with us. So Cheryl Rusa and I organized and planned all the events and prizes for the fans.

Prior to the Original *GLOW* Cruise, I had taken over twenty cruises. Ryan and his band had been invited to go on many cruises by Sixthman, the folks responsible for all the KISS Kruises and many more. Ryan played on every single one of those, and of course I got to go with him. Yay for me! Great perks!

I knew a good cruise like the back of my hand, so I went to work and advertised the *GLOW* cruise on social media.

We took about twenty-five *GLOW* fans on a five-night Mexican Riviera cruise. Their hosts, in addition to myself, were Envy from The Soul Patrol, Royal Hawaiian, and Lightning (Cheryl).

The night before the cruise, we all stayed in Long Beach, California. We met at a restaurant bar, had dinner and drinks, took photos, and went back to our hotels dreaming of the high seas. In the morning, we boarded a Norwegian Cruise Line ship and set sail.

Our first stop, on September 9, was Cabo San Lucas. We left the ship in the morning and negotiated a price for all of us to get in a van and head to a resort where there was food, drink, and surfing. Cheryl rented a board and headed for the ocean. I went in a different direction and explored the caves with one of our fans and took photos. After four or five hours, our van came back, picked us up, and dropped us at the port to do some shopping. That night we boarded the ship, cleaned up, and all had dinner together.

Every night we had games and contests with our fans. One of the highlights was when we had fans dress up as their favorite *GLOW* girl. Vanessa dressed up as Dementia, Manny was Americana, and Greg was Royal Hawaiian. But Andrew and Chris won first place for dressing up as

The Heavy Metal Sisters, Chainsaw and Spike. They did a great job of wearing the same makeup as the originals, and their wigs were fantastic!

We had lots of fun on board the ship with our fans, but we also explored as much as possible on excursion days!

On September 10, we visited Mazatlán. A few of us went on a snorkeling cruise and laid out on the beach. I can't remember where the others went that day, but we had plenty of options to pick and choose from.

On September 11, we finally reached Puerto Vallarta, where some of us decided that we would do a jeep ride/tequila distillery excursion. Cheryl was appointed our designated driver because she doesn't drink. We were in a caravan of ten red Jeeps, and it was so, so hot that day.

Our first stop was on top of a hill overlooking the beautiful Pacific Ocean. We could see our cruise ship from there. On that same stop, we learned how to make guacamole. But actually I already knew how to make it since my mother made the best authentic Mexican food anywhere.

Next, we took the Jeeps back down the hill through the city. We stopped at our tour guide's abuela's house. She had bottled water for sale and a clean bathroom for the patrons. Unfortunately, by the time I got to the front of the line, the cold bottled water was sold out! An ice-cold Coca-Cola wasn't going to do it for me, but it was better than nothing.

Our final destination was right around the corner from Abuela's house: a tequila distillery called Doña Engracia Hacienda. They gave us a tour, showing us the agave plants and how they cut them up to make the 100% agave tequila. We were escorted inside for the tequila tasting. Ron, Oyanka, Rick, Kim, Cheryl, and I indulged in the tequila tasting that day. Yes, even our designated driver, Cheryl, took a shot.

After the tasting, we were escorted into the restaurant for lunch. After all, we had been drinking some good tequila in the hot sun. Once we finished eating, they took us to our last hangout, a very cool hotel in the marina that had a big pool. We laid out for another few hours and drank more before we were escorted back to our ship. It was a long day, but it was fun!

While in port we found a Walmart where we bought snacks and waters to bring back to the ship. Oyanka bought a very cool doll for her daughter.

I did a second *GLOW* cruise in March 2024. This was in the Eastern Caribbean and included stops in Puerto Plata, Dominican Republic; St. Thomas, U.S. Virgin Islands; Tortola, British Virgin Islands; and Great Stirrup Cay, The Bahamas. Fortunately, it was just as successful as the one in 2019! Again, we went through Don Goodlin, and Cheryl and I made the whole itinerary, activity plan, and contests for our fans by ourselves. I had canvas beach bags made that said "Original *GLOW* Girl Cruise 2024." Inside, they had personalized Turkish towels and items the fans would need for the beach and cruise. The cruise also included free Wi-Fi and an unlimited drink package.

On March 2, I flew from Nashville to Miami and went out to dinner with all the *GLOW* fans that evening. But Cheryl had gotten delayed and didn't get in until after 8:30 p.m.

We checked out at 12 noon on March 4 and headed for the Port of Miami, where we embarked on the NCL's *Norwegian Encore*. I hadn't been on this ship before. It had huge waterslides and the Norwegian Encore Speedway go-kart track, which, I think, was the largest race track at sea, with over 1,100 feet of pedal-to-the-metal action. Cheryl went on this four or five times! There was a laser tag, but we never got to that.

The first stop was Puerto Plata, where we got on an air-conditioned bus and headed to a beach with food. We stopped at a store on the way, where Adrian bought me Dominican Republic coffee. It was delicious!

The next stop was St. Thomas. While entering the port, I noticed that there were many yachts – so many that it reminded me of Nice in

France, only smaller. But it was absolutely beautiful. A few of us checked out the beach to the west. We hired a van to take us there and stayed for about two and a half to three hours.

That evening we headed to Tortola. The beach here was absolutely beautiful, and there were fewer people.

I don't always do ship excursions. I just look up what I want to do, then hop in a taxi and go! That way, you can go places where there aren't so many tourists.

The next day, we were at sea and did our costume contest.

The following day, we disembarked on a man-made island called Grand Stirrup Cay that the cruise ship company owns. I had been there before, but it had been a while, and they had added a zip line. Cheryl was in heaven! She and one of our fans, Rick, could not wait to try the zip line. While I was lying in the sun, I could hear Cheryl screaming and see Rick waving to me as they zipped across the sand.

Every night we would all have dinner together. The days we were at sea, we had contests (costume, art, trivia, etc.), autograph signings, and photos with fans. It was another great cruise for the original GLOW girls!

I'd like to plan another one for the future … maybe to Europe or maybe just hang out someplace in Southern California, where we could go to the beach one day, go to Disneyland the next, then head to Vegas! The sky's the limit!

Chapter 45: The COVID Pandemic

A few months after the first Original *GLOW* Cruise returned from our seven-day Mexican Riviera trip in September of 2019, we started hearing about a new virus called COVID-19 originating in Wuhan, China. A cluster of patients in the city of Wuhan began to experience the symptoms of an atypical pneumonia-like illness that did not respond well to standard treatment. What happened next is history none of us will ever forget.

January 23, 2020
Wuhan, China, a city of 11 million people, was placed under lockdown due to the 2019 Novel Coronavirus outbreak.

January 24, 2020
The CDC confirmed a travel-related infection of the SARS-CoV-2 virus in Illinois, bringing the total number of cases in the U.S. to two.

February 10, 2020
Worldwide deaths from the 2019 Novel Coronavirus reached 1,013. The SARS-CoV-2 virus had now killed more people than the Severe Acute Respiratory Syndrome (SARS-CoV-1) outbreak, which claimed 774 lives globally from November 2002 to July 2003.

February 18, 2020
Due to the high caseload and numbers of asymptomatic individuals testing positive for COVID-19, all passengers and crew of the *Diamond Princess* cruise ship were quarantined off the coast of Japan, placed under travel restrictions, and prevented from returning to the U.S. for at least 14 days after they left the *Diamond Princess*.

March 6, 2020
The *Grand Princess* cruise ship was stranded off the California coast after officials learned that a California man who had traveled on the ship in February contracted COVID-19 and died. The California Air National Guard dropped off a limited supply of testing kits by helicopter. More

than 3,500 people were aboard the ship, but only 46 could be tested and 21, mostly crew members, tested positive.[1]

People on cruise ships were being detained out at sea, with many passengers getting very sick. Passengers were secluded in their cabins. I thought, *Wow, we were lucky our cruise was scheduled in 2019 and not 2020.*

February 29, 2020 - March 5, 2020
Ryan and I headed to Cozumel with our friend Phil and his gal for five nights. We were having the time of our lives in this beautiful warm paradise, not knowing that in just a few days – March 11, 2020, to be precise – after more than 118,000 cases in 114 countries and 491 deaths, the WHO would declare COVID-19 a pandemic.

We also heard that a terrible tornado hit parts of Nashville. The Basement East, a favorite spot Ryan had played several times, was completely destroyed. We live about twenty minutes south of the area that was hit, but being out of the country, we had no idea if our friends were OK and what had actually been destroyed. Our friends were posting photos. It looked like a war zone.

March 13, 2020
The Trump administration declared a nationwide emergency and issued a travel ban on non-U.S. citizens traveling from 26 European countries due to COVID-19.

March 14, 2020
The CDC issued a "no sail order" for all cruise ships, calling for them to cease activity in all waters that the U.S. holds jurisdiction over.

May 28, 2020
The recorded death toll from COVID-19 in the U.S. surpassed 100,000.

June 10, 2020

The number of confirmed COVID-19 cases in the U.S. surpassed 2 million.

September 22, 2020

The reported death toll in the U.S from COVID-19 surpassed 200,000.

October 2, 2020

President Trump tested positive for the SARS CoV-2 virus and was treated at Walter Reed National Military Medical Center with antiviral drugs, including remdesivir.

November 16, 2020

Moderna's COVID-19 vaccine was found to be 95.4% effective in its clinical trial.

November 18, 2020

Pfizer-BioNTech's COVID-19 vaccine was found to be 95% effective in their 44,000-person trial.

January 18, 2021

The reported death toll from COVID-19 in the U.S. surpassed 400,000.[2]

☆ ☆ ☆

Shortly thereafter, another tragedy hit. Our beautiful Maine Coon cat, Elvis, passed away. I woke up and he wasn't in his usual spot, which was on my bed or near the bed. I got up to look for him and found him in my office, lying down. I stopped in my tracks. He never took naps on the floor in my office. I cried out to Ryan and said, "Come and see if Elvis is dead."

Ryan picked him up and said, "Yes, he is."

I bawled my eyes out for the next three days.

I will never forget that day. I had never seen one of my animals dead before. I was a mess.

Because of the pandemic, we had to drop him off at the front door to get him cremated. It was pretty tough to say goodbye at the door and not be able to go into an office and say goodbye to my Elvis properly. I picked up his ashes a day or two afterwards and brought them home in a nice box they had picked out for me.

Life became so different with everything shut down. I remember the news saying, "Don't wear a mask," and then a few months later saying, "Yes, wear a mask." It was a confusing time.

I was not doing any conventions or signings, but with my production company, I was able to do a few custom matches with three or four people that I trusted, knowing that if they were sick, they would not work. I was one of eight to ten passengers on a big jet plane going back-and-forth from Nashville to Los Angeles, California. I thought, *Wow, this is great. Nobody is on these flights. I have rows and rows to myself.*

There was not a lot of work for me and absolutely none for Ryan. But with my new soap line, NashvilleBotanika, I was selling soap like crazy.

I was happy to receive the $1,200 check that we all got from the government. There were certain loans called PPP loans that you could also get from your bank. Ryan had a pretty good amount that kept him going for the whole year. Mine was much less. Then, if you were lucky enough, you were able to collect some kind of unemployment for part of the year.

It seemed like every day I was glued to the TV. I couldn't help myself. More and more people were dying. The death toll was going up drastically.

My Aunt Barb and Uncle Ben, my dad's brother, contracted the virus in early February 2021. They were both still on the waiting list to get their vaccinations. Aunt Barb was released from the hospital, but Uncle Ben was not. After many tests, he was put on a ventilator. We all knew what that meant. My uncle did not receive the vaccination in time and sadly passed away from COVID complications on February 24, 2021. He was the first person that I personally knew that had died. My father also lost a cousin from COVID-19.

After that incident, I made sure to wear my mask on all my flights, regardless of who was looking or who was judging me. I have received all my vaccinations to date.

Chapter 46: Bullying: The Painful Truth

"Bullying is an ongoing and deliberate misuse of power in relationships through repeated verbal, physical and/or social behavior that intends to cause physical, social and/or psychological harm. It can involve an individual or a group misusing their power, or perceived power, over one or more persons who feel unable to stop it from happening." [1]
– From "Understanding bullying," Australian Education Authorities/The State of Queensland

When I was a young girl, the concept of bullying never crossed my mind. In fact, I didn't realize what bullying was. I was just being a kid, being me, and minding my own business. I had many, many friends, and while I'm sure most of us had heard the term "bully" at some time or another, it wasn't considered as prevalent of a problem as it is today. While they did exist, an aggressive individual, or bully, certainly didn't have the types of opportunities or outlets to bully others as they have in recent years, particularly with the advent of the Internet and social media.

Now, as I look back, the first time I can remember being bullied was when I was in the third grade. Around that time, my hair had become curly and unruly, so my parents decided it was best to keep my hair short. One day, two boys at school made fun of my haircut. I just ignored them, hoping that if I didn't respond, they would get bored and stop. Unfortunately, they decided to chase me home from school. I remember running as fast as I could to get away from them, and at one point hiding in bushes so they couldn't find me. I waited until they passed so I could walk home freely.

The boys didn't give up and had a tomboy named Tracy S., whom they had also bullied, chase after me one day. I'd seen them tie her to one of the poles at school using her long hair. It's hard for me to be mad at Tracy, I guess, because she was probably just glad they were picking on someone else for a change. Throughout fifth grade, a bully named Cary would punch me in the arm. I know that boys that age do dumb things to get girls to like them, but even if he was trying to get my attention, to me, it still felt like he was bullying me.

Then came junior high. Oh boy, oh joy! Ever wonder why so few adults have positive memories from junior high school? One of the main reasons is that kids at that age can be so mean, especially 13-15 year-old girls! The best-looking boy at my junior high was named Tony, and we had started dating. Obviously, the other girls in my grade were jealous, and I remember these girls making fun of me and saying things like, "Dream on, Jeanne." when they passed me in the halls. It didn't hurt me physically, like being punched in the arm, but it definitely hurt my feelings.

Some of the boys used to make fun of me as well – I remember two of them in particular – but, really, they were flirting with me because they liked me. Since I'm part Hispanic and part Italian, they combined the slurs spic and wop into an oh-so-junior-high-school insult: "spop." Worse than that, they dragged me into the boys' locker room one day. It may have been funny to them, but I was both scared and humiliated. Thank goodness that only happened on one occasion.

I blossomed once I got out of junior high and into high school. My hair was longer and straighter, my braces were gone, and I had started to fill out in ways the boys definitely noticed. They never made fun of me after that. Some of those junior high girls were nicer, but still were very cliquish. Whatever I did or didn't do, there were groups of girls that were always going to be catty and petty. At some point I just accepted it. I guess I put them all in their place eventually, as I was voted "Best Looking" in my senior class in high school.

I thought all the bullying was behind me once I left high school, and for a while, it was. When I joined *GLOW* I got along with all the other girls pretty well. We were young; we were beautiful; and we were on TV ... what was there to complain about? After season two ended, I went on that modeling tour of Japan with eleven other women. Even though there were different cliques of girls who, just like in high school, didn't exactly get along, my motto was always, "Just be nice to everybody."

Fast forward to 2012. Bret Whitcomb and Brad Thomason had written, filmed, and produced *GLOW: The Story of the Gorgeous Ladies of Wrestling*. The film was a great trip down memory lane for a lot of us

GLOW girls, and we had a chance to see people we hadn't seen in years. Up to this point, I think all of the girls had gotten along pretty well. After the documentary came out, there was talk of Netflix doing a show about *GLOW*, and that was when all hell broke loose. Some girls were upset that they weren't going to be involved and weren't going to be stars.

Some were upset that Ursula Hayden, the owner of the *GLOW* trademark, was the only one making money, which she got from licensing the trademark to Netflix. They accused Ursula of screwing the other girls out of millions of dollars. I totally get that, but the way I saw it, the trademark belonged to Ursula. She could do whatever she wanted with it.

As for the millions, I doubt she received that much money for the deal. Even if she did, she owned the trademark. She licensed it to Netflix. It's just business. Ursula never had any issues with us *GLOW* girls using her trademark to design *GLOW* merchandise. I guess that was the payoff.

That being said, I thought the show would've been enhanced by having the original girls do cameos. In 2017, after some of the original *GLOW* girls had just come back from a cruise, there was a lot of talk about the Netflix show. That particular cruise was noteworthy because the cruise leader, a former *GLOW* girl, was already proving to be difficult at times. In fact, a *GLOW* girl from season one ended up getting into an argument with the cruise leader. Why? She thought the idea of a filmed, onstage Q&A for our *GLOW* fans was goofy, and she did not want to do such an event. There were some choice words said by the cruise leader's daughter, and that was that.

There was even some negativity surrounding the airing of the first season of *GLOW* on Netflix during the summer of 2017. Some of the original *GLOW* girls were saying that the actresses couldn't act. Some complained that Marc Maron's character was shown doing cocaine in several scenes, even though our director, Matt Cimber, never did drugs. One of the girls filmed another girl providing these honest opinions at a Netflix viewing party that year. I don't think anybody understood that the Netflix series revolved around fictionalized characters and gimmicks from our show. It was never meant to be a carbon copy of our original

GLOW. In my eyes, I thought anything that promoted our brand would benefit all of us, whether we were in the show or not.

And that's exactly what happened. Once the Netflix series aired, we got a lot of publicity from different media outlets wanting to interview the original *GLOW* girls. The series had put us back on the map. I was doing interviews left and right. *The New York Post* gave me a two-page spread, and there were articles in *The Hollywood Reporter*, *US Weekly*, *Variety* and *People* magazine.

In May of 2017, the Cauliflower Alley Club (CAC) – a well-respected, benevolent organization for wrestlers established back in 1965 – honored the women of *GLOW* in recognition of our personal and professional accomplishments in the field of pro wrestling. They dedicated that evening to all of the ladies, and we were honored.

But I heard there were a few wrestling professionals in the audience that night who didn't agree with us receiving that honor. Some even wanted to give their own awards back to the CAC as a form of protest. That whole story has always bothered me. How do you judge people you don't even know? Don't listen to rumors.

There were some female pro wrestlers there who were saying that *GLOW* made fun of wrestling. *GLOW* never made fun of pro wrestling. That was never our intention. We had comedy sketches, and Matt came from a film background, but we combined those elements with the traditional pro wrestling that David McLane pushed for. We put women's wrestling on television. We promoted women's wrestling harder than any other professional wrestling promotion ever did before us. Let's make that very clear. *GLOW* was never about "making fun" of wrestling. If anything, it opened doors for women wrestlers to achieve new things.

But from there, things only got worse.

Certain *GLOW* girls went about trying to get whatever dirt they could find on anyone who might be getting more media attention than they were. Even worse, these girls attempted to use *GLOW* fans to damage other girls' reputations. I was the target of a great deal of this abuse, which I found unprofessional, junior high-like, and despicable. Any time I got more attention – or more conventions, tours, or interview requests – there seemed to always be snarky comments and ugly posts on social media. It was petty, it was sneaky, and it was the result of jealousy. Many of these comments were posted on other girls' social media pages, but my fans are pretty loyal. They kept sending me screenshots of all the nasty things that other girls were saying about me.

It was hurtful, for sure, but at least I was glad to know which girls were going out of their way to ruin my reputation. In this business, you learn pretty quickly who your friends are and who is out to get you. I couldn't believe that these women, who were pushing 60, were acting like they were 16 again! It was even worse than the bullying in junior high school because the stakes were higher, and these "adults" should have been above that type of behavior.

Another "adult bullying" incident took place when Cheryl Rusa and I had the chance to be part of a possible reality show written by one of the GLOW ladies. Shatner Universe, the production company owned by the legendary actor William Shatner, wanted to pitch this show to Netflix. The show's producers offered to have dinner with any GLOW girls who were interested while all of us were at CAC.

Cheryl and I were the only two girls to take them up on this offer, so we went to dinner. The next minute, there were all sorts of rumors that Cheryl and I had slept with the producers. This blatant lie took things way too far. In show business, it is not uncommon for women to use sex to get roles. However, I have always been professional in my career, starting on Day One with GLOW ... turning down this offer, turning down that offer, not getting the GLOW crown. Since the very beginning of my career, I've always felt that it was OK to say no.

I guess these ugly rumors had been flying around for a while, because finally one of the girls enlightened me as to the specific things two of these women were saying about Cheryl and me. Both of us were furious. Really, can you blame us? Ryan knows all about this bullying situation, and when I told him to guess what lies these ladies were spreading at the time, he repeated them word for word before I could even finish my statement. Unbelievable! My relationship with Ryan is way too strong to be disrupted by these types of childish rumors, but they still represent the type of ugly, petty behavior that grown-ups should be above.

Not getting to see Matilda the Hun before she passed will always haunt me. At a Shatner Universe meeting, I was talking with one of the producers and the *GLOW* girl who was pitching her reality show. When the subject of my memoir came up, I mentioned that I would need an editor for my book, as I didn't want it to mimic Matilda's book, *Glamazon Queen Kong: My Life of Glitter, Guts & Glory*. It wasn't my intention to demean Matilda's book in any way. I just wanted my book to be unique, and I had no qualms about reaching out to someone whose writing and editing skills were superior to mine. That's just good business, in my opinion.

Unfortunately, that comment was taken way out of context by the other *GLOW* girl at the meeting. She went and told Matilda that I had trashed her book, which was absolutely not true. She also told another *GLOW* girl, who was suffering from a serious illness, that I made fun of that illness at that same meeting.

Seriously? I'm not the kind of person who goes around making fun of someone else's health. The truth is that, at that meeting, I was not involved in a particular conversation between the producer and the *GLOW* girl pitching the show. I was looking at my phone at the time. When I turned back and heard the producer laugh (based on a different conversation altogether), I simply gave the benefit of a "courtesy laugh" without having any idea what was being discussed. That's fairly common social behavior in a group where multiple conversations are taking place, and obviously not done with malicious intent. My nephew is autistic. My heart is to help, not make fun of.

To add even more context, even before this meeting and without the other *GLOW* girl's knowledge, I had already had a few phone calls from the people at Shatner Universe. After she found out about them, she accused me of going behind her back. This was ridiculous because I was just a cast member like the other girls. The people at Shatner Universe just happened to be very interested in the character of

Hollywood. They even ended up putting Hollywood in the center of a promotional graphic for the proposed show, which likely added to the other *GLOW* girl's resentment. I was even accused of trying to steal her show idea. Not my style. I would never do that to anyone. Again very hurtful and sad.

I always wondered why I could never get in touch with Matilda, but when I heard about the lies these girls were telling, it all made sense. They had brainwashed a 70-year-old woman into thinking that I neither liked nor respected her – shameful behavior on their part, and totally untrue as well. People get over yourselves. I read right through you.

I worked with Matilda for two seasons. Vine and I were her seconds in the ring, and we did countless matches, sketches, and songs together. We spent a ton of time together and we always got along well. Certainly, I respected her as a wrestler, as a person, and for all her other accomplishments, which included roller derby, acting in numerous films and TV shows, and marrying the love of her life, Ken (whom she called "Poopsie"), and having a great son, Dean. Matilda's even in the Smithsonian Institution Archives in Washington, D.C.! All of these facts made it difficult for me to NOT be able to talk to Matilda during this ugly time.

Even worse, I later found out that, during the COVID-19 pandemic, the girls arranged a group FaceTime call with Matilda and went out of their way to exclude me (and several other girls) from the call. Sadly, Matilda passed on January 7, 2022. I never got my opportunity to say goodbye, all because of some mean-spirited, vindictive exaggerated lies. And despite the fact that I've made it known that my feelings have been hurt by all of these behaviors, I have yet to receive an apology from any of the girls who have spread lies about me behind my back. To me, this silence speaks volumes. But they have not hurt my fond memories of Matilda. I miss Matilda very much and think of her often. I still have my journal that Matilda and all the *GLOW* girls signed at our reunion in 2010. "Hollywood, My sweet sister of bad girls. Love & Body Slams Always! Queen Kong Matilda"

The years since 2012 have been very stressful and disappointing with regards to some of the ladies I once considered friends and coworkers on a very cool little show called *GLOW*. Is this junior high school-type bullying still happening? Unfortunately, yes. And while I'm over the initial shock that middle-aged adults still behave like spiteful teenagers, it still hurts to have people spread vicious lies behind your back.

I suppose it's true that somebody will always try to rain on your parade. Somebody will always try and tear you down. People will "gaslight" you for no other reason than jealousy or their own unhappiness. But it sure would be nice if these people could mind their own business, stop worrying about what others are doing or not doing, and stay positive. It's a whole lot healthier to smile and be kind than to frown and be miserable.

Am I perfect? Hell, no. I never said I was. We are only human, and we all react to certain events in certain ways. And sometimes it is difficult to bite your tongue, especially when people are coming at you with salacious lies and rumors. If you want to know something about me, please just ask. Communicate with me; don't judge me based on your (usually false) assumptions. I will always tell you the truth, whether you like it or not. (And if you aren't going to like it, I'll be sure to say it in a way that doesn't hurt your feelings for no good reason.)

You have to stand tall and be strong, especially in the world we live in today, and especially when social media can be used to spread so much misinformation and innuendo.

So thank you, fans, for always having my back, and for knowing exactly who the real heels are.

Chapter 47: Remembering Ursula

As I was writing this book, Ursula Hayden passed away. She died from cancer on December 3, 2022. While many fans remember her only as Babe the Farmer's Daughter (or The Princess of Darkness, or Donna Matrix), Ursula was more than just a pretty face in wrestling boots. She had passion and deep love for *GLOW*. She not only kept *GLOW* in the spotlight, but also helped *GLOW* to find more respect. After purchasing the *GLOW* brand from Meshulam Riklis in 2001, she worked hard to make the original *GLOW* episodes available. She also worked on the *GLOW* documentary, and she consulted on the Netflix *GLOW* series.

A funny memory that I definitely cannot forget is the time where Ursula and I were flying back to Los Angeles from Las Vegas on a Saturday. We often flew together and usually her mother would come and pick us up.

On this occasion she was going to be house-sitting in the Hollywood Hills Sunset Plaza area for a friend. She asked if I would house-sit with her for the night.

We drove up Sunset Plaza to this home tucked away in the hills. The bedroom and bathroom were the most beautiful rooms in the house. It looked like I just stepped into Henry VIII's bedroom — the huge dark wooden canopy bed was an ornate and beautiful sight – the bathroom was spectacular and everything was very neat and in its place.

Since we were already in West Hollywood, I asked her if she would like to go to The Rainbow with me that evening. Before we left we wanted to have a few drinks. We didn't see any alcohol anywhere except inside the refrigerator where there were several bottles of wine. I saw a smaller bottle of wine and I told her why don't we just open this bottle since it's small — I am not a huge wine drinker. We had a glass and were on our way. A week later back in Vegas, she told me that according to her friend the bottle that we opened was the most expensive one in the lot. So here's the thing: we didn't even *like it*! And we didn't have to pay for it.

I could tell you more about Ursula and myself, but I'd rather let her daughter, Alaska Hayden, share what her mother means to her.

ALASKA HAYDEN: My mama homeschooled me and was my absolute bestest friend. We spent a lot of time together. More time than most kids get to spend with their parent, and I'm very grateful for that.

I will never forget growing up watching her work on *GLOW* and wondering why some lady on the TV dressed in a crazy costume was body slamming my mom. It was wild, to say the least.

She worked a very long time – 16 years – to get *GLOW* rebooted. There were a lot of ups and downs, and it felt like a beautiful miracle when all her hard work paid off. She was able to license the trademark that she owned for Gorgeous Ladies of Wrestling to Netflix for the three seasons their show aired.

I'm very proud of her and everything she has done. She is the strongest person I know and forever my everything. The biggest love of my life, and I look forward to the day we reunite.

Another Perspective: Dr. Mike Lano (Photographer, Wrestling Historian, and Podcaster)

Jeanne is one of the hardest-working wrestlers and artists I know. From all of her *GLOW* work as a total original for all the years of the show from day one, to later finessing and continuing wrestling and working in the business, to supporting and attending many wrestling-centric charity annual reunions like Cauliflower Alley Club and multiple conventions and fanfests, speaking up positively about the wrestling industry and more, there's no one like Ms. J. She was a big star at the *Busted Open* WrestleMania weekend radio show party at the famed Los Angeles Whisky a Go Go on April 1, 2023, and she's run and promoted many wrestler cruises and other special events each year, in addition to all of her years of TV and film and stunt work. She was also a lead red-carpeter for the *350 Days* pro wrestling documentary gala on the opening night in New York City.

Jeanne always delivers on-camera, no matter the role or project, and equally radiates when public speaking. She's long been well respected by her Hollywood peers as a perfectionist.

And, of course, she has her famous artisan soap business, HollywoodBotanika. She's also still constantly in demand on radio shows and podcasts around the world and has quietly helped the careers of many other female and male wrestlers with her kind advice, support, and guidance. Even though she was initially inexperienced ring-wise when she started in *GLOW*, she's traveled the world since she started wrestling and is constantly speaking out for the industry.

Ms. J wouldn't remember me from the few times I shot and covered the original *GLOW* tapings for wrestling magazines. Press for the most part were kept away from talent, and instead we had reasonable access to Dave McLane, whom we knew as broken-in by Dick "The Bruiser" Afflis in Indianapolis. Years later, at Jeanne's very first Cauliflower Alley Club reunion in L.A., Cheryl "Lightning, Lil Mo" Rusa formally introduced us.

I was impressed circa 1993 at how well versed and knowledgeable she was of most of the people there, such as female wrestling legends like Cora and daughter Debbie Combs, Mae Weston, Gladys "Killem" Gillem, Ella Waldeck, and of course Penny Banner, June Byers, Moolah, and Johnnie Mae Young. Also, male workers, from our then CAC President Lou Thesz to Fred Blassie, Danny Hodge, Red Bastien, Nick Bockwinkel, Larry Hennig, Harley Race, and more. J, Cheryl and I also went to a few of those totally different women's wrestling "Jackpin" reunion/conventions in San Diego in subsequent years, where I introduced them to a long-time pal of mine, Nicole Bass, then fresh off quitting WWF and well after her ECW success as part of Pete/Justin Credible's collective group of heels.

Jeanne's done my various national radio shows a record number of times and is always funny, topical, and we love hearing about her rockstar spouse and their world travels, in addition to J's award-winning, handcrafted soap line! Rock On and Devil Horns Up on your first book! And I always hang with her a bit at comic cons and more traditional, mainstream fanfests, where she's usually a mega center of attention, as everyone loves Hollywood. Hollywood might be in Tennessee now, but no one can take the Hollywood out of Jeanne. And she looks progressively younger every year, proving that Benjamin Button thing is legit and not a work.

Retired dentist Dr. Mike Lano has been a professional photographer and writer for newsstand magazines since time began. He's been CAC's photographer since 1990 and still does his weekly newspaper column and radio show, plus two weekly podcasts on the wrestling biz. And he still works for the few remaining global newsstand wrestling genre magazines we have left, including the "better than ever" *Pro Wrestling Illustrated* here in the U.S. He's looking to return soon to photo-graphing wrestling and sumo in Japan, where he had such a blast in 1991 on multiple tours.

Chapter 48: Hollywood Worldwide: Vive la France!

In June 2023, I went to Paris with my friend Amanda. I had been to France before, but I had never been to the French Riviera.

Before we even left the States, our flight from Nashville to JFK Airport in New York was delayed by two hours, which meant that we were going to miss the Paris connection from New York. They put us on a 12:30 a.m. flight, and we almost missed that one, if you can believe it! The air train was not working from Terminal 4 over to Terminal 1. We had to run downstairs, follow the signs outside, and look for one of the buses that would transfer us to Terminal 1. We had maybe 20 minutes before the flight was supposed to take off.

We ran as fast as we could off the bus with our luggage and had to go through security again. There was a line! So I politely asked the folks in front of us if we could please go ahead of them because the doors were going to close in about five to ten minutes. Fortunately, all of them said yes.

We were the last ones to board. But before we got on the plane, Amanda noticed that her backpack was not with her. She ran back to security and found it, and we were just able to board the plane.

Our flight landed around 11 a.m., and we took a taxi to our hotel. Our driver seemed irritated and couldn't find the address, so we made him drive until he found it. Tired but excited, we walked around looking for something to eat and drink.

We walked over to the Eiffel Tower, took photos, and had dinner, where I drank my first Aperol Spritz. We got back to the room around 8:00 p.m. I laid down at 8:30 and was out like a light.

Amanda got up earlier the next day and walked around to get some pastries while I took a shower. We took the subway over to the Louvre and Notre-Dame. I had seen the church before, but it had recently suffered a major fire. Since they were still rebuilding the church, there were barriers all around it. It was sad to see this, as it's such a beautiful place.

We walked around in that district, had a snack and a drink, and then headed back to the hotel. Later that night, we walked to a nice restaurant and sat outdoors. I ordered escargot and a wonderful Caesar salad.

☆ ☆ ☆

The next day, we woke up around 6:00 a.m. and took the subway to the Gare De Lyon train station. From there, we took the 8:20 a.m. train bound for Nice. Unfortunately, a family had a child who didn't stop crying until the fourth hour of our trip.

The train stopped in Cannes for a few minutes to let passengers off and on. We saw a golf course and the beaches, which were very busy. We also stopped in Antibes before arriving in Nice at 2:00 p.m.

Using our GPS, we walked to the Hertz Rent-A-Car and picked up our little black Peugeot, which had a stick shift. OK, no problem. I know how to drive a stick shift like the back of my hand. However, while we were in the car, I could not put it in reverse. I was used to an old-school stick shift, where you press down and then over to the right or left, depending on where the reverse is. I was getting pretty frustrated and was ready just to put the car in neutral and push it back. Fortunately, a car with a family in it pulled in next to us. I waved over to the man that was driving and pointed to the R on the stick shift. They did not speak any English at all, but he understood what I meant. He showed me I had to pull up, not down, on the shifter to move the car into reverse. I felt pretty stupid, but hey … I just did not know. We put on our GPS and headed straight for the hotel, which was about five miles away. We had a pretty big room with two beds in it.

Our concierge mentioned that we could take the train that comes every few minutes into Central Nice because we probably wouldn't find any parking. That turned out to be so much easier. We headed into Central Nice and checked out the beach. We sat in a very nice outdoor cafe, ordered our spritzers and dinner, and then strolled through the streets, looking at all the shops.

The next day, we were on the road at 8:30 a.m. We arrived in Èze right before 10 a.m. – the perfect time before the crowds hit. This was truly one of my favorite places. As we walked through this little village, founded in 200 BC, we saw restaurants and luxury hotels that I really want to stay at in the future.

Èze has been described as an "eagle's nest" because of its location overlooking a high cliff 427 meters (1,401 feet) above sea level. At the very top, there is a nice exotic garden with great views of the surrounding area. It's one of the prettiest towns on the French Riviera.

From Èze we drove to see Monte Carlo and it's beautiful casino. Established in 1863 by Charles III, Prince of Monaco, it's the most famous casino in the world, with only the most expensive cars parked out front. I definitely felt out of place in my tourist shorts and rock T-shirt!

In Monte Carlo the products in the shop windows do not have any price tags. People that are wealthy don't need to see the prices. Mandarin oranges grow on the roadside trees. It is the world of the rich! Every year in May, the streets of Monaco and Monte Carlo are turned into a Formula One race track. Needless to say, we didn't stay very long and headed towards Italy.

Since we started so early, we decided that we would drive into Italy and visit the city of Ventimiglia, about four-and-a-half miles from the French-Italian border. It didn't take long to get there, but we drove around at least fifteen minutes before we found a place to park close to the beach.

We decided on a nice cafe, Il Gattopardo, and had lunch that consisted of capricciosa pizza, Insalata Caprese, and Aperol Spritzes. We walked to the beach and stayed there for two hours. I did not know that there were so many pebbles (not sand!) on their beaches. It was around 80 degrees and perfect. We definitely put in a twelve-hour day and got lots of sun!

When we got back to our hotel, we went for dinner in Central Nice at Bistro d' Aqui. I had a Caesar salad and onion soup.

The next morning, we were up at 7:30 a.m. and on the road by 9:00 a.m. Our next destination was Antibes (pronounced "an-teeb") fifteen miles away. We parked our car on a side street and started walking to find some breakfast. I had Eggs Benedict at Cafe Milo that tasted so fresh!

It was a Monday, and unfortunately the museums are not open on Mondays, so we only got to see the outside of The Picasso Museum. We did a little bit of shopping, walked through the farmers' market, and headed to the beach. The beach in Antibes has sand that has been imported, but the water has all the pebbles. You get used to walking on them eventually.

We stayed in Antibes for two hours before heading to Cannes (pronounced "can"). We walked up to an old church, Notre-Dame de l'Espérance ("Our Lady of Hope"). Cannes is home to one of the biggest film festivals in the world. They have a big white sign that says CANNES, pretty much like the HOLLYWOOD sign above the Hollywood Hills. We walked down from this beautiful view, looking out at the sea and hundreds of yachts, to do some shopping before getting a little snack and some spritzes at an outdoor cafe.

Because the sun stays out until almost 9:00 p.m., we decided to stop back in Antibes and visit Fort Carré, one of the first fortified strongholds to be built in the Renaissance under the orders of the King of France, Henri II. It sits up on the hill overlooking the sea and Port Vauban and was used to guard the nearby border with the County of Nice and to defend the town of Antibes. In pop culture, Fort Carré appears as the villain's fortress in the 1983 James Bond film *Never Say Never Again.*[1]

The fort has a fascinating history that sheds light on the whole of the region. Its beautiful architecture is based on mathematical principles. The rampart walkway (43 meters high) offers unbeatable views. The 4 hectares of protected gardens with typically Mediterranean flora and fauna make this monument a place well worth discovering. We could not do the tour inside because it was after 6:00 p.m. when we got there. It was starting to become overcast and a bit chilly for us, but we took some beautiful pictures.

We drove back to our hotel, got on the train, and went back into Central Nice for dinner at a very nice restaurant on one of the cozy streets.

The next morning, we took the train into Central Nice for breakfast at Le Liber'tea. Our waiter and waitress were rude because we sat down in the wrong area. "You cannot sit there," the waiter said. "That area is for lunch. It is breakfast now." So we moved to the other side. I had some scrambled eggs, hot chocolate, bread with jam, and orange juice for 15.90 euros.

This was our last day in Nice, so we started shopping again. I bought a bikini top. Amanda bought a T-shirt. We went to PAUL to get pastries and sandwiches for the train ride on The Ouigo, a high-speed train service. We returned to the hotel to change, and after gassing up our rental car, we headed to the train station.

The train station is located next door to Nice Villa. We were two hours early, so we sat in a cafe with Wi-Fi and went into PAUL's pastry shop to get a few more things for the ride.

Our tickets were for Car 4, seats 405 and 406. We sat in 405 and 406, only to find out we were not in Car 4, but Car 14! Oops!

We had to run the other way to get in Car 4, but then we were told by the conductor that we were sitting in the wrong seats again! Oh, well … it happens. It was five hours and 50 minutes to the Paris train station. We arrived around 8:40 p.m., and the sun was still very bright in the sky.

We took an Uber to the hotel, which was about 40 minutes from where we caught our Uber and would be only a 5-minute ride in the morning to the Charles de Gaulle Airport. We arrived at 9:25 p.m. and went upstairs quickly to drop off our luggage. We went downstairs and had some appetizers and Aperol Spritzes. We finally went to bed around 12:30 a.m.

☆ ☆ ☆

We got up at 5:30 a.m. and were out the door at 6:30 a.m. We ate a wonderful breakfast at the hotel, caught our Uber, and headed to the airport. Security took quite a while, but we were on time for our Delta flight back to the good ole USA.

I had the window seat and Amanda had the aisle. Unfortunately, we discovered we had a larger girl sitting between us who smelled like she hadn't taken a shower in five days. We asked if we could move, but were told no because the flight was totally sold out.

Once the air conditioning started, it was much more doable. I've traveled a lot, and sometimes I wonder if people even know they might smell bad.

We had nine hours ahead of us, so I had a little snack and some champagne. I fell asleep and woke up an hour before the flight landed. We went through customs easily in Atlanta and got to visit one of our fans/friend Adrian Duarte, who works at the airport. Then we caught our second flight back into Nashville.

I would highly recommend Cannes, Antibes, Nice, Monte Carlo, Èze, and the Italian Riviera! I certainly did not want the trip to end. It was so beautiful with perfect weather. And the food! Oh, man! It is farm-to-table everywhere. Unbelievably fresh.

I will be back to the French Riviera again someday for sure!

Chapter 49: Conventions

Since that first NATPE convention with *GLOW* in January 1986, I've attended many conventions and continue to do so. In the '90s, a lot of promoters were hiring me for independent wrestling conventions, and I moved on to comic book conventions and other types of conventions after that.

I have attended a number of wrestling shows, such as The Big Event in NYC and the Cauliflower Alley Club (CAC) convention in Las Vegas; car shows; comic cons, including the L.A. Comic Con, Rhode Island Comic Con, and ConnectiCon in Hartford, Connecticut; as well as E3 (a video game show in L.A.), PAX East (a gaming convention in Boston), and RuPaul's DragCon in L.A. I was even able to attend the famous San Diego Comic-Con this year (2024) as a guest of Limited Run Games.

Meeting fans at the conventions is such a blast! Signing pics and taking photos with them is awesome. I always enjoy listening to their stories about when they first started watching *GLOW* and hearing comments like, "You were my favorite!" That always puts a smile on my face. If it were not for the fans, I would not be doing what I am today, or even writing this book.

Believe it or not, I have occasionally met fans who watched *GLOW* and went on to become wrestlers themselves. One of the most noteworthy was Kia Stevens, who wrestled in Total Nonstop Action (TNA) Wrestling/ Impact Wrestling under the name Awesome Kong. I met her at a CAC convention years ago, and she told me she had watched *GLOW* as a kid. Kia also played the character Tammé "The Welfare Queen" Dawson in Netflix's *GLOW* series.

Of course, I am proud to say that I am a fan myself, and there are a number of "celebrity guests" I have enjoyed meeting at conventions over the years. Gil Gerard and Felix Silla (RIP) from TV's *Buck Rogers in the 25th Century* were always great. Clayton Cardenas and Richard Cabral from *Mayans M.C.* and Ryan Hurst and Emilio Rivera from *Sons of Anarchy* were super cool, too. I'm hoping to meet Charlie Hunnam from *Sons* and J. D. Pardo from *Mayans* in the future. Of course, I also love to see my fellow wrestlers at conventions, such as Ric Flair, Ricky

Steamboat, Tugboat, Koko B. Ware, and Melina Perez. I've even seen The Smashing Pumpkins' Billy Corgan, who is the owner and president of the National Wrestling Alliance (NWA), at some conventions and other events.

Conventions are great for networking, too. In fact, I met John Crowther, a comic book writer, at a convention. That led to a Hollywood comic book released by Squared Circle Comics in 2020.

The main *GLOW* items I sell at conventions include 8x10s, posters, trading cards, comics, T-shirts, hats, pins, and patches. I also sell a variety of glamour shots and copies of my *Playboy* magazine.

While I sign mostly 8x10s, I have gotten some interesting requests to sign other things at the shows. For example, some fans have asked me to sign their arms so they could get my signature inked in later as tattoos!

Of course, many fans bring items they have kept for years, such as *GLOW* magazines and the posters inside them.

If you can't make it to a convention, you can still get items from my Etsy page at https://www.etsy.com/shop/glowhollywoodmerch/ and my personal website, http://www.jeannebasone.com.

Another Perspective: Tommy Bell (Artist)

My first real artistic focus was on the female figure when I was in high school. Fortunately for me, *GLOW* was hitting the mainstream hard, and I quickly found a muse in the multiple photos of Hollywood I was finding. She became a main focal point of mine as I began to sharpen my pencils and skills. I loved all of her fights, especially with Sally the Farmer's Daughter, and especially one where I don't think either fighter made it into the ring! Instead, they were all over the audience! I would've given anything to be in that front row!

Fast forward almost 30 years later, and I'd finally picked up my art pencils again, after many years away from them. Through the luck of social media and showing some new artwork on my platforms, Hollywood and I connected and even made plans to collaborate on a drawing or two! This was a huge moment for me, and so well worth the wait! After featuring her in a drawing for another production company, I had the idea of reimagining the look of "The Mummy" with Hollywood as my muse. Knowing her love for Halloween, I knew this would be the perfect project to do with her! I'm happy to say it was! She was even gracious enough to be a special guest on my drawing show, "Sketchy and Funny."

And what's next? Perhaps another great nod to the Universal horror films by combining two icons together in "The Mummy versus The Bride"? Who can say? It's been an absolute honor of mine to work with Hollywood on this incredible project! She's now not only a favorite artistic muse of mine, but also a great friend!

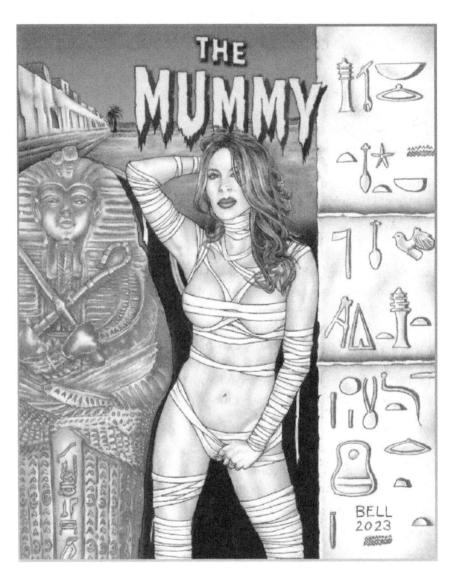

Artwork by the amazing Tommy Bell.

Chapter 50: Cleaning Up in the Soap Business

Ever since I was a kid, I have loved homemade soaps, incense, and oils. Growing up, I would collect and buy beads and seashells and make leather chokers and necklaces for myself and my friends, storing my supplies in an old egg carton. I was always drawn to music stores, head shops, and spiritual/New Age stores. The smell of the incense always drew me in. I also loved astrology and would look up my birth sign (Taurus, the bull) to see whom I would be compatible with. Maybe the answers were in the stars. But it was always soap that intrigued me the most.

In December 2018, I was at the mall and saw a huge display of homemade soap. I looked at all the shapes and colors and sniffed all the unique fragrances. There was even a description of what essential oils were and what they were used for.

I thought, *Why can't I make soap myself? I can do this!*

I gathered up as many reading materials as I could and started researching. I watched videos, bought the materials I needed, and finally got up the courage to make my first soap. I was so very nervous because I was afraid of the lye. Lye is extremely caustic. It can cause burns to the skin and can do a lot of damage if ingested or inhaled. I was afraid I was about to play mad scientist and have some deadly chemicals blow up in my face! I didn't know what to expect. Books don't really explain it well enough, and the people in YouTube videos have been making soap for years. Most of them were wearing goggles and gloves while mixing the ingredients together, which made me even more hesitant.

I tried to learn as much as I could about the whole introduction of cold processed soap. Cold processed soap is really making everything from scratch. It has no added detergents, which can strip our skin of its natural oils, which is one of the reasons I love making soap. No preservatives, either.

Cold processed soap is made by combining oils and sodium hydroxide (also known as lye), which causes a chemical reaction called saponification. In this process, you get to choose the oils, scents, colorants, and any other ingredients you want to add. Sounds easy enough, right? Nope.

A former *GLOW* girl once commented on my Facebook page, saying that anybody could make soap. Sorry, but that just is not true. There are a lot of trials and errors before you get perfect soap – and honestly, becoming a pro doesn't happen until at least a couple years of doing it. Like anything else, it takes work and effort if you want to do it well.

There is another word they factor in called "trace." What does trace mean? Well, you need to look at videos and figure out how thinly or thickly or how much to mix everything before you put it in your mold. I made a lot of errors, let me tell you.

I keep track of all my notes and recipes, and right now, I have three full notebooks of everything I've made since December 2018. At first, I was just making soap for myself and a handful of friends. But soap-making really became a passion, especially once the COVID-19 pandemic began in 2020. With so many things and places closed during the shutdown, I was able to spend more time learning the craft of soap-making. I find it extremely relaxing. It's an enjoyable pastime, and I put my heart and soul into it.

My homemade soap hobby has developed into a nice side gig, especially with everyone frequently washing their hands to combat the spread of the virus. Talk about being in the right place at the right time! I launched HollywoodBotanika (aka NashvilleBotanika), an artisan small business creating natural and handmade soaps without the harsh chemicals that are used in many mass-market products. And none of my soaps are tested on animals, which is extremely important to me. I have made soap for Billy Corgan's tea shop, Madame Zuzu's, in Highland Park, Illinois; Rhonda Shear's upscale consignment boutique shop, (re)treat, in St. Petersburg, Florida; and a handful of spas and boutiques throughout the United States. Most recently, my soaps began appearing on the shelves of the Nashville Jam Session store at the Nashville International Airport. I honestly feel blessed to have entered this exciting new phase of my career and contribute a portion of the sales to certain charities, such as:

Maui Humane Society (2023)
HairToStay
Children of the Night
Gilda's Club Middle Tennessee
UNICEF (for Ukraine)
Hurricane Harvy, Irma, Maria - Related Charities
Ruth Ellis Center (LGBTQ+)
The Life After Project
The ALS Association

Check out my soaps at https://www.hollywoodbotanika.com/ and https://www.etsy.com/shop/hollywoodbotanika/.

Amy and John Billings, owners of Nashville Jam Session at Nashville International Airport.

Chapter 51: Hollywood Worldwide: Turkish Edition

Istanbul was a big one on my travel wish list. The adventure kicked off as Ryan and I flew out from Nashville on the evening of Saturday, February 10, 2024. Since it was off-season in February, we lucked out with plenty of space on the plane – kind of like snagging a business class feel without the hefty price.

Touching down at Istanbul Airport at 5:40 p.m. on Sunday, February 11, we were met by a driver in a slick, black SUV that was a total surprise inside. It had fancy white leather seats and twinkling black and blue neon lights on the ceiling. The 40-minute ride took us to our place, the Vital Fulya Hotel, where we tucked into a great dinner after checking in.

Back in our room, we got geared up to watch the Super Bowl, an exciting time (especially while in a foreign country!) that stretched into the wee hours of the next day as the Kansas City Chiefs snagged the win against the San Francisco 49ers in overtime.

Before crashing for the night, I set up an appointment online for a "traditional Turkish bath" at the ancient Kalic Ali Pasa Hammam, which has been around since 1580. The next morning, I ordered an Uber and made it to the hammam in about 20 minutes.

Stepping into the hammam, I was greeted by the warmth of hot Turkish tea, sweet like apricots, in the reception area. Guided to the "hararet," the hottest part of the bath, I was treated to a thorough rinsing from head to toe with warm water, followed by a relaxing lie-down on a heated marble platform called the "gobek tasi." The friendly attendant then took me to another serene spot for a gentle exfoliation with a "kese," a soap-free scrub, leaving my skin feeling refreshed. After a sudsy bath (with foam created from a cloth bag) and a light massage, I was led to a cooler area and given a dry wrap before savoring a drink in the grand hall.

Later on, I strolled through the maze of the Grand Bazaar, an incredible experience with its endless array of goods. From gleaming jewelry to rows of sneakers and knock-off designer handbags, the bazaar was a real sight to behold. The spice shops were a highlight, and I ended up picking up some delightful teas.

Amid the wonder of the bazaar, I made time to visit the awe-inspiring Blue Mosque, making sure to cover my head with a scarf as a sign of respect.

Looking back on these experiences, I can't wait for the chance to return to this incredible city, a testament to the allure of Istanbul.

Chapter 52: The Road Ahead

So there you have it, the story of my life ... and what a long, strange trip it's been! I hope you've enjoyed the ride as much as I have.

It took a long time for me to put down all my thoughts into this book – over 30 years, in fact. I started my notes a year or two after season four of *GLOW* finished in 1990. I always knew I wanted to write about my upbringing and how I was chosen for the Gorgeous Ladies of Wrestling and other roles. Maybe there's a girl or woman – or even a boy or man – reading this now with a similar story and new opportunity in front of them.

My good friend and writing mentor, Bob Harris, had a lot to do with helping me understand how all of this works. We spent hours on the phone, with many pages of notes. I definitely learned a lot from that.

I did go through quite a few ghost writers to find "My Voice" and spent thousands of dollars in the process. I was really lucky at first and even had Writers House, a famous literary agency in NYC, sign me. They liked my story, so they hooked me up with one of their *New York Times* bestseller writers, who took my notes and hopes and turned them into ... a self-help book, which was a popular literary trend at the time. I wondered, *Will that even sell?* My gut instinct told me NO. But what did I know? Writers House told me the publishers loved "My Voice" and *GLOW*, but they did not want it as a self-help book.

So I started all over again with my notes and my friend, Rob Vogt's, writings. Rob helped me a lot, and I loved his voice because it was my voice. He got me right away. But Rob was going through some personal stuff and could not continue with the book, so more time went by.

Then one day at a Cauliflower Alley Club (CAC) convention in Las Vegas, I saw a book about women's wrestling written by Dan Murphy. We were acquaintances, as I had been going to these conventions for years with Cheryl Rusa. I asked him if he would help me with my memoir and he said, without a pause, "I'd be honored to!" What a great job Dan did with some of this book!

But then there was COVID, which slowed everything down. This was not any of the writer's fault. Keeping me onboard was tough, too.

Dan was getting married and had finished writing all his parts, so he suggested another writer focused on wrestling, John Cosper, to help with the editing/publishing, and I was on my way ... finally!

Then came the title, *Hooray for Hollywood!*, which was suggested by a fan I met via my Etsy page, Ken Davis. Ken is a self-described *"GLOW* geek" who watched in the '80s. He offered to help, and I thought another pair of eyes would be very good. Ken helped me to breathe even more life into the book that you are holding in your hands now.

So where do I go from here? Well, there are always new challenges ahead. Traveling the world is my thing now. I have a number of items on my bucket list. As I mentioned in the previous chapter, one that happened this year was visiting Istanbul, Turkey.

But it's been fun looking back on how I got from being a typical kid and music fan in Southern California to here: from "The French Fry Queen," to a phlebotomist, to a *GLOW* wrestler, *Playboy* model, actor, stuntwoman, business owner, artisan soap maker, and now, writer.

And it felt good to face up to each of these challenges and come out successful. After all, success breeds success.

And who knows? Maybe I'll even get to present that Oscar someday!

I had wondered at the beginning of this book if the world was ready for Jeanne Basone. Well, ready or not, Jeanne Basone is what they got.

I hope they at least found me entertaining.

Now ask yourself: Is the world ready for YOU?

Traveling with Ryan.

I love attending events like the Mid-Atlantic Wrestling Fanfest. It's a great opportunity to meet fans and legends like Malia Hosaka, Jim Ross, and Martin Tmart Damato.

From wrestling to video games. I still meet a lot of fans of Plumbers Don't Wear Ties!

A few pics of me and Ryan, along with Ryan's sleeve tattoo with the ring image.

Top: The Mouth of the South Jimmy Hart. **Bottom:** The pop-up 9/11 memorial.

Top: The haunted lighthouse at Heceta Head. **Bottom:** In Chile with Jennifer and Liz.

Hollywood and Lightning and Babe in Russia.

Hollywood in Paris.

Top Left: Hollywood in Paris. **Top Right:** Hollywood in Ireland. **Bottom:** At CAC Little Egypt, Matilda the Hun, and Billy Corgan of the NWA and Smashing Pumpkins.

My friend and book mentor, Bob Harris with some interesting reading
material in London.

The infamous cover of *FIGHTING Females* by Tony Weltzin.

Poster for the highly acclaimed *GLOW* documentary, and some fun
reunions at documentary film festivals.

Top: Fun times from the first and second original *GLOW* cruises that I hosted. **Bottom:** Photo by Terry Rylee.

Top: Amanda Girard, Matilda the Hun. **Bottom:** Lala and Zoe.

Top: Ursula and Alaska; in Paris with Amanda. **Bottom:** In Istanbul; my Nashville Botanika logo.

Top: *GLOW* in Hawaii. More *GLOW* action.

Top: Keith Main. **Bottom:** PR agent Gabe Elias, Godiva and me on *Family Feud.*

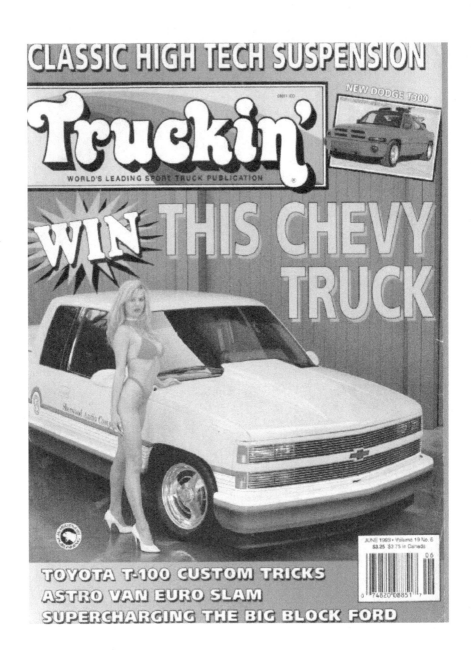

On the cover of *Truckin'*.

Top: With Lightning and Lady O. **Bottom:** Ace Frehley.

Top Left: With Ryan. **Top Right:** Laura, me, and Jon Abeyta. **Bottom left:** Dave LaGreca. **Bottom Right:** Ryan, me, and Neil Zlozower.

With the *GLOW* Championship Belt.

This book would not be complete without acknowledging some of the great photographers who have taken my picture over the years.

Dr. Mike Lano took these snaps featuring **Top:** David Arquette and RJ City. **Bottom:** Kevin Sullivan.

Photo by Craig Greathouse.

Photo by Jon Abeyta.

In the old west.

Photo by Julie Strain.

Venice Beach Postcard by Leverette.

Photo by Michael Strider.

Photos by Neil Zlozower.

Photo by Jon Abeyta. Laura, Dita Von Tease, and me.

Photo by Craig Greathouse.

The Hollywood Report: My GLOW Career by the Numbers

Total Aired Matches: 61 in 104 episodes of *GLOW* and the 1993 PPV. This includes 8 battle royals and a scheduled match that never took place in which Hollywood attacked Sally before the bell. It does not include matches in which Hollywood interfered, acted as a lumberjack, or appeared as a second to Matilda the Hun or Big Bad Mama.

☆ ☆ ☆

Total Singles Matches: 15. 8 wins, 5 losses, 1 double count-out, and 1 match that never took place against Sally.

Singles Match Wins: 8. Defeated Sally, Tiffany, and Vicky Victory once; Babe twice; Tulsa three times. The third victory against Tulsa was for the United States Championship title on the 1993 PPV.

Singles Match Losses: 5. Lost once to Sally, Justice, and Daisy; Lost twice to Roxy.

Singles Match Double Count-Out: Ninotchka.

Out of 14 singles matches, Hollywood won 53% of the time (8 out of 14).

☆ ☆ ☆

Total Tag Team Matches: 20. 4 wins (with Vine), 13 losses, 2 double count-outs, and 1 match against the Showgirls that was stopped.

Total Tag Team Matches with Vine: 12.

Tag Team Wins with Vine: 4. Defeated Tammy Jones and Ebony; Sally and Olympia; Tina and Ashley; California Doll and Amy.

Tag Team Losses with Vine: 6. Lost to Tina and Ashley twice; Americana and Susie Spirit; Americana and Debbie Debutante; Susie Spirit and California Doll; Sugar and California Doll.

Double Disqualification with Vine: One match against Cheyenne Cher and Sunny. This was aired in season four as "Another GLOWing Moment," Vine's only appearance after season two besides the filmed raps.

Total Matches with Vine as a Partner including Battle Royals: 24.

Total Tag Team Matches with Broadway Rose: 5. Lost to Tiffany and Roxy; Liberty and Justice; Sally and Babe; Thunderbolt and Lightning; Vicky Victory and Cheyenne Cher.

Total Matches with Broadway Rose as a Partner including Battle Royals: 8.

Total Tag Team Matches with MTV: 3. Lost to Tiffany and Roxy; Babe and Tulsa. One double count-out against Tiffany and Roxy.

Total Tag Team Matches with Godiva: 1. Lost to Sally and Babe.

☆ ☆ ☆

Total 2 vs. 1 Handicap Matches against Mt. Fiji: 3. Partnered with Vine, Broadway Rose, and MTV. Lost all matches.

Total 3 vs. 2 Handicap Matches against Mt. Fiji: 2. Lost with Vine and Attaché against Mt. Fiji and Little Fiji; Lost with MTV and Big Bad Mama against Mt. Fiji and Zelda.

☆ ☆ ☆

Total Tag Team Elimination Battle Royals: 3. Lost with Vine, Broadway Rose, and MTV.

Total 3 vs. 3 Matches: 7. Defeated Little Egypt, Tara, and California Doll in an Alley Fight with Vine and Attaché; Lost against Mt. Fiji, Thunderbolt, and Lightning while with Big Bad Mama and MTV in a 2 out of 3 falls match; Lost 2 Russian Roulette matches: against California Doll, Sally, and Tammy while teaming with Vine and Attaché; against Tina, Ashley, and Little Fiji while teaming with Vine and Angel; Lost 1 Gestapo Match with Matilda the Hun and Vine against Mt. Fiji, Little Fiji, and Americana; Lost to Tina, Ashley, and Amy while with Vine and Attaché. The Caribbean Cruise Match with Big Bad Mama and MTV against Mt. Fiji, Zelda, and Lightning was canceled due to no prize because Johnny C. was planning to take Babe instead.

Total Street Fights: 2. Lost to Tina, Ashley, Sally, and California Doll while with Vine and The Soul Patrol; Lost to Tiffany, Roxy, Sally, and Babe while with MTV, Godiva, and Beastie.

Wrestlers with the Most Matches against Hollywood in any Type of Match (not including Singles Battle Royals, but including Tag Team Battle Royals):

- Sally: 10.
- Babe; Mt. Fiji: 8.
- Roxy; California Doll; Tina; Ashley: 7.
- Tiffany; Lightning: 6.
- Tulsa: 5.

I love books – browsing retail book stores and books online. When I'm traveling to Europe, one of my passions is to search out old book stores and flea markets.

Sisterhood of the Squared Circle: *The History and Rise of Women's Wrestling* - Pat LaPrade and Dan Murphy (2007, ECW Press) * See pp. 175-178 *GLOW: Gorgeous Ladies of Wrestling*

Business Is About To Pick Up!: *50 Years of Wrestling in 50 Unforgettable Calls* - Jim Ross (2024, Audible Studios)

The Woman Who Would Be King: *The MADUSA Story* - Debra Miceli and Greg Oliver, Paul Heyman (Foreword) (2023, ECW Press)

The Queen of the Ring: *Sex, Muscles, Diamonds, and the Making of an American Legend* - Jeff Leen (2009, Atlantic Monthly Press)

Fabulous Moolah: *First Goddess of the Squared Circle* - Lillian Ellison with Larry Platt (2002, Regan Books / HarperCollins Publishing)

The Great Inimitable June Byers - John Cosper with Kailey Farmer (Foreword) - (2023, Eat Sleep Wrestle, LLC)
Website: eatsleepwrestle.com

Banner Days: *Autobiography of the First A.W.A. Women's World Wrestling Champion (1954–1977)* - Penny Banner with Gerry Hostetler (2004, A Flying Mare Publication)

Missy Hyatt: *First Lady of Wrestling* - Missy Hyatt with Charles Salzberg and Mark Goldblatt (2001, ECW Press)

Chyna: *If They Only Knew* - Joanie Laurer with Michael Angeli (2001, Regan Books / HarperCollins Publishers)

LITA: *A Less Traveled R.O.A.D. – The Reality of Amy Dumas* - Amy Dumas with Michael Krugman (2003, World Wrestling Entertainment, Inc. (P) 2003 Simon & Schuster, Inc.)

Through The Shattered Glass - Jeanie Clarke, Bradley Craig and Neil Cameron, Kevin Von Erich (Foreword), Missy Hyatt (Introduction) (2016, self-published on CreateSpace)

Trish Stratus Yoga: *Balanced Body, Balanced Life* - Trish Stratus (2013, Robert Kennedy Publishing)

Our Fight: *A Memoir* - Ronda Rousey (Author) and Maria Burns Ortiz (2024, Grand Central Publishing)

Crazy Is My Superpower: *How I Triumphed by Breaking Bones, Breaking Hearts, and Breaking the Rules* - AJ Mendez Brooks* (AJ Lee of WWE) (2017, Crown Archetype / Penguin Random House)

Incomparable - Brie Bella, Nikki Bella (2020, Gallery Books)

The Rise of Jade Cargill: *From Grass to Stardom* (2023, Heavenly Court Press)

Becky Lynch: The Man – *Not Your Average Average Girl* - Rebecca Quin (2024, Gallery Books)

HELL IN BOOTS: *Clawing My Way Through Nine Lives* - Saraya-Jade Bevis* (2025, Gallery Books) * Former WWE Champion as Paige (Pre-order available)

An Encyclopedia of Women's Wrestling: *100 Profiles of the Strongest in the Sport* - LaToya Ferguson (2019, Union Square & Co.)

Women Love Wrestling: *An Anthology on Women & Wrestling* - Jason Norris (2020, self-published)

The Ballad of Cousin Elvira - John Cosper with Jeanne Basone (Foreword) (2020, Eat Sleep Wrestle, LLC)

The Girl With the Iron Jaw: *The Amazing Life of Mars Bennett* - John Cosper, Victoria Otis (Foreword) (2022, Eat Sleep Wrestle, LLC)

Princess Victoria: *A Tale of Tears, Triumphs, and Turnbuckles* - Vicki Otis and John Cosper (2022, Eat Sleep Wrestle, LLC)

Rolling Thunder: *A "HammerHead" Jed Mystery* - A.J. Devlin (2020, NeWest Press) - Website: ajdevlin.com

Glamazon Queen Kong: *My Life of Glitter, Guts, and Glory* - Deanna Booher (2017, QK Enterprises)

Hammer of the Gods: *The Led Zeppelin Saga* - Stephen Davis (1985, William Morrow and Company)

No One Here Gets Out Alive: *The Biography of Jim Morrison* - Jerry Hopkins and Danny Sugerman (1995, Warner Books Publishing)

ED by ZLOZ: *EDWARD VAN HALEN - Photographs By Neil Zlozower* (2022, Neil Zlozower) - Website: Zloz.com

My Favorite Horror Movie 2: *The New Blood* - Edited & Curated by Christian Ackerman, Felissa Rose & Chuck Foster (2019, Black Vortex Cinema) * See p. 109 for *The Shining* (1980) by Jeanne Basone.

Alice's Adventures In Wonderland: *And Through The Looking-Glass* - Lewis Carroll (1913, Reprint - London: Macmillan & Co., Ltd.) * My favorite book. I bought it in London.

Neldas Recipes & More: My first recipe book - Jeanne Basone (2016, Lulu Publishing Services)

Holding my beloved copy of *Alice in Wonderland*.

Photography Credits

Jon Abeyta
John Chennavasin
Jeff Riley
Loren Franck
Nick Douglas
Mike Lano
Michael Strider
Neil Zlozower
Tony Weltzin
Julie Strain
Photo provided by Bob Harris
Noelle Rose
Craig Greathouse

Easyriders, April 1995: Raiko Hartman
Playboy, December 1989: Richard Fegley

Playboy's Book of Lingerie, January/February 1993: Richard Singer
Playboy's Book of Lingerie, May/June 1993: Richard Singer

Truckin', June 1994: Brian McCormick
Tongue, "Headlock Hotties," Spring 2003: David Safian

GLOW Rap Credits

PART I page 7 written by Ken Davis.
PART II page 69 written by Ken Davis.
PART III page 186 written by Ken Davis.

Chapter 19: My *GLOW* Raps page 146
* Co-written with Steve Blance and Jeanne Basone.
** Written by Steve Blance.
All other raps written by Jeanne Basone.

Reference Notes

Chapter 2: Growing Up

1. Edut, Ophira and Tali ("The AstroTwins"). "Taurus: All About This Zodiac Sign's Personality Traits, Compatibility and More." *Astrostyle.com*. astrostyle.com/astrology/zodiac-signs/taurus/. Accessed 21 Jul. 2024.
2. Edut, Ophira and Tali ("The AstroTwins"). "Gemini: All About This Zodiac Sign's Personality Traits, Compatibility and More." *Astrostyle.com*. astrostyle.com/astrology/zodiac-signs/gemini/. Accessed 21 Jul. 2024.

Chapter 40: Hollywood Worldwide: European Edition

1. "Karlštejn." *Wikipedia, The Free Encyclopedia*, Wikimedia Foundation, 15 Jun. 2024, en.wikipedia.org/wiki/Karlštejn.
2. "Clifden." *Wikipedia, The Free Encyclopedia*, Wikimedia Foundation, 8 Jun. 2024, en.wikipedia.org/wiki/Clifden.
3. "San Gimignano." *Wikipedia, The Free Encyclopedia*, Wikimedia Foundation, 13 Jul. 2024, en.wikipedia.org/wiki/San_Gimignano.
4. Ibid.
5. "Nyhavn." *Wikipedia, The Free Encyclopedia*, Wikimedia Foundation, 2 May 2024, en.wikipedia.org/wiki/Nyhavn.

Chapter 45: The COVID Pandemic

1. Centers for Disease Control and Prevention. "CDC Museum COVID-19 Timeline." *David J. Sencer CDC Museum: In Association with the Smithsonian Institution*, 15 Mar. 2023, www.cdc.gov/museum/timeline/covid19.html.
2. Ibid.

Chapter 46: Bullying: The Painful Truth

1. Australian Education Authorities/The State of Queensland. "Understanding bullying." *Bullying No Way*, 19 Jun. 2023, bullyingnoway.gov.au/understanding-bullying.

Chapter 48: Hollywood Worldwide: Vive la France!

1. "Fort Carré." *Wikipedia, The Free Encyclopedia*, Wikimedia Foundation, 3 Jun. 2024, en.wikipedia.org/wiki/Fort_Carré.

Acknowledgements

I always knew I wanted to write my story about *GLOW*, my life, and beyond. Writing may come easy for some, but certainly not for me. Nevertheless, I thought, *I'll take a shot at it!*

I began writing soon after the show closed. I continued for years until the pandemic slowed me down.

There are so many people to thank. I know I won't be able to mention all of them, let alone thank them individually.

Thank you to my wonderful parents, Nelda and Pete. They brought me into this world with unconditional love, joy, support, happiness, and the common sense that I would need along the way. They let me think for myself and I learned independence, honesty, and sympathy.

To my very beautiful sisters: Julie May, Joelle Nelson, and their families. Thank you for your support of my craziness on the rollercoaster of my life.

My Writing Team:

I am so very grateful to Dan Murphy, a professional magazine writer and author on wrestling. He never flinched a bit when I pitched him to come on board as my co-writer. When chatting with him at conventions, I loved the way he spoke so positively and elegantly on every genre of wrestling. You are one of a kind, Dan. You polished my writer's voice perfectly. Thank you.

Ken Davis is a huge *GLOW* fan who reached out to me in 2023 and offered help fact-checking and proofreading my manuscript. His contribution of *GLOW* knowledge and editing input rounded out my story. Thank you, Ken, for your kindness and generosity.

John Cosper, an accomplished author of many books, formatted the manuscript and assisted in organizing the photo sections. John honored my writing aspirations when he had me write the Foreword for *The Ballad of Cousin Elvira*, the story of 1940's professional girl wrestling star Elvira Snodgrass. Thank you, John, for your expertise, patience, goodwill and spirit.

A special acknowledgement to Rob Vogt – college writing instructor, tennis coach, and wrestling fan – who I've known for 20 years. We spoke about my dream of writing a memoir. He offered help. Rob, I am incredibly thankful to you for nailing my writer's voice in the early drafts.

My Canadian friends:

I am enormously grateful to Bob Harris, my mentor, wordsmithing engineer, and a good friend. Bob is a wrestling historian, a promotion genius, jack of all trades, and my partner in crime. He held my hand through the "book process", giving me unique ideas, wisdom, and purpose. I learned decades ago, when Bob speaks, don't interrupt him, just let him talk. But I still interrupt all the time. LOL!! Bob, you are a sweetheart of a person, wise, and a great source of inspiration to me. There are no words to tell you how much I appreciate you. Much love and thank you!

A big thanks to award-winning writer A.J. Devlin, author of wrestling's "Hammerhead Jed" comedy-mystery series. He honored me in his second book *Rolling Thunder* with placement of my praise blurb on the back cover. He was also my beta reader for *Hooray for Hollywood!* I'm so grateful and very happy to be friends with these two wonderful guys. They give me confidence and strength.

I also have to thank Vanni Barbon for his friendship, guidance, and answers to my many business questions. And to Bob's business colleague Marc Crimeni, thank you for investment opportunities.

To Winona Kent – award-winning mystery author and Chairperson of the Crime Writers of Canada – thank you for helping me understand the self-publishing process.

My special friends:

Christian Ackerman is a writer, director, and film producer. He published my first essay in *My Favorite Horror Movie 2: The New Blood*. Thank you for the opportunity.

My gratitude to John Arezzi. I first met John at the CAC and realized we were neighbors. John always took time out to meet for coffee and answer my book questions. He's featured me on his podcast and YouTube show, *Pro Wrestling Spotlight*.

Thank you to Todd A. Kaylor, a good friend for many years, producer, and an awesome writer.

William Patrick (Billy) Corgan Jr., frontman for The Smashing Pumpkins, owner/president of the NWA, husband, and father. Billy has always taken time out of his busy schedule to chat.

Connections:

Some of my stories are about connections, and I am extremely pleased to have met these awesome people along the way:

ECW Diva "The Queen of Extreme" Francine, a beautiful, smart woman inside and out. We immediately became friends while appearing at many of the same wrestling conventions.

Lori "Ice" Fetrick, a beautiful, strong woman from the 80s/90s TV show *American Gladiators*, public speaker, and *Chillin' with Ice* podcaster.

Dave LeGreca, who I met through mutual friend and Skid Row guitarist David "Snake" Sabo. Snake loves his wrestling! Dave is a super cool dude! I always have an open invitation to his SiriusXM *Busted Open* radio show. I am so appreciative of you and the Sirius XM family.

And a shout out to icon Jimmy "The Mouth of the South" Hart who I met through Johnny Cafarella. Jimmy reminded me to "always kill them with kindness." I hold that close to my heart, Jimmy. Thank you.

To my photographer friends:

Jon Abeyta, what can I say? You *are* my favorite! The one and only fabulous makeup artist and photographer I have ever shot with – thousands of photos, 1996 to present date. Thank you for my awesome cover shot. Luv ya, my friend.

Much appreciation to Jeff Riley and Loren Franck from *GLOW* magazine. You really made that magazine shine and me, too.

Michael Strider a fabulous shoot in NYC. You really capture some dangerous looking shots! Thank you, Michael, for your kindness and featuring my images in your first book *STRIDER - The Stories I Can Tell*. Can't wait for book # 2.

Big shoutout to Dr. Mike Lano. Mike always makes sure to include me with all the great wrestling celebrities and actors that he photographs at events. He makes me feel like a celebrity, too. I get ink in his column for the CAC mailer.
Email: Wrealano@aol.com

Neil Zlozower. Zloz! The man, the myth, the legend! Have you seen any of his legendary photos or coffee table books? If you are an Eddie Van Halen fan, you must check out his 384-page hardcover book titled *ED by ZLOZ*! Thank you Zloz, you are always incredibly kind with your time. I have all your great shots: Page, Plant, David Lee Roth, Mötley Crüe, Ted Nugent, and Led Zeppelin. They're all up on the wall. Website: zloz.com

Tony Weltzin, a photographer paralyzed from the waist down, but he never let that get in his way. Whenever I wanted to shoot, Tony's door was wide open. He also shot two of my front covers for *FIGHTING Females* magazine.

The glamorous Julie Strain and I met a few times – once on HBO's *Judge Julie*, and another on set in her home with other models. May your beautiful soul rest in peace.

Craig Greathouse – a good friend and fan of *GLOW*. Thank you. It's always a pleasure working with you.

Limited Run Games – one of my favorite companies to work for. They took the 90's *Plumbers Don't Wear Ties* 3DO video I starred in as Jane, reformatted it to Nintendo Switch, PlayStation 5, and re-released it. Thank you, Brian, Alena, Josh, Audi, and the whole family at Limited Run. You rock!

Thank you to the event promoters:

Thank you to Cauliflower Alley Club (CAC), President Brian Blair, and the CAC family for your continuous support.

In 2015, Rudy Garcia, production coordinator of the RuPaul DragCon in Los Angeles, invited me to attend their first convention. This was *GLOW*'s first big convention, with the most *GLOW* ladies in attendance since the show had ended. The following year *GLOW* appeared at L.A. Comic Con. Since 2015, I have been appearing at these fabulous cons.

Thank you, Sandy "Gremlina" Manley, from *GLOW*, who invited me to attend Rhode Island and Hartford Comic Con.

Always a pleasure to work for:

Marty "Tmart" Damato, (Big event and Legends); David Campbell (Big Event NYC); Tommy Fierro (80s WrestleCon); Jerry Sorrentino (80s WrestleCon); Nicholas Masci (Albany, New York); and John Crowther (Daytona Comicon and Squared Circle Publishing). John interviewed and wrote an autobio comic for me. He is always a delight to be around.

Doug Emkhe (Super Retro Con); Jim Davis (Super Retro Con); Dan Kawa Jr (Indiana); Marc Ballard (Nashville Comicon); Chris Czynak (Nashville Podcasters Convention); Jason Maples (EWF Pro Wrestling); Josh Baker (Celeb Fest); David Gomez (The Wrestling Guy Store, Los Angeles, California); and Casey Hart.

Big thank you to Vic Sotelo (Wrestle Con, LAX Fan Fest), who always has my back. The beautiful *GLOW* wrestling championship belt I own is a thank you from Vic for having me at his tables. Vic then introduced me to Jules from Oaktown Sports (West Coast Collectors Show) where I attended a signing in Las Vegas. Much appreciation to Ricky Lee (Sandra Lee Memorial Car and Bike Show in East Moline, IL).

Many thanks to:

Keith Ishii - author. You can find many of his books on Amazon. Mark Chervinsky - friend, director, editor. Pete Rosen, Esq., Huge thanks to Jeff Urband, my videographer since the '90s. Thank you to my friend Mike Rand. Mike also has a YouTube channel, @OfficialMikeRand, Tarryn J. Hoff, @GoTarryn on YouTube.

Sincere gratitude to Brian Hopson – actor, filmmaker, ghost hunter, podcaster, director and host of "Footsteps in Attic." Brian wrote me an 85-page horror script titled *Death Match at Diablo* from an idea I had with *GLOW's* writer Steve Blance.

Thank you to Evan Ginsburg, host of "The Evan Ginsburg Show."

The *GLOW* Family:

So thankful to Steve Blance, our head writer, referee, and commissioner from *GLOW*. Steve has been a good friend since our show. He is also a wrestling historian. Oh, and trust me when I say this: Steve does have a photographic memory!

Big thanks to Johnny Cafarella, our producer and "The Announcer" on seasons three and four.

Thank you *GLOW* girls and these ladies and gentlemen who allowed me to tell their *GLOW* stories: Janice Flynn, Sandra Margot, Ku'uipo, Cheryl Rusa, Debi Pelletier Miller, Dana Felton Howard, Dawn Maestas, Lauri Thompson, Jody Haselbarth, Andrea Janelle, Jayne Adams, Eileen O'Hara, Lily Crabtree, Michelle Duze Finney, Helena LeCount, Angelina Altishin, Michelle Jean Javas, Christy Smith, Norniece Norment, Nadine Higgins, Trisha Marie, Noelle Rose, Douglas Dunning, Ursula Hayden (R.I.P.), Matt Cimber, and Lynn Fero (Matt's wife).

374

Close Girlfriends:

My true friend Amanda Yarnell will always be my best travel buddy. Laura Bennett, you will always be my greatest friend and first partner in crime. Oyanka Collazo, I am grateful for our friendship and the soap ads you post once a week on social media. Special thanks to Marijane Cole and Cheryl Rusa.

A big thank you to Lee Bechley, who helped me get wrestling gigs when *GLOW* ended.

Much gratitude to these friends and fans and those who took the time to give me testimonials:

Tommy Bell, Rick Vincent, Amy Beth, Manny Briano, James Maher, Rick Howard Jr., Stephen Fenner, Ray Divelbiss, Adrian Duarte, Terry Rylee, Donald Goodlin, Shawn Campbell, Dave "Jackpin" Jackson, Al Burke, Kim Krieger, Alaska Hayden, Andrew Zeranick and Chris, Vanessa Bello, Telisa McKinney, Rick Martinus, Ron Lupton, Michael Karr, Keith Main, Adam Soper, Aaron Kettle, Thomas D. Bruff, Rod Swindle, Justin Michael Bernard, Stanley Karr, Robby Vegas, Lee Martin, Gary Laird, Jasmine St. Claire, Vince Minniti, Evil Zebra, Robyn Nelson, Another Wrestling Podcast, Supertramp, Mark Buckingham, Janna Hines, Heather Stevens, JJ Garcia, Teresa Lebrocq, GB Hettrick, Mark Bodek, Sal Sessa, Webster Ware, DeAnna DaSilva, Sylvester Boler, Joey Cassata, STJ, Christopher Annino, Fred Ottman, Robert Michael Avery Marshman, Jennifer Chiola, Patrick Keegan, Jennifer Ott, Les Muir, Jim Ross, Brett Whitcomb, Brad Thomason, Chuck Yeko, Calvin Yawn. Chris Taft, Carlos Perez and Royal Belts. If I have forgotten anyone I apologize.

Web Designers:

Jackson Presley and Joe DaVello

LA Crew:

Christian Cage, Kat Charrette, Elizabeth Cochrell, Lisa Danielle, Leonard Davila, Kristie Etzold, Suzie Johnson, Scott Kalb (R.I.P.), Darnell

Mayfield, Oliver, Cheryl Rusa, Jennifer Thomas, Jeff Urband, and Alan White.

Girls who worked for Hollywould Productions:

Lee Betchley, Belinda Belle, Jessie Belle, Lynn Burke, Oyanka Collazo, Lisa Comshaw (R.I.P.), Helen Cooper, Marc Duncan, Lisa Farrell, Candice Fleeman, Shannan Fredricks, Lindsey Howery, April Hunter, Rachel Iverson, Jennifer Knight, Tomiko Madoff, Kristine Martin, Mimi Lesseos, Christie Mathis, Allie Parker, Sue Sexton, Sybil Starr, Erika Sherwood, Donna Spangler, Sabrina Turkal, Claire Vaughan, and Tina Hollimon (R.I.P.).

Thank you to the DT Girls:

Kristen Andreotti, Shelly Berg, Diane Berry, Patrisha Beyeler, Tylene Buck, Ashley Clark, Mark Clausen, Donna Collins, Gina Davidson, Tara Deffenderfer, Yoland Edwards, Yvonne Garst, Christina Gonzalez, Vanessa Harding, Joanna Kemsley, Megan King, Amy Moran, Nicole Norris, Quisha Page, Tanya Panko, Sarah Pledger, Alyssa Reese, Marilyn Saint-Denis, Coral Sands, Mackey English Somer, Brinke Stevens, Dana St. Pierre, Elizabeth Tran, Tasha Welch, Sandy White, Julie Winchester, and Frankie Zappitelli.

The Vegas Crew:

James Brattoli, Marc Duncan, Richard Novick, and J.M. Rolen. A shout out to the fine folks who provide the professional rings that I wrestle and box in: Darnell (HTM), Ed Hunter (STJ), Alex Knight, and Kristie Etzold.

Very special thanks to Helene Bleich at Tribeca Publishing and her staff at *FIGHTING Females* Magazine for 4 front covers and articles, and video retailer Larry Druss at L. Scott Sales.

Thank you to Amy and John Billings who sell my artisan soap in their Nashville Jam Session store at the international airport.

Hugs to my fur babies Lala and Zoe who sit and watch mamma write and make sure I tap the right keys, and observe my artisan soap making routine in the kitchen. When I come in off a road trip, the first thing I do is pick them up one at a time, put them over my shoulder, cradle and kiss them like they're my own kids. I love them very much!

A very special thanks to Ruta Sepetys, award winning writer of historical fiction, who introduced me to her literary agent. And to Jonathan Merkh, my Nashville neighbor. Thank you for your friendship and publishing industry advice. So grateful to Julee Brand at W. Brand Publishing for all your wonderful knowledge, advice, friendship, and a badass book cover!

A sincere heartfelt thank you to Rudolph Chavez for overseeing the trademark filing for Hooray For Hollywood! for my Hollywood merchandising catalog, journals and blogs and the final wordsmith polishing.

To Ryan, my life partner, my everything. Thank you for your strength, understanding, and compassion. I don't always make things easy, I know – but what I do know is I love you very much. (oh and did I mention he's super hot!)

And, of course, to all the fans – without all of you, there would be no career and no *Hooray for Hollywood!*

PEACE AND LOVE,

Jeanne Basone

About the Author

Jeanne Basone is a professional wrestler, actress, model, stuntwoman, author, and artisan soap maker best known by her ring name **Hollywood** in the women's wrestling syndicated television show *GLOW, Gorgeous Ladies of Wrestling.* Jeanne was the first *GLOW* girl hired, and the only one to appear in all episodes of the show, from the pilot through the final fourth season. She and her co-stars were honored by the Cauliflower Alley Club, a fraternal professional wrestling organization, for their achievements in helping break the glass ceiling in the sport. She resides in Nashville and Los Angeles with her partner Ryan, and their two cats.

Affiliations

SAG (Screen Actors Guild-American Federation of Television and Radio Artists)
CAC (Cauliflower Alley Club) - Life Time Member
Crime Writers of Canada - International Associate Member
Alliance Of Independent Authors - Associate Member
Class of 2025 Women's Wrestling Hall of Fame (WWHOF) inductee

JeanneBasone.com
Instagram: OfficialGlowHollywood
X: GlowHollywood
Facebook: Basone Jeanne Marie